DATE DUE

MAY 16 1999	

Searching for the Sunbelt

Searching for the Sunbelt
Historical Perspectives on a Region
Edited by Raymond A. Mohl

The University
of Tennessee Press
KNOXVILLE

Chapter 10 was originally published in the *Journal of Southern
History* 50 (Nov. 1986): 597–628

Library of Congress Cataloging in Publication Data

Mohl, Raymond A.
  Searching for the sunbelt: historical perspectives
on a region / Raymond A. Mohl.—1st ed.
      p. cm.
  ISBN 0-87049-640-9 (cloth: alk. paper)
    1. Sunbelt States—Politics and government.
2. Sunbelt States—Economic conditions.
3. Regionalism—Sunbelt States—History.
4. Sunbelt States—Emigration and immigration.
I. Title.
F787.M63   1990
973—dc20   89-77169   CIP

201834

Contents

Tables

Preface

This volume of essays grew out of an interdisciplinary research conference on the Sunbelt held in Miami in November 1985. Funded by grants from the National Endowment for the Humanities and the National Science Foundation, the conference focused on the theme of "The Sunbelt: A Region and Regionalism in the Making?" Stanley D. Brunn of the University of Kentucky and Peter O. Muller of the University of Miami (both geographers) and I served as conference organizers. Our goal was to bring together for a mutual exchange of information and ideas historians, geographers, and other social scientists researching varied facets of the American Sunbelt. To a certain extent this objective was achieved, as historians and geographers talked together, listened to one another, and shared differing perspectives and methodologies over the four days of the conference.

Conference participants probed, explored, and investigated the Sunbelt from many different angles. This new regional concept, which achieved widespread popular currency in the 1970s, was debated, dissected, mapped, illustrated with slides and photographs, and subjected to rigorous statistical analysis. Few agreed on Sunbelt definitions: was there one Sunbelt, or two? The Sunbelt included Mississippi, Alabama, Tennessee, and Arkansas—or did it? It encompassed Colorado, Idaho, Washington, and Oregon—but perhaps not. There was no consistent Sunbelt, according to several analysts, but rather "sunspots and shadows." The Sunbelt was really a "sweatbelt" for low-income wage earners, an "undocumented belt" for illegal immigrants, or a "Latin belt" for the growing Hispanic population of the nation. How did the Sunbelt look from the perspective of the elderly, new immigrants from Asia and the Caribbean, blacks in southern cities, northern migrants to warmer climes, or women workers in the Southwest? What did Sunbelt landscapes look like from the interstate highways, or from the Mexican-American barrios of the Southwest? What was distinctive about the Sunbelt's economy, city politics, or presidential and congressional elections? What of the impact of federal policies, new technologies, agriculture, energy availability, or environmental issues? And what would the Sunbelt be like in the future?

With such a variety of definitions, approaches, and perspectives, it was difficult to find common threads or themes that might give a better sense of the Sunbelt as a region. In fact, the conference ended on a note of disillusionment as participants came to recognize the slippery and elusive nature of the Sunbelt concept.

The essays gathered in this volume are revised versions of the historical papers presented at the Sunbelt conference, and as such they suggest the diversity of definitions and conclusions that pervaded the conference as a whole. These essays also present the recent thinking of historians actively involved in research on Sunbelt-related themes. As the title of the volume suggests, these scholars have been engaged in a search for what is distinctive about the Sunbelt as a region. Individually they illuminate important aspects of change in the recent history of the American South and West and add to our knowledge and insight about American regionalism. Taken together, however, they suggest that the concept of the Sunbelt is as elusive as ever. The introduction, by Blaine A. Brownell, and the epilogue, by David R. Goldfield and Howard N. Rabinowitz, place the research papers into a larger, interpretive context. We hope that the varied perspectives offered here will help summarize some of the current historical knowledge about the Sunbelt. We also anticipate that the conclusions presented will help advance the research agenda on regionalism in productive directions.

I would like to thank my conference co-organizers, Stanley D. Brunn and Peter O. Muller, for their energy, insights, and cross-disciplinary collegiality. As editor of this volume, I am appreciative of the sense of common scholarly purpose developed over several years among the historians engaged in this project. Any endeavor of this sort, involving the work of several individuals, inevitably entails more time and effort than anyone initially anticipated. But my twelve colleagues have been unusually prompt, patient, and good-natured during the gestation period of this book. *Searching for the Sunbelt* is a collective effort vastly improved by the active involvement of all concerned.

A few other aknowledgments are required as well. Cynthia Maude-Gembler, acquisitions editor at the University of Tennessee Press when the idea for this book first emerged, consistently demonstrated faith and conviction in the project. Several readers for the Press made numerous valuable suggestions to improve the manuscript, which we have tried to incorporate in our revisions. At Florida Atlantic University, student assistants Christina Wood and Karen Milano were extremely helpful in the preparation of the final manuscript. As for me, this project has been, mostly, a lot of fun.

Raymond A. Mohl

Searching for the Sunbelt

1   Introduction

Blaine A. Brownell

Substantial changes occurred in the United States following World War II. Among the most widespread was the dispersal of population and economic activities across the country, and the concomitant rise of new metropolises and centers of decision making and production. This much seems obvious to everyone, but the precise consequences are described with far less certainty, especially when they involve complex notions of region, place, and culture.

None of these shifts was entirely new. Urban growth had occurred at a relatively greater pace in the South and West for most of the twentieth century, although much of it was admittedly subsidiary to economic developments in the North and Midwest. Cities had expanded along their edges since the mid-nineteenth century, impelled by each new wave of technology from horsecar to automobile. The construction of state highways and the beginnings of a national highway system were well underway by the 1930s. The war greatly accelerated developments in aeronautical engineering and, most importantly, stimulated the movement of millions of Americans into other parts of the country, for military service or factory jobs. By 1945 the country was poised at the brink of one of the most sustained booms in new housing construction and community building in its history, as veterans entered or resumed their careers and started families.

The presumed somnolence of the 1950s was quite deceptive. The interstate highway system, launched in 1956, forever transformed the American landscape, and sizable commercial airports were built or expanded in virtually every large or medium-sized city. Political infighting was well underway in Congress over the increasing location of new defense plants and military bases in the South and West. Older, multistory, downtown factories with outmoded machinery became less and less cost-effective, and the appeal of low-cost land on city peripheries, easily accessible by rail or highway, was too much for most manufacturing companies to resist. Many new plants were built not only outside

1

the central city but increasingly in a different part of the country, in the South or West, where land, labor, and living costs were even cheaper. These moves were accompanied by the movement of young workers and retirees to warmer or drier climes outside the nation's industrial belt. And as people and economic activities spread into other parts of the country, so did many corporate headquarters and administrative services.

In cities across the country, but especially in the Northeast and Midwest, housing and urban renewal programs reinforced decentralization, eliminating many downtown slums as new commercial and civic complexes were constructed, but also undermining established neighborhoods and older business districts. Inner-city populations became increasingly black, Hispanic, and poor, and metropolitan areas were fragmented into a patchwork of socioeconomic enclaves and independent governments. These trends continued into the 1960s, when serious questions arose concerning the social and economic consequences of government policies; but the trends already in evidence were far too deeply rooted in economic prospects, social anxieties, and technological possibilities to be deferred or deflected.

By the mid- and late 1970s downtown redevelopment was well underway in most cities, and satellite commercial nodes, new residential subdivisions, and industrial parks stretched out along wide freeway belts surrounding the urban cores. These trends were most evident in the newer, smaller southern and western cities. The Census Bureau revealed that nonmetropolitan areas were actually growing faster than metropolitan areas, to the point where Frank Lloyd Wright's utopian vision of "Broadacre City," a sort of endless dispersed suburb, seemed almost possible. Culturally the power of television and national franchising created an unprecedented degree of standardization across the country in terms of popular images and symbols, as well as products, services, and common reference points. Popular writers and scholars alike worried over the emergence of mass society and consumer indoctrination—and the passing of local and regional distinctiveness.

The ironies in all this were numerous, and quickly captured the attention of popular writers and commentators. The South and West—so long the economic colonies of the nation's industrial heartland and the northeastern financial and media nexus—were now the sites of new jobs and industries, the most sophisticated technologies, and the latest fashions in homes, dress, and recreation. Redistricting following the 1970 and 1980 censuses translated this demographic phenomenon into more congressional seats and electoral college votes.

The term *Sun Belt* was in fact originally used in 1969 by Kevin Phillips, in his book *The Emerging Republican Majority*, to describe a major conservative shift in national politics. Shortly thereafter, this and many other terms (e.g., the "southern rim," introduced by Kirkpatrick Sale in his 1975 book, *Power Shift*) began to appear in feature articles in newspapers and magazines and even on television specials. Scholars joined the chorus, adding interpretations of the latest census data to public opinion polls to trace the emerging pattern. Inevitably, the focus shifted from broad national patterns to specific regional references, and particularly to the ways in which the South Atlantic, the Southeast, the Southwest, and Southern California were blending, basking together in newfound wealth and attention. Meanwhile, the previously dominant Northeast and Midwest—now known as the Frostbelt—languished in population declines, factory closings, and inclement winters.

Relating this dispersal of national economic power and population to the formation of a new region was probably where the trouble started. Region plays a vital role in individual and community identity. The North, South, and West have a particular resonance in American history, literature, and culture. The idea of a new region that somehow combined South and West was both compelling—as an explanation for new trends—and confusing, because the images and identities simply would not mix. Another problem was that the phenomena supposedly carving out the new region were hardly uniform. As various writers put it, "sun spots"—specific places marked by economic success—were surrounded by much larger areas hardly touched by the new trends. Large populations of poor, unskilled workers were unaffected by the growth in skilled jobs and heavily automated factories and by the influx of better-educated workers from other regions. In the 1980s the identity of the Sunbelt became less compelling when the fall in oil prices and new initiatives in the North brought unemployment to Houston and successful high-tech industries to Route 128 around Boston.

The fact was that most residents of the Sunbelt were not aware of their new regional identity or good fortune, and even the prime beneficiaries of the new trends did not recognize the Sunbelt as a real place. One interesting feature of the 1985 conference at which these papers were initially delivered was a fundamental difference in approach to regions. Some scholars tended to rely much more insistently on objective patterns—trade flows, transportation and communication patterns, financial connections, and obvious similarities (as in the profusion of new and virtually identical shopping malls across the Sunbelt landscape). Others put more stock in subjective criteria, such as imagery and perceived identity, even to the extent of my own claim that unless most people actually consider themselves residents of a region—as southerners and westerners—then the region does not, in a very real sense, exist. By this standard, the Sunbelt was a figment of the objective imagination.

The papers gathered here mostly take a somewhat skeptical view of the Sunbelt as a new and well-defined region, even as they wrestle with efforts to make this definition more precise. Carl Abbott has offered in his own work some of the most thoughtful attempts to identify the major characteristics of the Sunbelt phenomenon and to locate these characteristics in particular geographical areas. Instead of an unbroken swath below the 37th parallel, he has detected a discontiguous "region," or the territories surrounding certain metropolises or clusters of cities (including such nonsouthern cities as Denver and Seattle). Abbott explores in his chapter the ways in which these new developments conform to traditional notions of region, and especially how they affect the South and the West.

James C. Cobb, a leading authority on industrialization and industrial promotion in the South, offers a complex but essential historical analysis of precisely how modernization affected this most rural and traditional of America's regions. His contribution examines not only the different ways in which the South industrialized and responded to industrialization but also the similarities between these processes in the American South and in Third World countries marked by traditional rural cultures, rapid industrialization, and dependence on dominant financial and information centers.

Defense industries and military bases constituted a major impetus for economic development in the South and West after World War II, and are often charged with the strong political influence of these regions in Washington. Roger W. Lotchin, who has examined the impact of defense installations in urban and regional development, here provides an assessment of the origins of the Sunbelt-Frostbelt struggle, especially as it relates to cities. Specifically, he discusses the military's role in decentralizing American industry as early as the 1950s and the emergence of defense spending as a national political issue, primarily pitting the older industrial core against formerly less industrialized portions of the South and West.

Even more dramatic were the internal political changes in the Sunbelt, especially in the major cities. The established (but largely different) elites that had governed southern and western cities and states before World War II were severely buffeted by dramatic changes in the postwar years. Among other things the civil rights movement, suburbanization, the impact of various newcomers (from foreign immigrants to northern urban professionals), and increasing federal influence in local affairs changed the entire political landscape—especially in the South. Richard M. Bernard traces the general outlines of these changes in his chapter, while Amy Bridges looks more specifically at the metropolitan Southwest and Southern California. Ronald H. Bayor examines one of the most crucial and visible dimensions of postwar urban change, in "Models of Ethnic and Racial Politics in the Urban Sunbelt South."

The shifting ethnic patterns in Sunbelt cities were, in many instances, tied directly to patterns of foreign immigration—legal and illegal. Interestingly enough, southern and western cities became, especially after 1960, the main centers of the new Latin American and Asian immigration to postwar America. Miami, Los Angeles, and Houston—rather than New York or Chicago—were the archetypes for this new immigration, and their politics, economies, and characters were likewise more substantially altered. The role of these international migrations in the formation of the Sunbelt is analyzed broadly in Elliott Barkan's chapter. The single most dramatic single case of urban ethnicity and biculturalism in the Sunbelt—and perhaps in the postwar United States—is covered in Raymond A. Mohl's "Miami: New Immigrant City."

The technologies most likely to be associated with the rise of the Sunbelt, by scholars and average citizens alike, are genuinely high tech: airplanes, telecommunications, microchips. But, as Raymond Arsenault reminds us in his contribution, the most critical technological innovation was probably air conditioning. Today it is virtually incomprehensible that investment banking, sales, or even light manufacturing could take place in the stifling, sultry heat of a southern summer. How could the modern pace of Houston or Dallas be maintained outside the sealed, controlled environments of downtown glass pillars and their connecting tunnels and overpasses? And might southern culture itself be desiccated by climatic standardization?

In "Searching for the Sunbelt," Bradley R. Rice recapitulates some of the central ideas and images behind the Sunbelt concept, and many of the responses, refinements, exceptions, and revisions to it. Like many other notions that reveal some basic realities, the idea of the Sunbelt has been obfuscated by definitions, suffocated in geography, and unable to sustain itself as a real location. In their epilogue, which they term more of an "epitaph," David R. Goldfield and Howard N. Rabinowitz review what these various essays have said about the Sunbelt and suggest how much more complex and challenging are the social and economic forces that have shaped America—and especially the South and West—since World War II.

If the Sunbelt cannot qualify as a true region, and if it has not eliminated regional distinctiveness, the traditional regions nonetheless have been fundamentally altered by the economic, social, and political forces that we associate with the power shift to the South and West. These areas, especially cities in the South, have experienced dramatic inmigration of people from outside that region, unprecedented communication with the rest of the nation and the world, and what is by any measure a pervasive standardization of entertainment, information, architecture, and expectations. And I suspect that the distinctive regional imagery still evident is less deeply rooted than it might appear, and too weak to sustain strong, distinctive regional identities. Texas barbecue, Alabama grits, Southern California health food, gun racks in pickup trucks, buckshot in highway signs, and the mania for football—which might indeed be the most widely shared Sunbelt characteristic!—are interesting, reassuring signs of place and identity. But they are, I think, a bit gossamer—and no longer supported by a strong undergirding of provincialism reinforced by isolation, tight family structures, deep religious commitments, and generational consistency. They are often cultivated nowadays in the pages of slick magazines, as an ersatz "yuppie regionalism" appealing to new arrivals fascinated by the exotic. The fact is that many Sunbelt cities do indeed look and function much alike, and something very fundamental has transpired to make them so.

This phenomenon cannot, however, be summarized or described in terms of a single new region. Like other popular symbols, the Sunbelt is shorthand—a useful abstraction—for a number of real phenomena, but as long as people do not identify with such a place, or even regard it as a place, it cannot be a region. But seeking to define it, tracing its implications, examining its characteristics, and reflecting on what it means for more traditional concepts of region and place provide useful and important ways of revealing what has occurred in postwar America, and the shape of things to come.

2 New West, New South, New Region
The Discovery of the Sunbelt
Carl Abbott

It is not often that a new term enters the American idiom to describe our economic and cultural regions. Americans have happily used *North, South,* and *West* since the beginning of the nation. *New England* dates from the seventeenth century. George Washington talked about the "Middle States." Even such a relatively new concept as the "Pacific Northwest" goes back a century, and the twelve states from Ohio to the Dakotas have been the "Middle West" since Theodore Roosevelt and William Howard Taft occupied the White House.[1]

In recent years people have been intrigued by new coinages such as those used by Joel Garreau to describe the "nine nations of North America," but few Americans sprinkle references to "the empty quarter" or "the foundry" into everyday conversation. Schemes to consolidate and redraw state boundaries to match natural and economic divisions have a long history but limited impact. Neither Rexford Tugwell's proposal to designate twenty "United Republics" nor Stanley Brunn's "Angelina" and "Tropicana" have penetrated the national consciousness. *Ecotopia,* introduced in 1975 by Ernest Callenbach's utopian novel, is used occasionally in the Pacific Northwest. In most cases, however, its use is mildly ironic rather than serious.[2]

One great exception to the generalization is the seemingly instant success of *Sunbelt.* In the 1970s *Sunbelt* became a sort of superstar of business and political journalism. It is, perhaps, our newest "Middle West." The term appears to be deeply entrenched in popular use and is essentially immune to criticism that the vernacular region does not coincide with important measurable patterns in economic activity or social and cultural behavior.

Given the speed with which we have embraced the Sunbelt idea and label, this essay attempts to explore several related issues. I will briefly review the process of introduction and acceptance of the term, and will then explore possible reasons for the "discovery" of the Sunbelt, its seemingly quick success, and its persistent use after achieving the status of cliché in national journalism. My underlying concern is to understand why Americans took the new terminology so readily to heart, by examining what it is that *Sunbelt* explains or implies that lies beyond the connotations of more traditional regional terms.

From Coinage to Cliché

In standard accounts, credit for introduction of the term *Sunbelt* goes to Kevin Phillips and his 1969 analysis of national politics in *The Emerging Republican Majority.* Phillips used *Sun Belt* and *Sun Country* interchangeably to describe a region characterized by conservative voting habits where Republicans could work to build their status as the new majority party. Phillips's Sunbelters were the mobile, leisure-oriented middle class, supplemented by a new generation of relatively affluent and mobile retirees.[3]

However, attribution of the term to Phillips is partially misleading. The idea of a Sunbelt has had at least two independent formulations. Phillips was unaware of any previous uses and considered the term his own, but U.S. Army Air Force planners as early as the 1940s had already defined and described a "sunshine belt" south of the 37th parallel as the acceptable location for new air training facilities.[4] It seems fair to suggest that the "sunshine belt" remained buried in Pentagon documents not only because it was intended for internal military use but also because it was an idea whose time had not yet come.

Phillips also used the term *Sun Belt* without clear definitions of either its territory or its characteristics. Given his basic concern with voting behavior, he was more interested in generalizations about the political and social consequences of Sunbelt growth than in its economic and demographic causes. Indeed, the book did not so much describe the *region* as cite four leading states. His prime examples were the "Florida-California Sun Country," the "new urban complexes of Texas and Florida," or the four boom states of California, Arizona, Florida, and Texas.[5] To a substantial degree, this analysis looked backward to previous studies of regional growth rather than forward to a new regional definition. It substantially restated classic work from the 1950s in which Edward Ullman and Harvey Perloff and his associates identified certain parts of Florida and the Southwest as benefiting from environmental amenities, resource endowment, and expanding local markets.[6]

Indeed, the time was no more ripe for the "Sun Belt" in 1969 than for the "sunshine belt" twenty-five years earlier. Perhaps because of the lack of innovation in its application, Phillips' new term languished for another six years. Political analyst Samuel Lubell tried it in 1970, but preferred to organize his discussion of voting trends around traditional regions.[7] The city of Austin, Texas, apparently pioneered the use of *Sunbelt* in promotional advertising in 1973, but national magazine articles on boom times in the old Confederacy continued to talk about "the South," "the new South," and "the new rich South" through the first half of the 1970s.[8] As has been widely noted, it was Kirkpatrick Sale's *Power Shift* (1975) and a series of *New York Times* articles in February 1976 that first popularized the idea of a Sunbelt (even though Sale used different terminology) and provided the rudiments of an operational definition.[9]

The term passed from coinage to cliché in 1976 and 1977. The *New York Times*'s seal of significance made it an instant hit in the press. One Sunbelt scholar has called the bicentennial year "the Golden Age of Sunbelt promotion," with articles on the Sunbelt's growing political and economic power and emerging image in nearly every trend-setting periodical.[10] Appearing at a time when many northeastern and middle western states and cities were finding it difficult to recover from economic recession, the idea that federal policy had long favored the growth of what was now identified as the Sunbelt became the pivot for a major policy debate from 1976 to 1978.[11] Although popular attention to the Sunbelt began to fade in the late 1970s, scholarship in the 1980s reflects the customary five-year lag between identification of a phenomenon and completion of substantial social science research. A set of social science and humanities data bases shows nine references to "Sunbelt" in 1976, an average of thirty-two per year for 1977–79, and an average of fifty-three per year for 1980–82. In a sure sign of academic respectability, *Sunbelt* has become a catchword used in scholarly titles where the less glamorous but sometimes more accurate *West* or *South* would do just as well.[12]

Sunbelt as a Regional Concept

The volume of attention has supported what can be called a "smoke and fire" approach that assumes the Sunbelt must exist if so many people are talking about it, writing about it, and using the term in promotional literature. The working definition is fuzzy at best, bundling together a wide set of characteristics that seem to be spatially associated. One identifiable set of traits relate to the Sunbelt as a regional development phenomenon resulting from a secular shift in the comparative advantage of regions. Specific explanations for the recent rapid growth of the Sunbelt variously emphasize locational decisions in response to amenities; locational decisions in response to regional market growth; migration and industrialization based on traditional agricultural and mineral resources; and migration in response to basic changes in the industrial mix of the American economy.[13] A second set of characteristics relate to the Sunbelt as a distinct sociocultural environment involving both lifestyle choices most easily expressed in low density, automobile-oriented communities with easy access to outdoor recreation, and distinct political values that support rapid growth.[14]

Taking a step back to reexamine the Sunbelt as a concept, however, one finds several peculiarities that throw doubt on its regional identity. Most obviously, it is difficult to use the presumptive defining characteristics to generate objective measures whose distribution coincides with the territory south of the 37th parallel—the consensual Sunbelt boundary as defined by journalistic convention and popular usage.[15] Key factors reflecting the emergence of a Sunbelt might include rates of metropolitan growth, location of national and regional metropolitan centers with high levels of producer services, and distribution of interrelated high-technology manufacturing, research and development, and military defense spending. None of these key regional development factors has been confined to the Sunbelt or distributed evenly within the consensual Sunbelt. I have argued elsewhere that these same factors allow division of the "census South" into a rapidly developing "outer South" encompassing the Chesapeake Bay states, Florida, and Texas-Oklahoma; a transitional "middle South" consisting of Louisiana, Georgia, and the Carolinas; and a more slowly growing "inner South" dominated by old industries. An extension of the same analysis suggests that the Texas-Oklahoma area can at the same time be viewed as part of a western-southwestern growth zone that includes Colorado, Utah, Nevada, New Mexico, Arizona, and all of the Pacific states.[16] An earlier study by Clyde E. Browning and Wil Gesler using 1970–76 data on federal spending, population growth, and economic well-being concluded that neither Maryland-Virginia nor Florida belonged with the South and that the West had "more characteristics associated with the Sunbelt than the Sunbelt itself."[17]

Cultural factors also show discontinuity rather than uniformity across the Sunbelt states. As one obvious example, ethnic mix and the resulting social and political tensions vary markedly from the eastern to western ends of the Sunbelt, with a divide in Texas west of Waco and Fort Worth. The South and Southwest have shown different patterns of ethnic assimilation and majority-minority relations. Religious affiliation links the entirety of the historic South and sets it apart from the West and Southwest. Tastes in magazine reading, however, place Texas and Oklahoma with California and Oregon and separate Florida and Virginia from the rest of the Southeast.[18] As a transitional subregion, Texas effectively functions with the dual identity of a southern and a western state.[19]

It is equally difficult to find a uniform set of political values across the Sunbelt. States tilt from liberal to conservative, or mix the two in odd local brews, on the basis of internal dynamics of personality, party organization, and parochial issues. Sunbelt voters have been inconsistent in enlisting in Phillips's emerging Republican majority. Charlotte, Nashville, Atlanta, Memphis, Little Rock, Corpus Christi, and Austin gave fewer than half their votes to Ronald Reagan in 1980. Miami, Tampa, Tucson, and Baton Rouge gave fewer than 51 percent. The typical Sunbelt politician of the last decade may have been Jesse Helms, Jeremiah Denton, John Tower, or Barry Goldwater. It may also have been Tom Hayden, Jerry Brown, Bruce Babbitt, Henry Cisneros, or Andrew Young.

In addition to lacking consistent defining characteristics, the consensual Sunbelt is less firmly fixed than it might at first appear. Many southeasterners use *Sunbelt* as another name for the South Atlantic and Gulf states, with a spillover into the Southwestern deserts. To many southwesterners, however, the real Sunbelt runs from California to Texas, with Florida as an outlier. We find similar results in comparing the Sunbelt images held by political journalists and college students in Chapel Hill; Grand Junction; Phoenix; and Davis, California.[20] Regional leaders also define partial Sunbelts. David Mathews, a former southern university president and Ford administration cabinet member, uses *Sunbelt* as a synonym for *South,* but Colorado governor Richard Lamm defines the Sunbelt as "the West and Southwest."[21]

All these problems of ambiguous definition return to the basic issue of why people have found the idea or terminology of a Sunbelt so appealing, even when they can't quite figure out what it is. Indeed, we have devised and accepted a term that reverses our customary pattern of regional coinage. In the past, Americans have either renamed the same region ("West" becomes successively "Northwest," "old Northwest," and

"Middle West") or responded to increasing population density and variety of development by subdividing a large region into subareas ("West" becomes "West Coast," "Pacific Northwest," "Southwest," "Mountain states," and the like). In the later 1970s, however, portions of regions were *recombined* that historically had maintained very distinct identities. Given the limited match with measurable factors and the continuing economic and cultural differences between the South and the West or Southwest, it is appropriate to ask (1) What purpose or need has been served by the identification and publicizing of a Sunbelt? and (2) What factors account for the time-specific acceptance of the new terminology in the later 1970s?

West, South, and Sunbelt: Growth and Change in Regional Images

One approach to these questions is to examine the historic regional images of the South and West, the components from which the idea of a Sunbelt has been assembled, utilizing the broad categories of economic growth and socio-cultural distinctiveness that are the chief pillars of the Sunbelt definition. In brief summary, such a review suggests that the definition of a Sunbelt has incorporated many characteristics long associated with the American West, but has required a substantial reappraisal of the South. Whereas the West has been able to evolve smoothly into the Sunbelt, the "Sunbelting" of the South has required a fundamental transformation of regional reputation and self-image.

The American West provides the easy case, for its historical image as a society reborn and remolded has in many ways previewed the bundle of traits associated with the Sunbelt. The New West beyond the 95th meridian has simultaneously epitomized American society and represented its future. A parade of writers in the mid-nineteenth century depicted the West as the logical extension and climax of American growth. Growth of the West, claimed a Chicago editor in 1856, was "laying the foundation for an empire of whose wealth, intelligence and power the sun in all his course has never seen the equal." The eccentric politician and promoter William Gilpin thought the Rockies to be "the keypoint of centrality . . . and unrivaled excellence" whose settlement would "stir the sleep of a hundred centuries . . . teach old nations a new civilization [and] shed a new and resplendent glory upon mankind." The West was a land of new beginnings open to individual initiative and social opportunity. The "Imperial Period of National Greatness," said John Wilstach, would rise in the Mississippi, Colorado, and Columbia basins, where there was "nothing to prevent the freest scope of the inventive and moral energies of man."[22]

A new generation of observers repeated the same themes at the end of the century. Charles Dudley Warner in 1888 reported the "joyousness of conquest and achievement" and the "marvellous building up of new societies" on the northern plains of the Great West. William Thayer's *Marvels of the New West* included "populous and wealthy cities that have grown into power and beauty as if by magic." In another hundred years, he predicted, western cities would surpass those of the East in enterprise and economic power, the result being "a national growth and consummation without a parallel in human history." The scholarly and always quotable James Bryce, after a series of visits in the 1880s, found the West "the most American part of America," a land of "passionate eagerness" where "men seem to live in the future rather than the present." Even Josiah Strong, who feared the impact of immigration, urbanization, Mormonism, Romanism, socialism, and whiskey on America's moral stability, was convinced by 1890 that the West held the key to the nation's future. With twice the population, wealth, and political weight of the East, its "preponderating influence" would soon determine "national character, and therefore, destiny."[23]

The new residents of the western mountain region and Pacific West shared the dominant view. Kevin Starr has documented in detail the "California Dream" of creating a new society in a new land. Hubert Howe Bancroft found on the Pacific Coast "the ringing up of universal intelligence for a final display of what man can do at his best . . . surrounded by conditions such as had never before befallen the lot of man to enjoy." Historian Gunther Barth has examined the dimensions of urban patriotism in Denver and San Francisco, whose residents shared dreams of economic success, an overweening confidence in their towns, and a faith that their growth made a direct contribution to the national purpose.[24]

The strongest counter to western optimism and confidence appeared during the 1920s and 1930s, when deep depressions in mining and agriculture reminded many westerners of their dependence on eastern capital and corporations. In particular, the Rockies and Great Plains produced a series of writers who described and deplored the "colonial" dependency of their states.[25] However, the literature was as much for the promotion of an internal political agenda as for external consumption.[26]

The concern largely bypassed the relatively prosperous oil regions of Texas, Oklahoma, and Southern California, where agricultural crisis co-existed with metropolitan boom.

The flush times after 1940 brought restatement and reaffirmation of the West's special status. Wallace Stegner and Earl Pomeroy, among others, argued that the West was the most typically American part of the nation. The Pacific Coast in particular was like the rest of the United States, only more so, expressing the national culture at its most energetic. It was urban, opulent, energetic, mobile, and individualistic, a region of economic growth and openness to change—a list of characteristics that matched America's favorite self-image and presaged the common description of the Sunbelt.[27] From the idea that the West was America at the extreme, it was only a short step to the belief that the West embodied the national future. The region in the postwar era, said historian Gerald Nash, anticipated economic and social trends by a generation. Neil Morgan asserted that "the West of today is very likely a close kin of the America of tomorrow." California, in turn, was the future of the West—Carey McWilliams's "Great Exception" and Morgan's "center of gravity in the westward tilt."[28]

The western image has also embraced several more specific subthemes that were established between 1870 and 1920 and reaffirmed after 1945. Like the broader enthusiasm about the region's future, they anticipate in detail some of the traits associated with the contemporary Sunbelt. The dry and benign environment of the Rockies and Southwest, for example, attracted tens of thousands of nineteenth-century health seekers and created a sanatorium belt that curved from Denver to Pasadena.[29] The same areas form the heart of a post–World War II retirement zone that has spread from a historical base in Southern California. They also offer prime examples of high-amenity areas that have grown because of their attraction for footloose industries such as electronics, where the original Silicon Valley has been followed by a silicon prairie in Texas, a silicon desert in Arizona, a silicon mountain in Colorado, and a silicon forest in Oregon.[30]

The West has also been a land of new starts. California, Colorado, and Puget Sound were all centers for utopian communities in the decades after the Civil War. Twentieth-century manifestations of the same impulse have ranged from Southern California's image as a haven for crackpots in the 1920s and 1930s to the diffusion of communes through California, New Mexico-Colorado, and the Pacific Northwest in the 1960s and 1970s.[31] Western states pioneered in the expansion of legal rights for women, such as suffrage and liberal divorce laws.[32] In the mid-twentieth century, the Mountain and Pacific states have ranked consistently high on indicators of social opportunity such as political participation and levels of health, welfare support, and education.[33] From the 1930s to the 1970s their metropolitan areas have scored relatively high on indicators of well-being.[34]

The South has had no such luck. For more than a century after the Civil War, the core of the southern image was backwardness. It was poor, it was rural, and it lacked major industrial development. A laggard economy implied a society that was only half modern, with strong agrarian values, high levels of violence, and limited attention to or investment in education. The racial caste system not only burdened the regional economy but also denied the concepts of individual opportunity and careers open to talent that formed the foundation of North Atlantic liberalism. From one perspective the South might be quaintly or reassuringly traditional. From another, its twin burdens of race and poverty made it the nation's great social problem. In either case, its defining characteristic was its failure to participate fully in the growth of the modern nation.

The counterimage of a New South was essentially rooted in the same negative comparison. As a prescription for regional change, advocates of a New South in the 1880s and of its various reincarnations in the twentieth century offered an agenda for industrialization in imitation of the North.[35] The idea of a laggard South converging on national norms dominated southern social science through much of this century. Although the degree to which southern manufacturing actually disturbed the political and social status quo was limited, its development was commonly presumed to be a transforming cause that would bring large cities, a cosmopolitan middle class, modernization of values, and a more open and tolerant society. Dozens of sociologists and economists stated the theory of convergence, analyzed its implications, and mined each decennial census for data on urbanization, occupational structure, health, income, and education that would confirm or postpone the "national incorporation" of the region.[36]

The popular image of the South as shaped by the news and entertainment media was equally negative. Jack Temple Kirby has traced the evolution from sharecropper and gothic novels and documentary photography in the 1920s and 1930s to the "tribal, passionate, and neurotic" South of the 1940s and 1950s. Civil rights agitation and reactive violence in the 1960s brought "neoabolitionist" dramas that confronted the evils of the "devilish South."[37]

At the start of the 1970s the South and West were still sharply contrasted in public image and public opinion. The same year that brought *The Emerging Republican Majority* to the bookstores also brought *Easy Rider* to the nation's movie theaters. In the film a pair of drugged-soaked buddies took a motocycle tour across the southern tier of the United States. They did not ride through a Sunbelt; instead, the movie contrasts a positive image of the West—an idyllic commune in the mountains of New Mexico—with increasingly negative and violent images of the South that include an acid trip in a New Orleans cemetery and a final confrontation with the deadly violence of the Deep South. The contrasting southern chic of the mid-1970s, which ranged from the television series "The Waltons" to the national popularity of country music, still functioned within the framework of negative comparison. The South supplied pastoral simplicity in contrast to the complexity of the North.

In a very different sector of the communications industry, *Wall Street Journal* articles on the South remained heavily negative through the first half of the 1970s.[38] A national survey during the same years found that southerners were relatively happy with their own region, but that only Florida was significantly attractive to outsiders. In comparison, the population of the Mountain states would have increased by 124 percent, and that of the Pacific states by 41 percent, if everyone desiring to live elsewhere moved to their region of preference.[39]

In the middle and late 1970s, in contrast, the public reputation of the South changed drastically with the discovery of the Sunbelt. For the first time since the Civil War, the idea of a Sunbelt allowed the newest New South to deny its dependence on and subordination to the North. Regional progress could suddenly be defined in terms of convergence or kinship with the dynamic West, as part of a new leading sector marked by fast growth and fast living. In a sense, the idea of a Sunbelt allowed the South to escape its own history and to transform instantly from a "backward" to a "forward" region.

The jump out of history was possible for two somewhat contradictory reasons. One reason, of course, was the culmination of the social revolution anticipated and applauded by the convergence theory.[40] Whatever its stand on issues of lifestyle, the South crossed the threshold of liberal society in terms of individual opportunity in the early 1970s. The relatively peaceful climax of the civil rights revolution and the peaceful school integration of the 1970s gave the South an unexpected reputation for racial moderation, as did the arrival of a more progressive political generation represented in the national media by the gubernatorial ABCs of Reuben Askew, Dale Bumpers, and Jimmy Carter. The reversal of black out-migration during the 1970s gained wide recognition as a reflection of both the realignment of the southern political system and the economic problems of the old industrial core.[41]

The second reason, ironically, was the previously mentioned divergence of economic fortunes within the South. Texas, Florida, and, secondarily, the South Atlantic states were changing so rapidly by the middle 1970s that the economic imagery of "the South" and "the New South" no longer seemed adequate. The result was the adoption of the Sunbelt and its associated imagery as appropriate for the booming periphery of the South, with the rest of the region drawn along by the force of the new terminology.

Conclusions

The discovery of the Sunbelt has created an enlarged vision for the South that is essentially an enlarged version of the West. The idea of a Sunbelt has meant more for the South than for the West. The West or Southwest did not really need the Sunbelt, since it has already had a positive regional reputation. California surfers and Texas "super-Americans" merge easily and directly into the idea of a Sunbelt. The South, however, is fundamentally redefined when it is viewed in terms of the Sunbelt. Having been historically defined in negative terms, the South has found a sort of rescue from its past riding on the coattails of the Sunbelt.

This result, and the history of the concept itself, strongly suggest the value of disaggregating the consensual Sunbelt among subregions and states. Very preliminary evidence indicates that the Sunbelt may have found its first and perhaps strongest home in Texas and Oklahoma, a pattern that may reflect both the ambiguity of their regional identity (cultural South and economic West) and their potential role in bridging perceived and real differences between Southeast and Southwest.[42] It would be useful to examine in more depth and detail whether Sunbelt imagery has been adopted more readily or extensively in some states and cities than in others, and whether there are subregional differences in the context or content of such use that reflect the different experiences and needs of the West, the outer South, and the inner South.

A related issue is the extent to which patterns of metropolitan growth, which lie at the heart of the processes associated with the development of a Sunbelt, confirm or deny regional identity. I suggest that patterns of economic and demographic change can no longer be understood in terms of the traditional South, however named, since the strongest growth areas are increasingly oriented away from the southern heartland.[43] In contrast, the same sorts of growth factors may well be operating to maintain unity between the northern and southern West. Several strings of cities that stretch north and south across regional and even international boundaries share certain growth histories, economic functions, and probable futures.[44] Indeed, much of the contemporary regional patterning of the West (and Sunbelt) can be understood in terms of the expansion and increased influence of greater Texas (extending from the Louisiana oil country and Ozark retirement zone into the oil regions of Colorado and Wyoming) and greater California (including Arizona, Nevada, Oregon, and Hawaii). Texan and Californian influence have deep historical roots and can be measured in patterns of finance and investment, permanent and seasonal migration, wholesale distribution, and recreational travel.[45] Florida, which maintains stronger ties with the Caribbean and the Snowbelt than with the interior South, appears to lack the same sort of regional "empire"—but it does fill a growing role in international commerce.[46] Atlanta is an important regional center but lacks the national standing of Los Angeles or Houston. Interestingly, it appears to have become relatively more oriented to the South Atlantic states than to the inner South over the last generation.[47]

Given the contention that the discovery of a Sunbelt has been of special significance for the South, a final question is the extent to which the Sunbelt idea may be seen as a denial rather than a vindication of the South. A number of specialists on southern history and society have recently called attention to the cultural distinctiveness that persists in spite of economic and demographic change. The broad reevaluation of what John S. Reed calls "the enduring South" has led historians, geographers, and sociologists to explore the continuing identity of the South as a cultural region. Southern cities, says historian David Goldfield, have remained peculiarly southern in many aspects of everyday life even while participating in the great postwar boom. The prototypical Phillips-Sale Sunbelter is a deracinated and isolated individual adrift in the suburbs of Dallas or the retirement communities of Florida. In contrast, the Goldfield-Reed southerner, rooted in networks of kinship and religion and committed to traditional patterns of social behavior, may enjoy some of the fruits of Sunbelt prosperity, but retains more in common with the nineteenth-century South than with contemporary La Jolla or Las Vegas.[48]

The basic uncertainty about the idea of a Sunbelt stems from the mismatch of regional need and regional performance. The emergence of the idea of a Sunbelt is tied directly to the modernization of the South; but California, Arizona, Texas, and the Florida peninsula are its centers of development and change. The traditional core South makes the smallest contribution to the consensual Sunbelt in terms of population growth, metropolitan development, leading economic sectors, or cultural innovation, yet the idea of a Sunbelt is of greatest potential benefit for states such as Mississippi, Tennessee, and Arkansas. We are left with the need for detailed research on the regional and subregional incidence of Sunbelt imagery, and for objective analyses of social and economic patterns. Taken alone, either approach gives us a partial view of the Sunbelt. Taken together, they can help us understand the emergence of the Sunbelt as a region *and* its discovery as an idea.

Notes

1. James R. Shortridge, "The Emergence of 'Middle West' as an American Regional Label," *Annals of the Association of American Geographers* 74 (June 1984): 209–220; Mitford M. Mathews, *Dictionary of Americanisms on Historical Principles* (Chicago: Univ. of Chicago Press, 1951).
2. Joel Garreau, *The Nine Nations of North America* (Boston: Houghton Mifflin, 1981); Rexford G. Tugwell, "Constitution for a United Republics of America," *Center Magazine* 3 (Sept.-Oct. 1970): 24–49; Stanley Brunn, *Geography and Politics in America* (New York: Harper and Row, 1974); Ernest Callenbach, *Ecotopia* (Berkeley, Calif.: Banyan Tree Books, 1975).
3. Kevin Phillips, *The Emerging Republican Majority* (New Rochelle, N.Y.: Arlington House, 1969).
4. Gilbert Guinn, "A Different Frontier: Aviation, the Army Air Force, and the Evolution of the Sunshine Belt," *Aerospace Historian* 29 (Mar. 1982): 34–45.
5. Phillips, *Emerging Republican Majority*, 273–74, 438.
6. Edward Ullman, "Amenities as a Factor in Regional Growth," *Geographical Review* 44 (Jan. 1954): 119–32; Harvey Perloff et al., *Regions, Resources, and Economic Growth* (Baltimore: Johns Hopkins Univ. Press, 1960).
7. Samuel Lubell, *The Hidden Crisis in American Politics* (New York: Norton, 1970), 269.
8. Larry D. Gustke, "Mental Images of the Sunbelt as a Travel Region" (Ph.D. diss., Texas A&M University, 1982), 183–84; Gene Burd, "The Selling of the Sunbelt: Civic Boosterism in the Media," in David C. Perry and Alfred J. Watkins, eds., *The Rise of the Sunbelt Cities* (Beverly Hills, Calif.: Sage Publications, 1977), 133.
9. Kirkpatrick Sale, *Power Shift: The Rise of the Southern Rim and Its Challenge to the Eastern Establishment* (New York: Random House, 1975).

10. Gustke, "Mental Images of the Sunbelt," 77.
11. Bernard L. Weinstein and Robert E. Firestine, *Regional Growth and Decline in the United States: The Rise of the Sunbelt and the Decline of the Northeast* (New York: Praeger, 1978); Jay Dilger, *The Sunbelt/Snowbelt Controversy: The War over Federal Funds* (New York: New York Univ. Press, 1982); James Cobb, *The Selling of the South: The Southern Crusade for Industrial Development, 1936–1980* (Baton Rouge: Louisiana State Univ. Press, 1982), 193–202; Carl Abbott, *The New Urban America: Growth and Politics in Sunbelt Cities* (Chapel Hill: Univ. of North Carolina Press, 1987), 2–5.
12. For examples of routine use, see Kathleen Butler and Ben Chinitz, "Urban Growth in the Sunbelt," in Gary Gappert and Richard Knight, eds., *Cities in the Twenty-first Century* (Beverly Hills, Calif.: Sage Publications, 1982), 97–111; Steven Ballard and Thomas James, eds., *The Future of the Sunbelt: Managing Growth and Change* (New York: Praeger, 1983); Franklin James, *Minorities in the Sunbelt* (New Brunswick, N.J.: Center for Urban Policy Research, 1984). It is interesting to note that academic adoption of the Sunbelt came at the same time that a number of influential journalists were consciously rejecting the term. John Naisbitt, in *Megatrends* (New York: Warner Books, 1982), removed the geographic core of the Sunbelt with a redefinition harkening back to the regional analysis of the 1950s, arguing that "the North-South shift is really a shift to the West, the Southwest, and Florida" (p. 234). Richard Louv, in *America II* (New York: Penguin Books, 1985), has rejected it as "a conceptual framework whose time has passed" because it cannot account for many of the important trends in American society (p. 29). Other journalists have ignored the Sunbelt entirely. Garreau, in *Nine Nations of North America*, writes about the Latin Americanizing of the United States. Peter Wiley and Robert Gottlieb, in *Empires in the Sun* (New York: Putman, 1982), focus on the rise of a super-Southwest.
13. For examples of different emphases, see Cobb, *Selling of the South*, 209–28; Walt W. Rostow, "Regional Change and the Fifth Kondratieff Upswing," in Watkins and Perry, eds., *Rise of the Sunbelt Cities*, 83–103; Alfred J. Watkins and David C. Perry, "Regional Change and the Impact of Uneven Urban Development," in Watkins and Perry, eds., *Rise of the Sunbelt Cities*, 19–54.
14. Richard M. Bernard and Bradley R. Rice, eds., *Sunbelt Cities: Politics and Growth since World War II* (Austin: Univ. of Texas Press, 1983), 15–18; Gurney Breckenfeld, "Business Loves the Sunbelt (and Vice Versa)," *Fortune* 95 (June 1977): 132–37; Sale, *Power Shift*.
15. Bradley R. Rice, "Searching for the Sunbelt," *American Demographics* 3 (Mar. 1981): 22–23.
16. Carl Abbott, "The End of the Southern City," in James C. Cobb and Charles R. Wilson, eds., *Perspectives on the American South*, vol. 4 (New York: Gordon and Breach, 1987), 187–218; Carl Abbott, "The Metropolitan Region: Western Cities in the New Urban Era," in Gerald D. Nash and Richard W. Etulain, eds., *The Twentieth-Century West: Historical Interpretations* (Albuquerque: Univ. of New Mexico Press, 1989), 71–98.

17. Clyde E. Browning and Wil Gesler, "Sun Belt-Snow Belt: A Case of Sloppy Regionalizing," *Professional Geographer* 31 (Feb. 1979): 66–74.

18. Leo Grebler, Joan Moore, and Ralph Guzman, *The Mexican-American People* (New York: Free Press, 1970); Robert A. Goldberg, "Racial Change on the Southern Periphery: The Case of San Antonio, Texas, 1960–65," *Journal of Southern History* 49 (Aug. 1983): 349–74; Edwin S. Gaustad, *Historical Atlas of Religion in America* (New York: Harper and Row, 1976); Charles A. Heatwole, "The Bible Belt: A Problem in Regional Definition," *Journal of Geography* 77 (Feb. 1978): 50–55; Wilbur Zelinsky, "Selfward Bound: Personal Preference Patterns and the Changing Map of American Society," *Economic Geography* 50 (Apr. 1974): 144–79.

19. Donald Meinig, *Imperial Texas* (Austin: Univ. of Texas Press, 1969); James S. Payne, "Texas Historiography in the Twentieth Century: A Study of Eugene C. Barker, Charles W. Ramsdell, and Walter P. Webb" (Ph.D. diss., University of Denver, 1972). There are also a number of continuities between the West South Central states and Southern California, many of which originated in the westward migration of Okies, Arkies, and war workers in the 1930s and 1940s. Expressions range from Texas-Pacific kinship networks among blacks to the diffusion of country music in the central valley of California.

20. Gustke, "Mental Images of the Sunbelt," 85–101; Abbott, *New Urban America*, 6.

21. David Mathews, "The Future of the Sunbelt," *Society* 19 (July-Aug. 1982): 63–65; Richard Lamm and Michael McCarthy, *The Angry West: A Vulnerable Land and Its Future* (Boston: Houghton Mifflin, 1982), 123.

22. *Chicago Democratic Press, Review of Commerce for 1856* (1857), 64; William Gilpin, *The Mission of the North American People: Geographical, Social, and Political* (Philadelphia: Lippincott, 1874); Jerome Smiley, *History of Denver* (Denver: Denver Times, 1901), 439–40; John Wilstach, *The Imperial Period of National Greatness: A Lecture on the Destiny of the West* (Lafayette, Ind.: n.p., 1855), 11.

23. Charles Dudley Warner, "Studies of the Great West: A Far and Fair Country," *Harper's New Monthly Magazine* 76 (Mar. 1888): 556–69; William Thayer, *Marvels of the New West* (Norwich, Conn.: Henry Bill Publishing Co., 1891), 404; James Bryce, *The American Commonwealth* (New York: Macmillan, 1912), 892; Josiah Strong, *Our Country: Its Possible Future and Its Present Crisis*, ed. Jurgen Herbst (Cambridge, Mass.: Harvard Univ. Press, 1963), 27–40, 182, 194, 198.

24. Kevin Starr, *Americans and the California Dream* (New York: Oxford Univ. Press, 1973) and *Inventing the Dream: California through the Progressive Era* (New York: Oxford Univ. Press, 1985); Hubert Howe Bancroft, *Literary Industries* (San Francisco: History Company Publishers, 1890), 2; Gunther Barth, *Instant Cities: Urbanization and the Rise of San Francisco and Denver* (New York: Oxford Univ. Press, 1976), 128–54.

25. Walter Prescott Webb, *Divided We Stand* (New York: Farrar and Rinehart, 1937); Joseph K. Howard, *Montana: High, Wide, and Handsome* (New Haven: Yale Univ. Press, 1942); Wendell Berge, *Economic Freedom for the*

West (Lincoln: Univ. of Nebraska Press, 1946); Morris Garnsey, *America's New Frontier: The Mountain West* (New York: Knopf, 1950).

26. For a review of this thesis and evaluation of its political intentions, see William G. Robbins, "The 'Plundered Province' Thesis and the Recent Historiography of the American West," *Pacific Historical Review* 55 (Nov. 1986): 577–97.

27. Wallace Stegner, "Born a Square: The Westerner's Dilemma," *Atlantic* 213 (Jan. 1964): 45–50 and "The West Coast: Region with a View," *Saturday Review* 42 (2 May 1969): 15–17, 41; Earl Pomeroy, "What Remains of the West?" *Utah Historical Quarterly* 35 (Winter 1967): 37–56.

28. Gerald Nash, *The American West in the Twentieth Century* (Englewood Cliffs, N.J.: Prentice-Hall, 1973), 296; Neil Morgan, *Westward Tilt: The American West Today* (New York: Random House, 1963), 26; Carey McWilliams, *California: The Great Exception* (Westport, Conn.: Greenwood, 1971).

29. Billie M. Jones, *Health Seekers in the Southwest, 1817–1900* (Norman: Univ. of Oklahoma Press, 1967); John Baur, *Health Seekers of Southern California, 1870–1900* (San Marino, Calif.: Huntington Library, 1959).

30. Ullman, "Amenities"; John Garwood, "An Analysis of Postwar Industrial Migration to Utah and Colorado," *Economic Geography* 29 (Jan. 1953): 79–88; Ann Markusen, Peter Hall, and Amy Glasmeier, *High Tech America: The What, How, Where and Why of the Sunrise Industries* (Boston: Allen and Unwin, 1986); AnnaLee Saxenian, "Silicon Valley and Route 128: Regional Prototypes or Historic Exceptions?" in Manuel Castells, ed., *High Technology, Space, and Society* (Beverly Hills, Calif.: Sage Publications, 1985), 81–105.

31. Charles LeWarne, *Utopias on Puget Sound, 1885–1915* (Seattle: Univ. of Washington Press, 1975); Robert V. Hine, *California's Utopian Colonies* (New Haven: Yale Univ. Press, 1959); Dolores Hayden, *Seven American Utopias* (Cambridge, Mass.: MIT Press, 1976), 321–47; James E. Vance, Jr., "California and the Search for the Ideal," *Annals of the Association of American Geographers* 62 (June 1972): 185–210; Frances Fitzgerald, *Cities on a Hill* (New York: Simon and Schuster, 1986).

32. Peter Gould, *Spatial Diffusion* (Washington, D.C.: Association of American Geographers, 1969), 63.

33. David M. Smith, *The Geography of Social Well-Being in the United States* (New York: McGraw-Hill, 1973), 79–103; Raymond Gastil, *Cultural Regions of the United States* (Seattle: Univ. of Washington Press, 1975), 117–36; Brunn, *Geography and Politics*, 323.

34. Edward L. Thorndike, *Your City* (New York: Harcourt Brace, 1939); Ben Chieh Liu, *Quality of Life Indicators in the U.S. Metropolitan Areas* (Kansas City: Midwest Research Institute, 1975); Smith, *Geography of Social Well-Being*, 104–19.

35. Paul Gaston, *The New South Creed: A Study in Southern Mythmaking* (New York: Knopf, 1970).

36. James Cobb, *Industrialization and Southern Society, 1887–1984* (Lexington: Univ. Press of Kentucky, 1984), 1; Cobb, *Selling of the South*, 265–67;

Rupert Vance, *Human Geography of the South* (Chapel Hill: Univ. of North Carolina Press, 1932); William H. Nicholls, *Southern Tradition and Regional Progress* (Chapel Hill: Univ. of North Carolina Press, 1960); Selz C. Mayo, "Social Change, Social Movements, and the Disappearing Sectional South," *Social Forces* 43 (Oct. 1964): 1–10; John C. McKiney and Linda Bourque, "The Changing South: National Incorporation of a Region," *American Sociological Review* 36 (June 1971): 399–412.

37. Jack Temple Kirby, *Media-made Dixie: The South in the American Imagination* (Baton Rouge: Louisiana State Univ. Press, 1978).

38. Cobb, *Selling of the South*, 183–86; Kirby, *Media-made Dixie*, 133–36; Burd, "Selling of the Sunbelt."

39. Philip Rones, "Moving to the Sun: Regional Job Growth, 1968–78" *Monthly Labor Review* 103 (Mar. 1980): 12–19.

40. Rebecca Roberts and Lisa Butler, "The Sunbelt Phenomenon: Causes of Growth," in Steven Ballard and Thomas James, eds., *The Future of the Sunbelt: Managing Growth and Change* (New York: Praeger, 1983), 1–36.

41. Numan Bartley and Hugh Davis Graham, *The South and the Second Reconstruction* (Baltimore: Johns Hopkins Univ. Press, 1975); Jack Bass and Walter DeVries, *The Transformation of Southern Politics* (New York: Basic Books, 1976).

42. Bernard and Rice, eds., *Sunbelt Cities*, 6–7, 28.

43. Abbott, "End of the Southern City."

44. The Great Plains gateways of San Antonio, Austin, Dallas, Fort Worth, Oklahoma City, Wichita, Omaha, and Winnipeg all lie within 100 miles of the 98th meridian. El Paso, Denver, Casper, Billings, Calgary, and Edmonton have grown as centers for the development of mineral regions in or along the Rockies. The West Coast ports from Los Angeles-Long Beach to Vancouver compete for the international commerce of the Pacific Rim.

45. For historical data or discussions, see Meinig, *Imperial Texas;* Earl Pomeroy, *The Pacific Slope: A History of California, Oregon, Washington, Idaho, Utah, and Nevada* (New York: Knopf, 1965); Gilman Ostrander, *Nevada: The Great Rotten Borough, 1859–1964* (New York: Knopf, 1966); Rupert Vance and Sara Smith, "Metropolitan Dominance and Integration in the Urban South," in Rupert Vance and Nicholas Demerath, eds., *The Urban South* (Chapel Hill: Univ. of North Carolina Press, 1954), 114–34. For aspects of contemporary data, see J. Dennis Lord, "Shifts in the Wholesale Trade Status of United States Metropolitan Areas," *Professional Geographer* 36 (Feb. 1984): 51–63; John F. Rooney, Jr., Wilbur Zelinsky, and Dean Louder, *The Remarkable Continent: An Atlas of United States and Canadian Society and Culture* (College Station: Texas A&M Univ. Press, 1982), 107, 126, 188, 207, 209, 239; Abbott, "Metropolitan Region."

46. In some interpretations, Virginia and Maryland are actual parts of Megalopolis, and Florida is a Megalopolitan outlier connected by migration, tourism, and popular tastes. See Jean Gottman, *Megalopolis: The Urbanized Northeastern Seaboard of the United States* (New York: Twentieth Century Fund, 1961); Wilbur Zelinsky, "Selfward Bound" and "The Roving Palate: North America's Ethnic Restaurant Cuisines," *Geoforum* 16 (1985): 51–72.

47. Lawrence W. Carstensen, Jr., "Time-Distance Mapping and Time-Space Convergence: The Southern United States, 1950–75," *Southeastern Geographer* 21 (Nov. 1981): 67–83.

48. John Shelton Reed, *The Enduring South* (Lexington, Mass.: Heath, 1972) and *One South: An Ethnic Approach to Regional Culture* (Baton Rouge: Louisiana State Univ. Press, 1982); George B. Tindall, *The Ethnic Southerners* (Baton Rouge: Louisiana State Univ. Press, 1976); Charles Roland, "The Ever-Vanishing South," *Journal of Southern History* 48 (Feb. 1982): 3–20; David Goldfield, *Cotton Fields and Skyscrapers: Southern City and Region, 1607–1980* (Baton Rouge: Louisiana State Univ. Press, 1982).

3 The Sunbelt South
Industrialization in Regional, National, and International Perspective
James C. Cobb

The Sunbelt South, consisting of the old Confederacy plus Kentucky and Oklahoma, is a region united by a common racial, cultural, and economic heritage. Variously described as a colony or as the nation's number one economic problem, since the Civil War the area has shown a common resolve to improve itself through economic progress, especially industrialization. Throughout its history it has been characterized by a persistent juxtaposition of concentrated wealth and widespread poverty. If the former has expanded considerably, the latter, while diminished, is far from disappeared. In the middle of the 1980s the Sunbelt South remains an enigma. With sixty-six of the nation's top seventy-five counties in terms of percent employed in manufacturing, and sixty-one of the nation's seventy-five poorest counties, the region has achieved its goal of industrialization—but without the prosperity that industrialization was supposed to bring.[1]

The key to solving this regional riddle, this paradox of poverty and progress, is to view the Sunbelt South from a variety of perspectives— regional, national, and international—and in a variety of contexts—historical, economic, and technological. The result is a complex picture, one that defies facile analysis and policy recommendations but that offers the best hope of understanding the economic odyssey of a region that remains as Charles P. Roland described it in 1970: "America's Will-o'-the-Wisp Eden . . . a land becoming and not become."[2]

Of all the contexts in which the Sunbelt South should be examined, the historical context may be the most important. In the antebellum South, so long as cotton profits were good, the exhortations of industrial advocates like J. D. B. De Bow and William Gregg fell on indifferent ears. The South's failure to develop an extensive industrial base, a failure made very apparent by the Civil War, led a number of observers to dismiss southern planters as woefully shortsighted and irrational in their preference for investments in land and slaves over factories and foundries. Critics who cite the failure of planters to invest more heavily in

25

manufacturing and a diversified agriculture are, in Edward Pessen's words, "applying unrealistic tests of rationality and farsightedness." Planters, after all, made a tidy profit from their land and slaves and, although the return was not as high as that projected from certain manufacturing ventures, neither was the investment as venturesome or intimidating. Perhaps affluent southern whites would have been better off to put more of their money into business and industry. Had they known the Civil War was coming, they probably would have, but plantation slavery nonetheless made average white wealth in the antebellum South considerably higher than in the supposedly more rational North. As Fred Bateman and Thomas Weiss have pointed out, southern planters might have improved their region's economic condition by diversifying their investments, but even in the best of circumstances the antebellum South's industrial sector would have been underdeveloped relative to that of the Northeast.[3]

If, overall, the Old South's mania for slaves and cotton was not the crippling obsession it seemed to be, its legacy was to become one of the true burdens of southern history. The antebellum demand for cotton, which had helped to offset the imbalance in the South's economy, did not survive in the postbellum era, and the productivity of free labor simply did not measure up to that of slaves. As cotton agriculture began to suffer, the absence of a diversified economy became far more serious. Southern industry weathered the war reasonably well, but it entered the postbellum period too underdeveloped to stimulate the growth of urban markets or the mechanization and diversification of agriculture. Whereas the strength of the South's agriculture had once compensated in part for the frailty of its industry, in the late nineteenth century the weakness of one simply made the weakness of the other more crucial.[4]

To a great many observers the solution was clear: the path to economic vitality led straight to the factory door. By the 1880s a large number of influential southerners were ready to embrace the gospel of industrialism as espoused by the young Atlanta orator and journalist Henry W. Grady. Grady made a persuasive case for industrialization and made it seem so simple—just a quick courtship and then a passionate coupling of southern labor and resources with northern capital and knowhow. By the time Grady had finished sketching his portrait of the vibrant New South rising from the ashes of the old, many a listener was ready to thank General Sherman for burning Atlanta, as Grady practically did on at least one occasion.[5]

Unfortunately it took a litte more than rhetoric and good wishes to build an industrial South. The region found itself both dependent on and competing with the dynamic industrial North, and a checklist of relative advantages showed few marks on the southern side. Grady was correct that the region could offer cheap labor and certain raw materials like wood and cotton, but except in Birmingham, the key mineral and fuel resources were lacking. The South's labor force was abundant and willing but unskilled and dispersed in comparison to the teeming labor pool clustered in the cities of the industrial North. Lacking indigenous capital or anything approaching an entrepreneurial tradition, the South could only look for assistance to the same North with which it also competed.

Again, the weakness and structural peculiarity of southern agriculture proved to be a decided disadvantage, because cotton needed relatively little processing and its cultivation and harvest required little in the way of supplies and subsidiary services. The population of the typical cotton-processing center seldom grew larger than 10,000, and the relatively good railroad connections afforded these towns denied most of the major cities the role of middlemen in the transfer of goods coming into and out of the Cotton Belt. This dispersal of industry in small towns accessible to large numbers of underemployed whites also retarded urbanization and stunted the growth of the urban markets needed to spur agricultural diversification or attract market-oriented industries.[6]

Given these realities, the leaders of the industrialization effort recognized the necessity of accentuating the South's short list of positives — cheap labor, untrammeled access to resources and raw materials, low taxes, and minimal, fiscally conservative government. To insure that incoming industry would not be concerned about tax costs, these leaders sponsored a move to minimize government expenditures, thereby starving or crippling public services and institutions. They also preached (and threatened to expedite) eternal damnation for all labor organizers and wage agitators, and obligingly provided huge chunks of land at practically no cost to railroads and timber companies.

In essence, what the leadership of the New South did was offer their region for exploitation as a means of spurring initial industrialization. The hope was that, once begun, the process would accelerate and sustain itself so the South would soon be enjoying northern-style prosperity and competing with the North for investment capital. These policies helped to encourage significant growth, dramatized by the humble beginnings from which southern industry sprang, but the South owed its growth largely to the less efficient, stagnating operations that were being cast off by the dynamic industrial economy of the North. Industries such as textiles could find new life in a region where labor and tax savings offset laggard technology and outdated management and organizational techniques.

The South took on the role of health spa for manufacturing industries in their declining years. Dominated by extractive, first-stage processing operations linked to the South's natural resources and agricultural products, these industries became the mainstay of the manufacturing economy of the New South. The economy grew and the South industrialized, but not very rapidly and certainly not at a pace sufficient to install the area below the Mason-Dixon line as a menace to northern prosperity. On the contrary, the New South's strategy for growth simply helped to confirm the region's status as a marketplace and a source of low-value goods, peripheral to or a colony of the northern core. Leaders of the New South received considerable criticism for their role in plotting this course, but given their commitment to industrialization and the realities of resources, markets, labor, and the national and world economies, they could have done little else.[8]

Only a massive restructuring and redistribution of human and natural resources and material wealth could have altered the course of industrial development in the late-nineteenth-century South. Still, by the twentieth century many of the South's leaders, while retaining their faith in industrial capitalism, decided to give the spirit of the marketplace a little help. During the first three decades of the twentieth century a number of southern states passed legislation aimed, at least in part, at accelerating the region's industrial growth.

Adopting a strategy common to "follower" societies hoping to vault over the earlier stages of economic development, growth-minded leaders argued that the key to accelerated progress was education. Between 1900 and 1920 per capita expenditures per pupil increased by 416 percent in the South while growing by less than 250 percent in the nation as a whole. The South also boosted its investment in transportation and public health and marshaled the resources of state government to the task at hand. Since the Grady era, growth advocates had contended that the South's racial problems were essentially solved and that the remedy for other worries like farm tenancy and the exploitation of labor actually lay in economic expansion. This belief in the rightness of economic growth and its effectiveness as a panacea for a host of social and institutional ills formed the core of a "growth consensus" that played an increasingly influential role in policy-making as the South emerged from World War I.[9]

A number of external events that helped to force a long-awaited trans-formation of southern agriculture also helped to confirm the growth consensus. Not the least of these was the invasion of the boll weevil, which ate its way across the cotton belt in the first two decades of the twentieth century, dropping cotton yields in some areas to fractions of previous crops. In 1924, with the state's cotton farms crippled by the boll weevil invasion, the Georgia legislature approved a provision per-mitting local tax exemptions for new manufacturing plants. The depres-sion also took its toll on the cotton economy, as did the New Deal farm recovery program created to relieve it. During the first seven years that Agricultural Adjustment Act (AAA) crop reduction programs were in operation, the South's sharecropping population shrank by one-third. Many of the sharecroppers were evicted illegally (under AAA rules). Still others fell victim to mechanization, as federal subsidies provided the capital for the purchase of tractors estimated by one study to have uprooted half a million Cotton Belt tenant families in the 1930s. The displaced tenants found their way into towns, from whence they returned only occasionally at chopping and picking times.[10]

Declining demand for farm labor created a number of problems for the business and professional classes in the South's towns and cities. This group had secured a good portion of its income by providing credit, goods, and services to the agricultural work force. Moreover, the exis-tence of a large, idle, relief-dependent population raised the prospect of crime and instability. With their communities and therefore their own, economic and social well-being at stake, the economic leaders of the South's small cities and towns joined their uptown brethren in an all-out effort to recruit industry as a means of employing a surplus popula-tion and reviving local commerce.[11]

This explosion of industrial recruitment enthusiasm translated itself into rampant buying of mobile, footloose industries that required little more than a roof and a cheap work force to put under it in order to be-gin operation. Some communities provided free buildings financed by deductions from workers' paychecks. Other provided free workers, at least during a training phase. This generosity was occasionally repaid by the manufacturers moving on when the training period expired or firing all the trainees when they became eligible for regular wages.[12]

Out of this chaotic, hell-for-leather scramble for industrial payrolls evolved a more orderly and businesslike (but no less enthusiastic) state-sponsored and supervised campaign for new industry that actually had its beginnings in Mississippi. In 1936 Governor Hugh L. White introduced his Balance Agriculture with Industry (BAWI) plan, which was modeled on a successful experiment with industrial subsidization in his hometown of Columbia, Mississippi. The BAWI plan utilized mucipal bond financing to provide cheap (often free) tax-exempt buildings to incoming industries willing to commit to a stipulated payroll. At approximately the same time, Louisiana began a statewide tax-exemption scheme to lure new industries. This idea spread rapidly across the South, provoking criticism from economists as well as northern politicians and labor leaders who saw in these subsidies an organized effort to pirate away northern industry. The proliferation of such state-sponsored programs went hand in hand with the creation of state development agencies and divisions, and paralleled the emergence of the governor, the legislature, and the entire state bureaucracy as agents of industrial expansion. Quickly, the responsibility for industrial development trickled down to local governmental officials and civic leaders.[13]

These efforts made some headway, but they fell far short of breaking the hold of low-wage, labor-intensive industries on the South. The expanded subsidy and recruitment programs of the postdepression years aimed at making southern locations more alluring, but they did little to alter the old pattern of development because they appealed primarily to the same kinds of operations the South was already attracting—those concerned with cutting costs (whether labor, tax, or building costs) as much as possible. To these competitive industries a bond-financed building or a tax exemption could be the proverbial new lease on life for which they had been searching when they initially turned their gaze southward. The invigorated, expanded effort to sell the South was successful primarily with those industries already shopping for southern locations. At midcentury a survey of southern industry was still basically a look at the nation's oldest, least efficient, lowest-paying industries. In 1946 average wages in the South stood at 86 percent of the northeastern average, roughly where they had been 40 years earlier.[14]

The real key to the South's economic upturn came not from industrial development efforts but from external influences that helped to make the South attractive to more and better kinds of industry. The transformation of southern agriculture induced by the depression and the New Deal accelerated the crusade for industry and expanded the region's labor surplus. The key contribution, however, came from World War II, which not only drew more labor away from the farm and encouraged more rapid mechanization but delivered a massive injection of capital into the southern economy. Nearly 40 percent of total expenditures for military facilities originated in the South. Trainees flocked to these facilities, and their paychecks sent a shock wave through local economies. Approximately $5 billion went into war plants, and southern industrial capacity expanded by 40 percent. Government spending at all levels doubled during the war. When the war ended, the South, although by no means affluent, had a great deal more purchasing power than it had enjoyed since the Civil War. Per capita income tripled during the 1940s, and the urban population grew by 30 percent.[15]

Market-oriented industries were quick to take note of these developments. Both General Motors and Ford saw Atlanta as a likely market and distribution center. Supporting industries supplying tires, windshields, headlights, and batteries fanned out across the region. Elsewhere, responding to the rapid mechanization of agriculture, farm equipment companies such as International Harvester and Allis Chalmers opened new facilities in the South.[16]

The most impressive postwar growth story belonged to Florida, where climate and lifestyle combined to create not only a haven for retirees but an attractive location for first the aeronautics and then the aerospace industries. Such industries found that managerial and engineering personnel were easy to recruit for Florida operations. They also found the state's tourism-supported tax structure and respectably conservative political climate to their liking. Florida's growth accelerated consistently in the postwar period, proceeding so rapidly that it outpaced the combined growth of twenty-one northeastern and North Central states between 1970 and 1976.[17]

Another growth hot spot was Texas, whose growth statistics during the 1970s would have been the envy of many nations. Energy was the key to Texas's growth, exemplified in speed and rambunctiousness by Houston, which gained 79,000 jobs and 1,000 residents per week in 1979. In Georgia, the population of the counties around Atlanta doubled in the 1960s while employment grew by 120 percent. In the South Carolina Piedmont, Spartanburg became a mecca for foreign investment, much of it textile related. By the 1980s middle Tennessee's hills were on an industrial roll as General Motors chose Springhill for its Saturn plant, following the lead of Nissan, which had moved into Smyrna a few years earlier.[18]

To be sure, this progress brought a host of problems. Forida's supersonic growth induced numerous environmental headaches. Houston faced high crime, snarled traffic, and a seemingly endless stream of job-seeking Rust Belt refugees, dubbed "blue platers" by locals because so many seemed to have Michigan license plates. Downtown Atlanta offered both convention-hotel glitter and ghetto gloom. Plagued like other Sunbelt South metropolises with white flight, Atlanta's inner-city population declined more rapidly between 1970 and 1975 than did that of Newark or Detroit.[19]

Many Sunbelt South leaders shrugged off such growth-related problems or took a certain secret pride in them as signs of economic maturity, indications that the region was finally catching up with the North. The Sunbelt South's major problem was not too much growth, but too little. The region's economic success stories were still exceptions in a region that claimed well over 40 percent of the nation's poverty population. In 1984, for the first time, the Sunbelt South had three states (Virginia, Texas, and Florida) hovering around the national average per capita income, but there were still six (Tennessee, Kentucky, South Carolina, Alabama, Arkansas, and Mississippi) that had not reached 85 percent of that figure. All states in this latter group were more than $2,000 below the absolute dollar figure, and Mississippi was close to $4,000 below it.[20]

No southern state had worked more earnestly (and with so little success) to attract industry than Mississippi, which in 1936 had pioneered its BAWI program of state-sanctioned subsidies for industry. The Magnolia State was consistently listed in the top ten in business-climate rankings and was ready to take southern hospitality to new extremes where incoming industry was concerned. Yet more than any other southern state, Mississippi had a number of areas so impoverished that the worst industry they could have attracted would have seemed terrific. Tunica, with its infamous Sugar Ditch Alley, the nation's best-known small-town slum, was a classic example. Tunica County's claim to be the poorest in the nation rested on a 45 percent poverty rate and a per capita income that was barely two-thirds of the average in Mississippi, the nation's poorest state. Government payments accounted for 27 percent of personal income, nearly three-quarters of the population received food stamps, and the infant mortality rate would have embarrassed some Third World nations. With unemployment climbing toward 20 percent and out-migration held in check only by the county's immobilizing poverty, the reality of Tunica's plight mocked the sign on Highway 61 reading "Welcome to Tunica—It's a Good Place to Live—Industry, Recreation and Agriculture." Local residents agreed industry was the answer, but the county's prospects were virtually nonexistent.[21] Like many once predominantly plantation counties, Tunica challenged the assumption that mechanization of southern agriculture would lead directly to industrial growth and economic diversification as investors moved in to take advantage of an area's labor surplus.

Conditions in Tunica seemed in keeping with Mississippi's reputation as the most backward state in the nation, but it was North Carolina that provided the best example of the difficulty of making the break with the low-wage tradition so evident in the Sunbelt South's industrial base. The Tarheel State led the nation in the percentage of its work force employed in manufacturing, but North Carolina workers received the lowest manufacturing wage in the United States, on the average about $2.15 per hour below the national norm; and the state's poverty rate was also five points above the national figure. North Carolina's heritage of catering to the low-paying, nonunion textile industry encouraged its publicly funded development organizations to accept the paradoxical mission of promoting progress by discouraging high-wage industries, particularly those that might bring unions with them. For a time, the Raleigh Chamber of Commerce adhered to a rigid, written policy of non-recruitment of industries that would not promise to resist unionization. The fear of unions and the drag effect of a low-wage industrial base cost North Carolina workers dearly. In 1981, when the executive of a British elastic firm cut the ribbon to reopen an abandoned zipper plant at Jamesville, he boldly announced that "pay scales at the company will be commensurate at least with those of the region of the state." What this meant, in effect, was that wages would probably amount to two-thirds of the lowest state-average wage rates in the nation.[22]

North Carolina's failure to break with its low-wage heritage was particularly striking because it had pioneered in efforts to do just that. Adhering to a pattern common to less developed regions, the South pressed its academic community into service by promising research and technical assistance to incoming industry. Under the leadership of Governor Luther Hodges, North Carolina led the way with the opening of the Research Triangle Park, a facility linking the expertise of the state's three major universities to the needs of more sophisticated research-and-development firms or firm components. The Research Triangle quickly made the Raleigh-Durham-Chapel Hill area the envy of a high-tech–mad region. Efforts to duplicate the North Carolina program reflected a desire to attract more desirable, better-paying firms to the South as a means of upgrading its industrial mix. The same was true of the South Carolina–inspired start-up training programs, in which the state, by utilizing its vocational and technical teaching facilities and staff, would provide incoming industries with a trained work force at no expense to the company.[23]

The logic behind the research and vocational-technical training emphasis seemed sound: better industries mean a healthier, more diversified industrial base. That logic failed, however, to take into account the changing structure and direction of the national and world economies. In the post–World War II era, the South began to claim a greater share of the superstar industries that formerly appeared only in southern developers' wildest fantasies. By the time these industries turned southward, however, their position in the world and national economies was considerably less secure. With the rise of foreign competition and the loss of American dominion over crucial raw materials, the high-rolling firms that once seemed to laugh off the labor and tax costs and expensive and troublesome regulations and restrictions they faced in the North developed a sudden enthusiasm for the savings and extra support afforded by a southern location. They took advantage of local wage scales, paying well enough to attract workers but not well enough to spark a bidding war for labor that would boost wage rates in the area. Tax exemptions were a welcome plus, although they were less important than the low overall levels of taxation.[24]

A case in point was Boeing Aircraft's 1985 announcement that it was opening a major repair facility at Greenville, Mississippi, a prototypical, plantation-agriculture, high-unemployment, largely black area in the Mississippi Delta. Not the least of Greenville's attractions was an abandoned air force base that was to be refurbished with the aid of federal grant funds; but the pot was also sweetened with $5 million in general obligation bonds from Greenville and as much as $10 million from the state of Mississippi, which also committed itself to a $577,000 vocational training program to provide Boeing with a made-to-order work force. Careful estimates put the total commitment of public funds at $18 million, a healthy subsidy for a firm whose profits totaled $390 million in 1984. Boeing promised to create 645 jobs in Greenville, but a company spokesman admitted that at least 60 percent of its employees would start work at less than $6.66 per hour, a starting wage about $0.53 below the state average for manufacturing workers and $3.00 per hour below what the company paid at its Wichita, Kansas, facility.

Thirty years earlier, Boeing would have had as much interest in Mississippi—or any other southern state except Florida—as in Mozambique. At mid-century most of the South was still maneuvering to provide a soft landing for the competitive, labor-intensive operations spinning off the still-dynamic northern industrial economy. By the mid-1980s more of these firms were heading south, but many were no longer prize catches.

Competition had made these industries more cost conscious, and the interstate scramble for the newly mobile big name industries made it a buyer's market where locations were concerned. "If you don't step up to the plate with a good financial package, the thing will pass you by," said a Greenville developer attempting to explain his community's generosity to Boeing. Elsewhere, Tennessee officials bragged that their state's educational progress had been the key to landing the much discussed and widely wooed General Motors Saturn facility, but the price tag for construction, training, and tax concessions ran to hundreds of millions of dollars. The story of Toyota's move to Georgetown, Kentucky was much the same.[25]

The increased mobility and competitiveness of desirable industries helped to alter the economic relationship between the North and the South. Historically a number of observers, both southern and nonsouthern, have cited freight-rate discrimination and other deliberate efforts at exploitation as reasons for the disappointing pace of southern industrial progress. Certainly the South's subordination to the North and its treatment by absentee northern investors were often disadvantageous, but the South's hopes for industrialization depended ultimately on external investment. To those who advocated industrialization, the South's position as an industrial colony of the North was preferable to its being an impoverished agrarian one.[26] So long as northern industrial growth was rapid, southern efforts to entice away laggard industry seemed more amusing than annoying.

By the middle of the twentieth century, however, industrial migration was no longer a joke to political and labor leaders in "manufacturing belt" states. These leaders first attacked and then adopted the various subsidy schemes employed by the South, and a war between the states for industry began in earnest. What started as an effort to curtail the use of municipal bonds to finance new industry became a multifront struggle that eventually involved the distribution of federal monies through a wide variety of programs. Losing industries and people to the South, a troubled North fought back through a number of agencies, including the New England Congressional Caucus. Meanwhile, the Southern Growth Policies Board, originally created to promote planning and intraregional cooperation, became the propaganda organ for the neo-Confederate industrial development effort. This battle also raged at the state and local levels as once economically secure northern and midwestern industrial states embraced a host of southern-style gimmicks and giveaways. Illinois, for example, surrendered $1 billion in tax revenue over a five-year period to allow industries accelerated depreciation write-offs.[27]

Stung by low business climate rankings, northern political leaders leaned on union officials to be more reasonable in their wage and benefit demands, thereby reducing somewhat the attraction of the South's nonunion work force. By the 1980s the old manufacturing belt relied on the same kinds of policies and tactics to hold on to industry that its leaders had once criticized the South for using to attract industry. In a dramatically altered economic context, what had once seemed desperate and insane became pragmatic and necessary. By the Sunbelt era, the South was far more attractive to industry than it had been a century earlier, but it was also facing a North unwilling to surrender even its most marginal industries.[28]

The term *deindustrialization* may conjure up visions of grimy northern towns with silent, locked factories, but the old manufacturing belt was not the only region that was deindustrializing. The villain was foreign competition—cheaper imports coming in from abroad and cheaper labor available in Third World countries. With the nation's trade deficit expected to reach $140 billion in 1985, with each $1 billion of that deficit costing about twenty-five thousand jobs, and with the South's economy laden with deficit-affected industries such as textiles and apparel, deindustrialization promised to be a continuing problem on both sides of the Mason-Dixon line. In 1982 an Alabama development official complained that "industrial jobs are going out the back door faster than we can get them in the front door."[29]

In 1978 Jonathan Logan employed 2,500 workers at its plant in Spartanburg, South Carolina, but the entire operation was shut down by the end of 1985. The story repeated itself again and again across the Piedmont textile belt as the industry cut more than 300,000 jobs between 1979 and 1985. In June and July of 1984 alone, the textile industry lost 9,100 jobs. North Carolina was the biggest loser, absorbing 3,500 job cuts, but the other southern states also took a beating. Jefferson County, Tennessee, was once home to six hundred garment shops but by 1985 could claim only one. With the textile industry running a $16 billion trade deficit in 1984, one dismayed North Carolina textile management executive predicted, "There won't be any textile labor in the U.S. by the year 2000 except for maybe novelty and specialty goods." There was a cruel irony in the fact that the industrial recruitment efforts of the

Sunbelt South had benefited from the rise of foreign competition in such industries as automobiles and electronics, but long before the region had its fill of footloose manufacturers, industrial mobility began to cut both ways. Complaints about industry moving to the Third World recalled similar laments a generation or two before about the migration of low-wage industries from the North to the South. After decades of such protests from Massachusetts, it was peculiar indeed to hear a Mississippi legislator suggest that turnabout was unfair play and cite competition with cheap foreign labor as "an abuse of the free enterprise system."[30]

For garment industry executives, the South had become a high-wage region in comparison to China, where apparel workers earned sixteen cents an hour; even Hong Kong's one-dollar hourly wage compared favorably to the five-dollar-per-hour rates in the South. Having found a competitor whose labor costs they could not underbid, developers in states like Mississippi could only assure industrialists eyeing Asian locations that catfish tastes better than squid.

There were further intriguing parallels in Third World, resource-poor nations like Hong Kong, Singapore, and South Korea, where cheap and disciplined labor were the primary assets. Like southern state governments in the early twentieth century, the South Korean government assumed responsibility for economic modernization, severely restricted labor's political influence, and prohibited strikes. As in the South, the apparel industry was attracted to Korea by a large pool of young women who were hard working, dexterous, and docile. South Korea took Japan as a model, much as the South did the North. The only slight consolation for the South was a final ironic Third World parallel: even as they pursued Japanese business, South Korean officials were already worried about competition from the cheaper labor markets of China, Thailand, and Sri Lanka.[31]

With the Sunbelt South losing some of its bread-and-butter industries, the likelihood of achieving the kind of prosperity foreseen by Henry Grady was greatly diminished. Moreover, the region had yet to transform itself into the more dynamic and progressive society that appeared to exist in the industrial North.

One structural characteristic accounting for the nature of the Sunbelt South's industrial growth was the dispersal of its manufacturing plants in small-town and rural locations. In the late nineteenth and early twentieth centuries, textile manufacturers built mill villages adjacent to small and medium-sized towns in locations with water power and an abundance of cheap white labor. With the introduction of electricity such operations could be even more widely dispersed to take advantage of a growing surplus of farm labor fed by mechanization and federal crop reduction subsidies. In 1969 nearly 40 percent of the South's manufacturing plants were in rural or small-town areas. By 1980 the percentage of the work force employed in manufacturing was 30 points higher in the rural South than in the nation as a whole.[32]

This ongoing pattern of nonmetropolitan manufacturing growth had several significant implications. First, it helped to explain low levels of union membership and labor unrest. Historically, industrialization that has failed to uproot the work force has allowed workers to retain their ties to the land and has instilled less class consciousness than has the concentration of industry in large cities. A great many southern industrial workers were able to remain on the farm, and many of them continued to farm part time to qualify for government crop reduction payments. With a number of workers commuting to jobs some distance away, there was less disruption of lifestyle and family ties than had been wrought by industrialization in the North and elsewhere. Not only was it more difficult for union organizers to reach small, dispersed southern plants, but once they arrived, it was a tough assignment to convince industrial workers to see themselves as such. If organizers did get the attention of small-town workers, they were subject to harassment by the media and local officials, who were in a position to rally the entire community against the outsiders. In New Albany, Mississippi, for example, the high school football team was pressed into service to hand out photographs of racially mixed union gatherings in order to thwart an organizing drive at a local furniture plant.[33]

Rural industrialization also reflected the region's historical dependence on low-wage, labor-intensive, slow-growing firms. To give but one example of a region-wide phenomenon, in the mid-1970s more than half of Georgia's manufacturing jobs were in industries like textiles, apparel, and food processing. In the 1980s, 62 percent of North Carolina's manufacturing jobs were defined as low wage. With such a concentration of labor-intensive operations, it is small wonder that the rural South's emergence as the nation's most industrialized subregion did little to threaten its long-standing status as the nation's poorest. The prospects for altering this status grew dimmer rather than brighter as job growth in the manufacturing sector slowed and the Sunbelt South grew increasingly dependent on service-sector jobs concentrated in metropolitan areas. During the first half of the 1980s, service jobs accounted for more than one-third or the region's total growth. Nearly 90 percent of this expansion was concentrated in Texas, Florida, and eleven metropolitan areas scattered across the South.

This growth imbalance, and the increased dependence on service-sector employment carry ominous overtones. Many service industry jobs are confined to low- or minimum-wage levels, yet with 90 percent of new jobs for the next decade projected to fall into this category, for southern workers they are figuratively the only game, and quite literally, in town.[34] The result may be a massive influx of job seekers that overwhelms service-dependent metropolitan economies and the educational and social welfare infrastructures they are struggling to support.

As a modern industrial society, the Sunbelt South has been a conservative capitalist's dream come true and a liberal social scientist's nightmare. In a 1984 Alexander Grant business climate survey, the thirteen Sunbelt South states attained an average ranking of 12.5, with seven of them in the top 13 states and all in the top 24. Although the importance of such rankings is in dispute, they do appear to correlate significantly with manufacturing growth. The Sunbelt South challenged the traditional liberal linkage between economic progress and the growth of a socially conscious support and service society. The list of qualities that made the region the apple of the industrialists' eye is by and large a litany of what generations of liberal observers had seen as examples of southern backwardness. The South's good business climate rested on a foundation of markedly lower wages, taxes, teacher salaries, and unemployment compensation. Surveys showed that the "worker climate" was inversely related to the business climate in the region. Despite a high poverty rate, the southern states spent considerably less on welfare than the rest of the country, and their lawmakers exhibited no particularly inspiring commitment to protecting the South's relatively unspoiled environment.[35]

Its impressive growth statistics notwithstanding, the Sunbelt South also rested securely at the bottom of educational achievement rankings. One of the most disappointing aspects of the paradox of industrial advance and apparent societal stagnation was the failure of industrialization to spur massive, sustained improvements in the South's educational system. Only vocational education had clearly prospered at the hands of industrialization and the industrialization crusade.

Some surveys indicated a generally negative relationship between education spending and manufacturing growth. These statistics were particularly disappointing because the need for improving public schools as a means of accelerating industrial expansion had long been the stock-in-trade of progressive politicians and liberal journalists in the South. This was a thorny issue because, as the debate over Mississippi's much-publicized education reform program showed, critics of higher spending for education could also cite it as a deterrent to industrial expansion. Here again, the matter of historical timing was crucial. Skilled industries, which the South once attracted in relatively small numbers, are most concerned with workers' educational levels. Other firms care more about worker endurance and dependability in less intellectually demanding jobs. As the South at last began to attract more sophisticated industries, movements toward increased spending on education were undermined by technological advances that resulted in the increased routinization of industrial work and thus decreased the need for highly trained or educated workers. In fact, one industrial location expert recently speculated that "firms may consciously locate and expand in areas with fewer educated and skilled workers because they will perform simple tasks with less resistance."[36]

Still dazzled by the glitter of high-tech firms, southern development leaders overlooked the low-wage, low-skill orientation of many high-tech plants. The official of one such firm described his production operation as "just like a poultry plant . . . you pay them as little as you can, give them a benefits package that's competitive in the community, and you hope [that workers do not join a union]."[37]

Just as changing economic and structural factors made certain types of industry less interested in public education, increased mobility allowed some firms to minimize their obligation to the communities in which they operated. The conservative political and social climate of the late 1970s and 1980s also encouraged industrial leaders to return to the cherished doctrine of laissez-faire. As civil rights, women's rights, and antipoverty and environmental movements began to wane, American industry relaxed its social welfare commitment and embraced the trickle-down theory that corporate earnings were the best medicine for any ailing society.

Certainly incoming industries accepted little responsibility for providing jobs for blacks. (Boeing's move into the Mississippi Delta, where the majority of the population was black, would have been an astounding exception had it not been underwritten by such a lavish subsidy.) One study showed that between 1977 and 1982, employment grew twice as fast in counties where blacks made up less than 25 percent of the population than it did in counties that were more than 50 percent black.

An industrial development specialist indicated in 1983 that "very few prospects would even look at" certain areas of Mississippi with large black populations. A recent case involving Amoco Fabrics Company's search for a southern plant location revealed that the company had an unwritten policy of avoiding areas where the population was as much as one-third black. Efforts to bring industry into the heavily black and impoverished northeastern counties of North Carolina met with a similar response. Industrialists admitted concerns about the trainability of black workers and their allegedly greater susceptibility to unionization. Another largely unspoken concern was the fear of black political takeover, which could lead to higher corporate taxes as a means of financing expanded services for the poor.[38]

Although policymakers cannot afford to ignore hard-core underdeveloped areas, they also must focus their attention on regions hit by layoffs and plant closings. One of the remarkable aspects of the Sunbelt South has been its ability to avoid the social and political upheaval that has accompanied industrialization elsewhere. In fact, its overall stability was a decided plus in industrial recruitment. The slow growth of southern industry and its dispersed locational pattern combined with the region's racial heritage to facilitate this relatively stable agrarian-industrial transition; but an apparent link between textile layoffs and the Ku Klux Klan resurgence in North Carolina, and the growing restiveness of residents of other deindustrializing areas, suggest that the South might not surrender its industry as quietly.[39]

In addition to trying to resuscitate local economies in the South, and to ignite dormant economies elsewhere, industrial development and political leaders face an even bigger challenge, one largely unmet in more than a century of vigorous campaigning for industry. That challenge, to paraphrase Big Jim Folsom, is to "put the big mules in harness" by making industrial development provide better payoffs in terms of wages, benefits, and tax revenues. Any one of these assignments would be a tall order. Taken together they are monumental, especially in an era in which industry is more inclined to go wherever it wants and, increasingly, to do as it pleases when it gets there.

If the prospect of dealing with the multitude of problems that come with progress southern-style is horrifying to policymakers, the complexity of these problems — their origins, persistence, and interrelatedness — is certain to occupy scholars for some time to come. The strengths and weaknesses of the South as an industrial region are rooted in a regional past whose economic implications remain little understood. Much work has examined the impact of slavery, the Civil War, and emancipation on the southern economy. We need now to look at the events stretching from the boll weevil onslaught of the World War I era through the Great Depression, the New Deal, and the Second World War. This was the turning period when the South began its move into an economic mainstream that was itself already undergoing transformation.[40]

It is now more apparent than ever that C. Vann Woodward was correct when he observed in 1952 that given its experience with poverty, tragedy, and defeat, the South was a more globally relevant society than the North. Granted, the Third World analogy can become strained. As a conveniently situated neighbor, the South benefited far more from its colonial relationship with the northern industrial core than did any other region of the world. The U.S. government was more of a sugar daddy to the South than to any other region, and it tied more reform strings to its aid programs in the South than anywhere else. Still, the predominant pattern in the South and elsewhere was to dispense this aid through the established power structure rather than provide consistent support for potentially destabilizing programs and activities at the grass-roots level. Another common phenomenon in less-developed regions was the mobilization of government as the sponsor of industrial development and the agent of labor control. The South was by no means unique in that some of its intellectuals served as propagandists for modernization whereas others steadfastly opposed it. The Nashville Agrarians encounter with the Chapel Hill Regionalists was replayed in a number of societies struggling to reconcile their cultural identities with the westernization of their economies.[41]

The comparative approach promises significant new perspectives on the unique experience of the Sunbelt South. It also promises to move the region out of the shadow of the North. Much of the attention directed at the South has set up the North as a model liberal, capitalist, industrial society. Persistent conservative agrarian influences are then blamed for the South's failure to follow the classic capitalist path blazed by the states above the Mason-Dixon line.[42] In the 1980s, however, it became clear that the North's reputation as a model industrial society, while of long standing, was nonetheless vulnerable to the same technological, resource, market, and productivity factors that had shaped the industrial South.

As the northern states began to face some of the economic problems that had tormented the South for nearly a century, costly social programs, government regulation, vigorous taxation, and labor-management neutrality began to fade from the northern political agenda. This ironic turn of events challenged the premise advanced by generations of liberal social scientists that the key to northern-style prosperity is a northern-style social and political climate. Insofar as the social and political climate of the South has played a role in its economic fortunes, the conservatism of that climate and its contrast to the North appear to have accelerated rather than impeded southern industrialization.

By rethinking the economic odysseys of the North and South and taking into account their relationship and their changing roles in the national and world economies, scholars may be able to revise some crucial notions, not only about those societies but about the economic system that pulled them first in different, and then in similar, directions. Such a rethinking can have important implications for regional and national economic planning, and also for a foreign policy that often simply assumes industrial capitalism can cure what ails any underdeveloped nation. To leaders of these nations, the experience of the Sunbelt South suggests that they approach industrial development with caution, lest by expecting too much they wind up demanding too little of it.

Notes

1. Bureau of the Census, *County and City Data Book* (Washington, D.C.: U.S. Government Printing Office, 1983), lvii.
2. Charles P. Roland, "The South, America's Will-o'-the-Wisp Eden," *Louisiana History* 11 (Spring 1970): 101–19.
3. James C. Cobb, *Industrialization and Southern Society, 1877–1984* (Lexington: Univ. Press of Kentucky, 1984), 5–10; Edward Pessen, "How Different from Each Other Were the Antebellum North and South?" *American Historical Review* 85 (Dec. 1980): 1126; Fred Bateman and Thomas Weiss, *A Deplorable Scarcity: The Failure of Industrialization in the Slave Economy* (Chapel Hill: Univ. of North Carolina Press, 1981), 163.
4. Cobb, *Industrialization and Southern Society,* 10–11. For an in-depth study of the South's economy, see Gavin Wright, *The Political Economy of the Cotton South: Households, Markets, and Wealth in the Nineteenth Century* (New York: Norton, 1978).
5. Cobb, *Industrialization and Southern Society,* 11–14; Paul M. Gaston, *The New South Creed: A Study in Southern Mythmaking* (New York: Knopf, 1970), 68–90.
6. William N. Parker, "The South in the National Economy, 1865–1970," *Southern Economic Journal* 46 (Apr. 1980): 1019–48; David R. Goldfield, *Cotton Fields and Skyscrapers: Southern City and Region, 1607–1980* (Baton Rouge: Louisiana State Univ. Press, 1982), 86–88.

7. C. Vann Woodward, *Origins of the New South, 1877–1913* (Baton Rouge: Louisiana State Univ. Press, 1951), 118; "The New South Fraud Is Papered by Old South Myth," *Washington Post*, 9 July 1961.

8. Cobb, *Industrialization and Southern Society*, 14–26.

9. Parker, "The South in the National Economy," 1045; Dewey W. Grantham, *Southern Progressivism: The Reconciliation of Progress and Tradition* (Knoxville: Univ. of Tennessee Press, 1983), 258; Reinhard Bendix, "Tradition and Modernity Reconsidered," *Comparative Studies in History and Society* 9 (1967): 334; George B. Tindall, "Business Progressivism: Southern Politics in the Twenties," *South Atlantic Quarterly* 62 (Winter 1963): 92–106.

10. Numan V. Bartley, *The Creation of Modern Georgia* (Athens: Univ. of Georgia Press, 1983), 170; Pete Daniel, "The Transformation of the Rural South, 1930 to the Present," *Agricultural History* 55 (July 1981): 231–48; Jack Temple Kirby, "The Transformation of Southern Plantations, c. 1920–1960," *Agricultural History* 57 (July 1983): 257–76.

11. Cobb, *Industrialization and Southern Society*, 34–37.

12. James C. Cobb, *The Selling of the South: The Southern Crusade for Industrial Development, 1936–1980* (Baton Rouge: Louisiana State Univ. Press, 1982), 5–8.

13. Ibid., 8–95.

14. Joseph Black, "Regional Wage Differentials, 1907–1946," *Monthly Labor Review* 66 (Apr. 1948): 375.

15. Cobb, *Industrialization and Southern Society*, 51–52; Morton Sosna, "More Important Than the Civil War: The Social Impact of World War II on the South" (Paper presented at the annual meeting of the Southern Historical Association, Memphis, Nov. 1982).

16. Glenn E. McLaughlin and Stefan Roback, *Why Industry Moves South: A Study of Factors Influencing the Recent Location of Manufacturing Plants in the South* (Kingsport, Tenn.: Kingsport Press, 1949), 35–36, 39–40, 42, 45.

17. Cobb, *The Selling of the South*, 179–81; Gurney Breckenfield, "Business Loves the Sunbelt (and Vice Versa)," *Fortune* 95 (June 1977): 133.

18. Cobb, *The Selling of the South*, 192; Bartley, *Modern Georgia*, 203; *New York Times*, 20 January 1977; Barry Bluestone and Bennett Harrison, *The Deindustrialization of America: Plant Closings, Community Abandonment, and the Dismantling of Basic Industry* (New York: Basic Books, 1982), 83; *Jackson Clarion-Ledger*, 12 Aug. 1985.

19. Bartley, *Modern Georgia*, 203; Goldfield, *Cotton Fields*, 193; Bluestone and Harrison, *Deindustrialization*, 86.

20. U.S. Department of Commerce, Bureau of Economic Analysis, "1984 State Per Capita Personal Income," 7 May 1985, typescript in possession of the author.

21. *Jackson Clarion-Ledger*, 15 Sept. 1985.

22. Jerry Hagstrom and Robert Guskind, "Playing the State Ranking Game— A New National Pastime Catches On," *National Journal* 16 (6 June 1984): 1270–73; Paul Luebke, Bob McMahon, and Jeff Risberg, "Selective Recruitment in North Carolina," *Working Papers for a New Society* 6 (Mar.–Apr.

1979): 17–19; Donna Dyer and Frank Adams, "The Lost Colony of North Carolina," *Southern Changes* 4 (June-July 1982): 7–8.

23. Cobb, *The Selling of the South*, 163–78.

24. John Hekman and Alan Smith, "Behind the Sunbelt's Growth: Industrial Decentralization," *Economic Review* (Federal Reserve Bank of Atlanta) 67 (Mar. 1982): 6–7; James S. Fisher and Dean M. Hanink, "Business Climate: Behind the Geographic Shift of American Manufacturing," *Economic Review* (Federal Reserve Bank of Atlanta) 67 (June 1982): 29–30. For a brief discussion of major industries accepting tax exemptions see Cobb, *The Selling of the South*, 49–50.

25. *Jackson Clarion-Ledger*, 25 Aug. 1985; Carter Garber et al., "Greasing GM's Wheels," *Southern Exposure* 14 (Sept./Oct.–Nov./Dec. 1986): 46; *Atlanta Journal and Constitution*, 5 October 1986.

26. Joe Persky, "The South: A Colony at Home," *Southern Exposure* 1 (Summer-Fall 1973): 14–22.

27. Cobb, *The Selling of the South*, 193–208; Tina Rosenberg, "States at War: Going Broke on Tax Breaks," *New Republic* 189 (3 Oct. 1983): 20.

28. Alfred J. Watkins, "Good Business Climates: The Second War between the States," *Dissent* 27 (Fall 1980): 476–85.

29. Donald H. Trautlein, "Where Have All the Factories Gone?" *Industry Week* 226 (19 Aug. 1985): 28; "When the Bubble Burst in Alabama," *U.S. News and World Report* 92 (19 Apr. 1982): 104.

30. "Textile Industry Faces Struggle for Survival," *Southern Exposure* 13 (Feb. 1985): 4; *USA Today*, 9 Sept. 1985.

31. James A. Caporaso, "The State's Role in Third World Economic Growth," *Annals of the American Academy of Political and Social Science* 459 (Jan. 1982): 103–11.

32. Richard E. Lonsdale and Clyde E. Browning, "Rural-Urban Locational Preferences of Southern Manufacturers," *Annals of the Association of American Geographers* 61 (June 1971): 262; Hekman and Smith, "Behind the Sunbelt's Growth," 8; *Virginian Pilot and Ledger-Star* (Norfolk), 14 July 1987.

33. Reinhard Bendix, "Tradition and Modernity Reconsidered," 341; F. Ray Marshall, *Labor in the South* (Cambridge, Mass.: Harvard Univ. Press, 1967), 314–18; Arthur G. McDowell to Roy Wilkins, 8 Jan. 1965, Congress of Racial Equality Papers, Addendum, 1944–1968, Microfilm, Series III, Reel 23, Library of Congress.

34. James S. Fisher, "Manufacturing Additions in Georgia: Metropolitan-Nonmetropolitan Differences from 1961 to 1975," *Growth and Change* 10 (Apr. 1979): 11; *Virginian Pilot and Ledger-Star* (Norfolk), 14 July 1987.

35. Hagstrom and Guskind, "Playing the State Ranking Game," 1270–73; Kenneth Johnson and Marylin Scurlock, "The Climate for Workers," *Southern Exposure* 14 (Sept./Oct.–Nov./Dec. 1986): 24–27.

36. Mississippi's Governor Bill Allain warned, "We're defeating the purpose of saying we must have a good education system to get good jobs when the funding method for the education is against the very jobs we need the education to fill." Oxford (Miss.) *Eagle*, 29 Mar. 1985; Thomas R. Plant

and Joseph E. Pluta, "Business Climate, Taxes and Expenditures, and State Industrial Growth in the United States," *Southern Economic Journal* 50 (July 1983): 113.

37. Marc Miller, "The Lowdown on High Tech," *Southern Exposure* 14 (Sept./Oct.–Nov./Dec. 1986): 36.

38. *New York Times*, 15 Feb. 1983; Dyer and Adams, "The Lost Colony," 7; Stuart A. Rosenfeld and Edward M. Bergman, *After the Factories: Changing Employment Patterns in the Rural South* (Research Triangle Park, N.C.: Southern Growth Policies Board), 27.

39. Memo, Bob Hall to NCEC and Interested Parties Re: Attached Charts and Maps on 1984 North Carolina Registration and Turnout, 1 June 1985, in possession of the author.

40. Parker, "The South in the National Economy," 1045–46; Numan V. Bartley, "The Era of the New Deal as a Turning Point in Southern History," in James C. Cobb and Michael V. Namorato, eds., *The New Deal and the South* (Jackson: Univ. Press of Mississippi, 1984), 135–46.

41. C. Vann Woodward, "The Irony of Southern History," in Woodward, ed., *The Burden of Southern History*, rev. ed., (Baton Rouge: Louisiana State Univ. Press, 1970), 187–212. See also Mary Matossian, "Ideologies of Delayed Industrialization," in Jason L. Finkle and Richard W. Gable, eds., *Political Development and Social Change*, 2nd ed. (New York: Wiley, 1971), 115.

42. See, for example, Jonathan M. Wiener, "Class Structure and Economic Development in the American South," *American Historical Review* 84 (Oct. 1979): 970–93. This literature is synthesized in Cobb, *Industrialization and Southern Society*, 143–64.

4   The Origins of the Sunbelt-Frostbelt Struggle
Defense Spending and City Building
Roger W. Lotchin

Introduction

The idea of the Sunbelt emerged suddenly onto the American scene in the 1970s. Despite the widespread use of the term *Sunbelt*, analysts and pundits were unable to reach a consensus about the economic and political shifts underlying the concept. Politicians blamed the phenomenon on discriminatory federal spending policies that redistributed the wealth of the northeastern, New England, and Middle Atlantic states to the South and West. Economists had a different set of answers, centering on such matters as energy prices, cheap labor, open spaces, truck and highway transportation, changing manufacturing processes, branch plant movements, interstate migration patterns, cheap land, climatic advantages, and rising farm prices. Commentators on the Left stressed the significance of good climates for investment and business, by which they meant weak labor unions and right-to-work laws. Others cited western and southern amenities; but almost everyone emphasized defense spending.

Besides their agreement on the military factors responsible in part for the Sunbelt, most commentators agreed that the phenomenon had emerged in the early 1970s. These analysts also shared the view that political influence had something to do with the shift and that representatives from the South and West had somehow garnered enough of it to help effect a historic regional alteration in American cultural patterns. This movement had produced an economic realignment from a developed to an underdeveloped region, or to two regions, each of which had long considered itself a colonial appendage of the North.[1]

Until the rise of the Sunbelt, no American region had ever been displaced in the hierarchy of American economic power. The East had been forced eventually to share some of its power with the Midwest, but overall it still held sway until the Second World War. The shift to the South and West, and its military underpinning, was thus a matter of

47

historical importance. If government expenditures were crucial in creating the Sunbelt, and if military spending has been the key to federal discrimination in favor of that region, then the event is all the more singular. No American region heretofore has been so dependent on military patronage.

Therefore the Sunbelt phenomenon, or the shift of power and wealth to the South and West, certainly has deserved all the attention it has received since about 1973. Yet explanations of this power shift leave something to be desired. Historians will suspect that such a fundamental alteration of the balance of power could not have taken place in such a short time without more long-range warning, indications of decline, or public controversy. Was there no warning of the outbreak of the "second war between the states" before the early seventies? Even more intriguing, how did the underlying process of military redistribution work? When and under what circumstances did this political coup take place? Did the West openly court the military, and did the East avoid this connection? Did only the Sunbelt states recognize the immense potential of defense spending for development? Did eastern centers like Detroit, Chicago, and Boston fail to note the huge defense contracts generated by the Second World War and again by the Korean conflict? Did the more liberal regions of the country simply shun the development and employment potential of defense spending? Or were the more populous regions of the United States, stretching along the industrial belt from New England to the Mississippi River, simply outmuscled by the South and West? Alternatively, were they outwitted, perhaps because they were caught napping or were distracted into other areas of political gain? If defense spending is indeed a crucial factor in the power shift to the South and West, these are important questions not answered satisfactorily in the literature on the Sunbelt. Perhaps a historical perspective can begin to address some of these queries.[2]

This investigation into the Sunbelt in general has already been initiated in a number of books, notably *Sunbelt Cities*, edited by Richard M. Bernard and Bradley R. Rice, and Carl Abbott's *The New Urban America*.[3] More particularly, Bernard and Rice and their contributors have documented the long-standing interest of western and southern cities in defense spending. San Diego, as a case in point, is discussed in *Sunbelt Cities* and in more detail in my own research; similarly for the San Francisco Bay and Los Angeles areas. From the 1907-1909 voyage of Theodore Roosevelt's Great White Fleet until the mid-1950s, these metropolitan regions competed vigorously for shares of the federal defense budget.[4] When half the American fleet was sent to the Pacific in 1919, each city struggled to become the fleet's home port, to acquire a great new naval base, or to get some portion of the defense installations and expenditures for their own areas. When World War I created new army and navy installations, these became an added source of gain for California cities. San Diego and Los Angeles also sought to acquire aircraft manufacturing firms, which were heavily dependent on military contracts from this early period. Moreover, some California universities began to abet this drive through campaigns of their own.[5]

When World War II broke out, the competitors fought for federal offices, defense highway spending, port-of-embarkation status, contracts of every size, and representation on the federal boards and panels that dispensed these assets. Each party sought to curry favor with the armed services by continually praising the military and by identifying their own cities with various service branches. They achieved this feat by advertising their defense production records and even by persuading the navy to name ships after particular towns. Los Angeles went further still, getting permission to hold special war bond referenda to finance the construction of five U.S. Navy ships, including the flagship of the Southland fleet, the cruiser *Los Angeles*. California cities continued these activities after the war ended.[6]

So did non-Sunbelt cities. Although these efforts are not pilloried in the literature on the maldistribution of military wealth, representatives of eastern and midwestern cities and states were neither morally superior to the contest for martial riches nor asleeep at the switch when the gravy train passed their stations. They too competed vigorously for defense contracts, defended their military bases with commendable enthusiasm, and remained wary of any Congressional legislation that might put them at a disadvantage in this struggle. In fact, the East and Midwest had never been unaware of the need for vigilance in this area or the potential to be gained from defense spending. As early as 1939, Chicago spokesmen had questioned the equity and strategic necessity of aircraft contract distribution. During the war the East and Midwest fought against industrial decentralization. In the name of defense, the South and West tried to deconcentrate the country's industries, supposedly to make them less vulnerable to Nazi attack. In truth, however, they were more interested in making themselves less susceptible to colonial control from the eastern power centers. The Frostbelt fought back just as forcefully; indeed, throughout the war the controversy over the urban geographic distribution of military spending continued to rend the fabric of national unity.[7]

So not only did the South and West gain military installations and contracts from the 1930s on, they also engaged in a sectional struggle for these assets with the older power centers of the country. This competition dates at least from 1939 and continued in some form or other through the 1950s.[8] The conflict was overt, explicit, and bitter; the contestants even employed many of the same charges and terms that surfaced in the Sunbelt debate of the 1970s and 1980s. This essay focuses on two case studies of this competition, one centering on industrial dispersal to protect against nuclear or thermonuclear attack, and the other concerned with federal government manpower policies. These are by no means definitive or even relatively complete studies of the controversy, but they can at least uncover some of the circumstances, timing, and origins of the later struggle and perhaps reveal some unexpected participants as well.

Industrial Decentralization

Industrial decentralization or dispersal became a reality before World War II. The American military concluded that the defense industries were too highly centralized in a few vulnerable places, especially along the coasts. For example, airframe production centered in Seattle, San Diego, and Los Angeles on the West Coast and suburban Long Island and Baltimore on the East Coast. A few enemy strikes could cripple much of this vital defense industry. Even before Pearl Harbor, which did nothing to lessen this anxiety, the government had moved to disperse the industry throughout the interior of the United States. Decentralization might lessen manpower shortages and would distribute defense contracts to previously unblessed cities. The coastal builders received large orders initially, but once they had reached capacity, the government built its new plants at places like Wichita, Dallas, Fort Worth, St. Louis, Kansas City, and Tulsa. This change did not hurt the coastal construction firms, since they usually built the inland branch plants. However, it did adversely affect the aircraft metropolises and threatened to establish new centers of production that would remain competitive in the postwar years. In the short run, this fear proved groundless. When World War II ended, the government did not have enough money to keep even the parent plants operating, much less the branch plants in places like Tulsa.[9] However, the advent of the Cold War and the development of nuclear and thermonuclear weaponry greatly enhanced the vulnerability of the industry. Once again, the government moved to reduce that threat. This move touched off a seven-year controversy that pitted the urban South and West, minus California and Washington, against cities in the Midwest and Northeast.

Both nuclear weapons and jet technology were prestigious products of California cities, which were certainly aware of the technologies' destructive potential. In 1946 a group of Los Alamos scientists presented Los Angeles Mayor Fletcher Bowron with a sample of sand fused together by the initial atomic test in New Mexico. Charged as he was with maintaining urban employment and protecting the citizens of his city, Mayor Bowron must have found this artifact of modern technology somewhat confusing. So did the federal authorities. If they seriously attempted to secure the country against nuclear and jet technologies, it would mean dismantling some of the concentrated Northeast and Pacific Coast military industries. On the other hand, emphasizing the economic side of defense, i.e., production, meant even more concentration.

Before civilian Washington could choose one of these alternatives, the air force touched off the battle. In 1948, it pressured Boeing into producing the B-36 bomber at a World War II Wichita plant rather than in the highly vulnerable Seattle area. Similar demands led to the migration of Chance-Vought from Connecticut to Dallas, the relocation of Consolidated Aircraft's B-36 production from San Diego to Fort Worth, the construction of General Electric's turbojet engine plant in Kansas City, and the "contemplated move to Lockheed Aircraft from Burbank, California, to Tulsa."[10] These real or threatened blows to the established defense centers forced them to protect themselves.

Puget Sound led the martial cities in defending against the policies of their own government. In 1949 Seattle interests, including the chamber of commerce and city hall, hit on the idea of dispersing military contracts *within metropolitan areas* in order to avoid decentralizing them *between geographic areas.*[11] In the meantime, the federal government continued to worry about "defense in depth," or dispersal. At that moment, Washington, D.C., discovered the Seattle plan and was so impressed by it that it became the basis "for the national industrial dispersion policy." The administration naturally turned to Puget Sound because of its expertise on the matter and brought several Seattle boosters to the nation's capital to work for the National Security Resources Board, the government agency then responsible for the dispersal program. Ethan Allen

Peyser, Presley Lancaster, Jr., and Jack Gorrie set about writing the federal guidelines for dispersal. Not surprisingly, these rules protected Seattle's economic interests more than they promoted the defense of congested areas from nuclear attack.[12]

California did not lag far behind Seattle in producing its own plans for urban defense in depth. The Los Angeles Metropolitan Area Industrial Dispersion Committee helped industry to find "safe industrial sites within that area."[13] Like Los Angeles, San Francisco contributed another model dispersal plan. It was worked out jointly by the Bay Area Council, "an organization dedicated to the economic interests of the nine counties that open on San Francisco Bay," and the Stanford Research Institute.[14]

The federal guidelines announced on 10 August 1951 specified that new defense plants or expansions of old ones could not be located within ten miles of densely populated or highly industrialized areas.[15] However, the rules contained many escape clauses, and the federal government did not directly administer them. It influenced them through the power to withold contracts, allocate materials, and grant tax breaks; but each plant had to be certified by a local dispersion committee, formed for each metropolitan area. Not too surprisingly, the defense cities found this plan congenial, and fifty-two metropolitan areas had formed dispersion committees by the beginning of 1952. The proponents of the plan always insisted that it meant dispersal within metropolitan areas rather than a geographic redistribution of defense monies to other sections. Events proved them correct. Of the nearly $8 billion in new plant or plant expansion contracts given out in the next six months, most went to the existing defense centers, with a bit more allocated elsewhere. Yet even this modest dispersal proved too much for central cities, which resisted the loss of any more industry to their already growing suburbs.

The Korean War tended to reinforce rather than reduce the concentration of military production. Dispersal policies were always torn between immediate production goals and long-range defense goals. Since the war presented an emergency, government officials felt that they must meet the immediate mobilization needs of the conflict rather than the long-range goal of protecting the United States from nuclear attack. Therefore, most of the Korean defense work took place in the established industrial martial metropolises. Between the urban insiders who wrote the guidelines, the local dispersion committees that enforced them, and the war emergency, the historic defense centers did not suffer in the short run. Nonetheless, in the long run, the Rains debate did help to bring about significant decentralization, which unfolded over the course of the 1950s. However, the conflict also created problems for these cities, and for the government as well.[16]

As during World War II, areas that did not share fully in the military bonanza resented that fact. These places had suffered population losses in the war and did not want to repeat the experience in the Korean conflict. Their bitterness and determination not to lose out on this latest defense boom injected a note of acrid sectionalism into the war. On 11 July 1951, Congressman Albert Rains of Gadsden, Alabama, offered an amendment to the Defense Production Act of 1950, under which the government fought the war. The amendment would have required the military, in bestowing defense contracts, to take into account the need for industrial dispersal in order to defend the country from atomic attack. Rains took his cue from the Truman dispersal guidelines and from numerous critics who favored dispersal. The southern and western legislators in Rains's coalition reasoned that if a little dispersal was good, a lot was better. After all, the air force had assured the country that seven of ten enemy planes would reach their American targets, and that each atomic bomb would create a crater three miles across. Not unreasonably, spokesmen from the South and West argued that nothing short of geographic decentralization would protect American defense industries from such a first-strike disaster. It would also give southern and western cities a larger portion of the defense pie.[17]

Both the rhetoric and the geography of this struggle are reminiscent of the contemporary Sunbelt controversy. Cities in the South and West had developed later than those in other parts of the country and, with the exception of the urban areas of the West Coast, were not heavily industrialized. The have-not cities therefore viewed the new defense industry as a surrogate for the factories that had so far passed them by. The cities of the Northeast, Midwest, and Pacific Coast also viewed the matter largely in economic rather than military terms. Thus, despite their protestations about national defense, the congressional debate turned a question of warfare into one of welfare. Overnight the issue became one of urban development—that is, urbanization versus de-urbanization.[18]

The congressional debate broke down along several lines. Generally speaking, less industrialized areas opposed heavily industrialized ones: the South and West, minus California and Washington, struggled with the northeastern, midwestern, and Middle Atlantic states; and depressed areas sought the economic means of thriving areas. The have-nots lost the opening round. Southern and western congressmen led but did not stand united against the rival sections, and the amendment lost. Apparently many southerners and westerners preferred to see the contracts go to the established centers rather than to interrupt defense production.[19]

At the conclusion of the Rains debate, the president acted. Perhaps to forestall further Congressional legislation and to placate what his successor would call the "military-industrial complex," Truman issued his own dispersal policy on 18 August 1951. This policy effectively protected the interests of the defense cities. It also carefully dissociated the administration's own formula from the more radical idea of industrial geographic decentralization. Truman's plan aimed at finding "dispersed sites around such existing industrial centers as Detroit, New York, Pittsburgh, and San Francisco." Nonetheless, this compromise did not reduce the vulnerability of defense production centers, and administration concern continued.[20]

The increasing destructiveness and technological sophistication of new weapons heightened this anxiety. Jet planes were proven in the Korean War; the hydrogen bomb was tested by the United States and the Soviet Union in 1952 and 1953; and intercontinental rocketry was literally just over the horizon by the end of the Korean fighting. These developments forced the administration to confront the dispersal problem anew. An atomic bomb would create an urban crater three miles across; a hydrogen bomb, a crater ten miles across. These facts made the Truman ten-mile urban limit obsolete, just as future limits were likely to be exceeded with each advance of the arms race. The Eisenhower administration shared these concerns, as did a number of people outside the government, such as those associated with the *Bulletin of the Atomic Scientists*. When the Korean truce eliminated the need for heavy production in established defense centers, the stage was set for a reconsideration of dispersal policy.[21]

Since 1950 government officials had employed the lure of accelerated tax write-offs for new and expanded defense facilities in dispersed areas. In addition, Secretary of the Air Force Harold Talbott and President Eisenhower publicly advocated the need for greater air defense. So did Marshall K. Wood, the chief of mobilization planning. Predictably, this campaign caught the attention of vested defense interests, such as the Los Angeles Chamber of Commerce, which began a countercampaign of their own. Undeterred by this clamor, on 11 January 1956, the Office of Defense Mobilization issued guidelines accepting the principle of *geographic as opposed to metropolitan* dispersal. This urging was all the encouragement that the South and West needed to mount another assault on the "congestion" of the established defense cities.

J. William Fulbright, who later led the fight against the Vietnam War, also captained this attack on the martial metropolises. The Arkansas Senator and his allies sought to amend the 1950 Defense Production Act by putting Congress on record as favoring geographic dispersal. Supposedly, congressional support would strengthen the hand of the Office of Defense Mobilization in its attempt to implement the January guidelines. The debate that followed echoed the arguments of the 1951 struggle over the Rains amendment. Fulbright's coalition warned of the destructiveness of the H-bomb, pointed to the greater vulnerability of American urban targets since the opening of the Circle Route over the North Pole, and argued that the United States should not put all its eggs in one basket. They also minimized the impact of their amendment by noting that it applied only to new plants and expansions, and reminded their opponents that every relevant government department supported the principle of geographic dispersion.[22] However, Senator Carl Mundt of South Dakota got closer to the real point when he reminded the Senate that the process of urbanization had long worked against certain parts of the country.

> California, the East, and other areas of the Nation are heavily populated with the sons and daughters of rural America, who were forced to leave their home states to secure employment in defense industries—a fact which up to now the Department of Defense has pretty well ignored. I repeat, the word is "ignored." The Middle West has been pretty well ignored in the locating of defense fabricating plants. The defense plants are supported by all the taxpayers, not merely the taxpayers of the coastal States which now have a plethora of defense industries.[23]

In the minds of Mundt and the decentralizers, "national defense and progressive development" were what the argument was all about. However, now national defense could be harnessed to the progressive development of their own previously neglected urban areas.

Mundt's opponents knew this fact quite well, and they marshaled the same arguments that had carried Congress in 1951. California led the charge, providing fully one-fourth of the speakers in the House debate and much of the vehemence as well. Geographic dispersal would amount to socialist planning, disrupt the flow of production, and raise defense costs by spreading out producers. Moreover, decentralization would politicize the economic life of the nation and necessitate massive new expenditures for infrastructure, like streets and utilities, in the new defense centers that would have to be built.

Despite this rhetoric, these speakers had much more prosaic concerns. "The idea of sectionalism is repugnant to me," said future House Speaker John McCormack, as he set out to defend the interests of New England. "I am not going to vote for anything that will put the great automobile business of Detroit . . . in a goldfish bowl and circumvent their expansion," threatened a Detroiter. With decentralization, "your labor will be forced to move, and your management will be forced to move," agreed Carl Hinshaw of Pasadena. This amendment would "result in the denial of defense-production contracts not only to our great industrial firms in Connecticut but throughout New England," agreed Horace Seely-Brown of Connecticut. Edward Boland echoed the same alarm for "Greater Springfield," Massachusetts. Albert Cretella of New Haven chimed in that there "is no question that this is a back door attempt to further pirate industries." Noting that the Defense Department would spend $5 billion on guided missiles in 1957, Gerald Ford asserted that decentralization would "mean that industrial States, including the State of Michigan, will be precluded from participating in this kind of production for the Armed Forces." Elmer Holland professed to see the decline of Pittsburgh, and especially the ruination of its Golden Triangle renewal project, in the amendment. Donald Jackson, of Pacific Palisades, California, echoed these sentiments for the aircraft industry of his area. The policy is "an outrage upon industrial areas of the United States," thundered Hinshaw of Pasadena. "It would make farm communities out of the industrial areas and industrial areas out of the farm areas." "Dispersal would disrupt the economy of all the large industrial areas in the Nation," agreed Gordon McDonough of Los Angeles. "Moving a plant out of St. Louis to a weed patch somewhere is no solution," echoed Lenoir Sullivan of that city. Thomas Kuchel and William Knowland of California protested equally vehemently in the Senate.[24]

But it was left to representatives of metropolitan Providence, Los Angeles, and Cleveland to bring the opposition arguments into clearest sectional and urban focus. "We in Rhode Island have long been suffering from the problems which necessarily attach to a one- or two-industry State. We know intimately the burden inflicted by the flight of the textile industry to mills in the South and the movement of the center of the machinery-manufacturing industry to the Middle West," explained John Fogarty. Decentralization could "deal a death blow to the hopes and aspirations of many of our Rhode Island communities which are so desperately striving to pull themselves up virtually by their own bootstraps to secure a place of economic stability." Chet Holifield of Montebello, California, pointed out that "the laborers in these industries live in urban centers. That is where they have lived for some time in connnection with our war production." Finally, Cleveland's Charles Vanik noted that American national defense was designed to protect its urban centers. "If we disperse defense production industries, it means that we are going to have to disperse and weaken national defense installations" and to *"develop new urban areas* which will require new military and civilian installations." That, of course, was exactly what the sectional coalition of small city, town, and agrarian military-industrial have-nots had in mind.[25]

The geography of the vote vividly revealed its sectional bases. In both houses of Congress, the electronics and aircraft states of Washington and California stood with most of New England and the urban industrial belt stretching to the Mississippi River. Sixty-four Senators favored the amendment, and nineteen opposed it. In the House it won narrowly by a vote of 210 to 207. Surprisingly, in the very house where the numerical advantage of the northeastern, midwestern, and Pacific Coast states was strongest, they failed to present a united front. Illinois, Indiana, Ohio, Michigan, Pennsylvania, and New York provided Fulbright's House allies with 29 of 210 votes, 9 from Pennsylvania alone. The switch of all of the yea votes in any one of these states would have reversed the outcome. On the other hand, the Frostbelt–Pacific Coast alliance gained scarcely a single vote in either house from states south of Virginia, west of the Mississippi River, and east of the Pacific Coast. Although this geographic section does not exactly fit all definitions of the Sunbelt, it does approximate much of the shift in national resources noticed in the 1970s.[26]

Ironically, despite the Sunbelt's supposed role in resuscitating the Republican party, Democrats usually accounted for most of the southern and western votes in these struggles. If one includes in the South and West those areas south and west of a line running from Maryland to the Ohio River, around Illinois and southern Iowa, and then along the western boundaries of Iowa and Minnesota, the Sunbelt had a senatorial bloc of sixty votes. Ninety percent of these Senators voted for dispersal. In all, 81 percent of Senate Democrats voted yes on dispersal, along with 53 percent of the Republicans. In the House of Representatives, the South and West had a total of 183 votes. Of this number, 75 percent voted for dispersal and only 21 percent voted against, most of them from California and Washington. From a partisan standpoint, 60 percent of the House Democrats and 33 percent of the Republicans voted for the amendment, while 33 percent of the Democrats and 60 percent of the Republicans voted against it. Thus the vote exemplified more sectional than partisan consistency; nonetheless, the Democrats were strongly identified with dispersal and therefore with the fortunes of the Sunbelt.

Both in its geographic bases, its rhetoric, its sectional overtones, its concentration upon the defense budget, and even in its sectional inconsistencies, the struggle was a preview of the better-known controversy of the seventies and eighties. By 1951, and certainly by 1956, Americans had come to see the defense budget as at least as much a matter of welfare as warfare. And the debate was more than just a rhetorical exercise. By the early sixties a substantial amount of decentralization had occurred, especially decentralization of new weapons contracts and capabilities. Fulbright and his allies won more than just a debate.

Defense Manpower Policies

Reliance on the Federal military budget is supposedly an already well-known Western and Southern behavior pattern. What about the Northeast and the Midwest? Was their struggle against decentralization merely defensive, or did they too have their own schemes to pirate industry from the South and West? They did indeed, and their freebooting took the form of Defense Manpower Policy Number Four (DMP No. 4). In fact, this attempt to pirate industry had even less of a defense rationale than did the idea of geographic decentralization. The Frostbelt scheme would have concentrated even more defense production in the prime urban target areas, in order to relieve unemployment and nourish sick industries.

The principle underlying DMP No. 4 dated back to the Second World War. During that conflict the government attempted to allocate its prime contracts and subcontracts so as not to exacerbate labor shortages in the arsenals of democracy or to worsen unemployment in cities receiving fewer contracts. With the onset of the 1949 recession, the Truman administration reverted to this policy. It tried to channel all government spending into the areas hardest hit by economic troubles.[27] The longstanding problems of the New England textile cities, and those recently created for the automobile industry by the Korean War, added intensity to this thrust. New England textile mills had lost ground because of management problems, higher labor costs, and foreign and southern competition. The Korean War caused material shortages, especially of steel, which forced a curtailment of automobile production and related employment. These developments brought about pressures to use defense monies to alleviate unemployment, revive industries, and aid the growth or maintenance schemes of city builders.

Defenders of these urban vested interests proposed various therapies. For example, Thomas Lane of Massachusetts sought to route "federal purchasing to jobless areas" and to extend unemployment benefits. He also tried to get the secretary of labor to enforce the Walsh-Healy Public Contracts Act to ward off southern textile competition, to channel defense monies into high unemployment areas, and to encourage the Defense Department to spend more on textile products—even to stockpile them, in much the same way it was already hoarding strategic minerals.[28] Representative John Dingell and Senator Blair Moody, both of Detroit, similarly attempted to increase the amount of federal monies available to pay unemployment benefits in areas particularly affected by the Korean War.[29] Others proposed different remedies, but DMP No. 4 became the favorite military spending panacea. In the case of Detroit, the Korean War did indeed disrupt automobile production for a time. However, the argument did not have much merit for the textile industry, because the South profited from the war while New England claimed to be hurt by it. In any case, most commentators admitted that New England textile problems stemmed from causes other than the war. Moreover, New England already enjoyed substantial defense spending, though not necessarily in textile towns.

Nonetheless, New England representatives led the fight for DMP No. 4. Their action brought both federal relief and sectional conflict. Fortunately for the urban centers of the Northeast, the defense mobilizer in 1952 happened to be Charles Wilson, formerly of General Motors. In February 1952 Wilson issued DMP No. 4 in final form. Under this arrangement, surplus-labor areas were informed of the low bid for a certain contract; their firms were then allowed to match that price and secure the award. This generated a chorus of protest that such a procedure was socialistic and violated the sanctity of secret bids. Worst of all, it showed economic favoritism to New England and the Northeast. The outburst apparently had an effect, for the Truman administration subsequently declared certain industries to be unaffected by its February ruling, among them textiles and shoes. New Englanders were furious.

Once again congressional rhetoric and votes revealed the sectional bases of the struggle. With the exception of California, these bases were the same as in the debate over geographic decentralization, which pitted the South and West against the Northeast and Midwest. This time the positions were reversed, with the Northeast and Midwest trying to steal the defense contracts of the South and West. Otherwise, both process and rhetoric were suggestive of the later Sunbelt controversy. "The Civil War is being fought all over again in the field of economics, and the South is gaining victories," Representative Thomas J. Lane of Lawrence, Massachusetts, assured his colleagues in 1952.[30] "In view of the much more rapid economic gains in the South, in view of the disproportionate gains in military outlays, new construction, and defense contracts generally in the South, some easing of the pressure on labor and other scarce factors would facilitate the carrying through of war contracts in the South," Seymour E. Harris, chairman of the Committee on the New England Textile Industry, told a congressional hearing. "Any labor released in textiles [in the South by the working of DMP No. 4] could much more easily find opportunities for work in defense industries in the South than in New England."[31]

As in the later debate, the South was accused of unfair competition, especially in regard to wages and unions. Representatives of New England cities and industries repeatedly charged that the South was in violation of the wage standards of the Walsh-Healy Public Contracts Act. Others said that the peculiar business climate of the region—that is, the absence of unions—created unfair competition for the others. Like their successors who charge unfairness when defense dollars for a given state do not equal its tax burden, these earlier representatives hammered away that defense expenditures discriminated against New England. William F. Sullivan, of the National Association of Cotton Manufacturers, even demanded a quota system to ensure fair treatment.[32] Solomon Barkin, of the Textile Workers Union of America, went further, proposing that "the procurement policy must be designed to aid civilian industries maintain their full health and status."[33] The mayor of Lawrence, Massachusetts, and an alderman followed capital and labor to the stand to reiterate the demand for "equal" treatment.

Massachusetts congressman John F. Kennedy made the same point. In 1952 Kennedy testified at a Surplus Manpower Committee hearing that "a substantial number of defense contracts could be channeled to these distressed areas through preferential negotiation as planned under the Defense Manpower Policy No. 4." He hinted that sectional pressures had caused the policy to be suspended.[34] In an April 1954 *Atlantic*

Monthly article titled "New England and the South: The Struggle for Industry," the future President reiterated this belief. He went on to outline a more comprehensive attack on the problem of regional decline and competition. Kennedy tried to avoid the kind of sectional rhetoric that had characterized the DMP No. 4 debate, but he did single out the South for criticism. He argued that low wages, anti-union activities, failure to provide welfare for workers, land grants to factories, and other alleged southern practices undermined rather than strengthened the long-term prosperity of the South. However, he admitted that these policies might produce jobs in the short run. The senator did not use the word "pirating," but he certainly implied it. The federal government was partly responsible for this situation, Kennedy argued, by its policy of lavishing monies on the South. Perhaps in a utopian mood, he urged an end to the unfair *artificial advantages* of the South so that the regions could indulge in a sporting competition for industry, based on their *natural advantages* and their developed skills and resources.[35]

Although Kennedy and other New Englanders eschewed any sectional animosity in their campaign, they certainly stirred up some through their rhetoric. Much of the controversy seemed to be between Massachusetts, especially the city of Lawrence, and North Carolina, with South Carolina and Georgia taking a lively interest as well. When northern representatives stressed the inequities of defense spending, Herbert C. Bonner of Washington, North Carolina, countered with statistics indicating that the New England states, primarily Massachusetts and Connecticut, had received three times as much money in defense contracts as other regions in 1950-51. Massachusetts alone received as much as the five southern states between North Carolina and Mississippi, and Connecticut gained one and one-half times as much.[36] Thurmond Chatham, of Winston-Salem, documented that the National Association of Wool Manufacturers, based in New York City, opposed the distribution of contracts on a negotiated basis to distressed areas. The group believed that this suspension of competitive bidding would lead to unemployment in efficient areas, which would lose defense awards to the original unemployment zones. This change would merely shift the distress from one locale to another, costing the taxpayers more and undermining the defense effort.[37]

Nor did southerners exactly agree to the charges of unfair labor competition. The *Raleigh News and Observer* reminded New Englanders that southern mill workers were not "a pitiful company of the outrageously exploited," and that despite the continuing wage differential between the sections, southern wages had risen markedly. Moreover, "the New England textile industry which now complains of the competition of the South maintained its profits and kept down its wages for years by importing successive waves of immigrants ready to work for almost any wage at all." The *Observer*, and others in the South, maintained that the region had developed its own industry rather than pirating it from New England.[38]

Southern representatives rejected charges of unfair competition and government favoritism and countercharged that DMP No. 4 itself represented sectional discrimination. Throughout the debate, sectional bitterness was both implicit and explicit, sometimes painfully so. Congressman Paul Brown of Elbertson, Georgia, argued that the textile problem was industrywide and not confined just to New England. "Why should one state in New England," he asked, "have a preference in law as against a State in the West or a State in the South?" Brown went on to point out, "We have in the South, it is true, a great many mills, but many of these are running less than three days a week."[39] DMP No. 4 "represents an outrageous maneuver of throwing people out of work in one section of the country in order to give jobs to another," thundered Representative Burr P. Harrison of Winchester, Virginia.[40]

Henderson Lanham of Rome, Georgia, charged that John F. Kennedy and the "CIO bosses" of Pittsfield, Massachusetts, had halted the transfer of a General Electric plant from Pittsfield to Rome by blocking the issuance of federal tax amortization certificates to the plant.[41] Mendel Rivers of Charleston, South Carolina, joined the fray to remind the New Englanders that "economic law moved their industries in some other direction," and to demand that these economic laws not be set aside. He would support a relief program for the communities adversely affected by the Korean emergency, but not any tampering with the principle of competitive bidding. "If you do this thing to us, you are creating wounds that will be aggravated in the future and we will not forget it," warned Rivers.[42]

Some very important western representatives joined this southern defense. Chet Holifield, William Knowland, Barry Goldwater, Dennis Chavez, Jack Shelley, and several others saw DMP No. 4 in the same light as did the historic South. Although this group was not a very tidy ideological mix, its members stood together against the principle of undermining competitive bidding. Shelley and Knowland, who faced each other across the San Francisco Bay and across an even greater ideological and partisan gulf, perhaps were typical.

Representative Shelley, the past head of the San Francisco Labor Council and the future mayor of that city, thought that DMP No. 4 had been issued long after the disruptions of mobilization had passed. Moreover, San Francisco shipbuilders could not be assured of getting a contract on which they were the low bidder until some surplus-labor area builder had a chance to meet the bid. Even though the local shipbuilders, like the New England textile industry, had long suffered through hard times, not being designated a surplus-labor area ruined the Bay Area's chances. San Francisco area electronics firms had suffered the same fate.[43] Although California had not fought with the Confederacy in the Civil War and labor leader Shelley did not share the southern view of unions, he did share its sectional perspective on DMP No. 4. "Only one area west of the Mississippi has been so approved [as a surplus-labor area]. Only one area in all of the Southern States is included," he complained. "These eastern and midwestern cities designated comprise relatively limited sections of their own States." Shelley felt that he had been tricked into supporting the retention of the policy when it was considered for congressional action.[44]

Shelley's conservative Republican neighbor William Knowland, the majority leader of the Senate, objected to DMP No. 4 just as vigorously. He opposed giving the president that much power to shift contracts around, and he felt that such a policy struck a blow at the free enterprise system by eliminating fair competition. Yet he also saw the sectional implications of the policy. When Burnet Maybank of Charleston, South Carolina, noted that under the policy "distressed areas will be able to take business from other areas," such as California, Knowland answered that "the Senator from South Carolina is correct."[45] Other westerners joined in, as Goldwater and Chavez fretted about the loss of parachute contracts for cities in Arizona and New Mexico.

They need not have worried. Senator Leverett Saltonstall put the matter to a vote on July 22, 1953, and lost; the count was twenty-five yeas to sixty-two nays. The vote, like the preceding rhetoric, had a strong sectional cast. Most of Saltonstall's support came from Pennsylvania, New York, and New England, in addition to Michigan, where he received fifteen of his twenty-five votes. Four more came from Illinois, Indiana, Kentucky, and Minnesota, and another five from Nebraska, South Dakota, Montana, and Washington. As in the concurrent struggle over dispersal, some sections were not monolithic, but the Frostbelt tended to support Saltonstall, and everyone else, to oppose him. DMP No. 4 did not get a single vote in the states of the southern Confederacy and received only four of thirty-four votes in the West. Moreover, the outcry against DMP No. 4 apparently contained the program in the implementation stage. As noted previously, the government deleted textiles and shoes from the distressed areas list and the total amount spent in distressed areas remained small. As one frustrated member reminded the House, the government had channeled only $52,000,000 to such areas by mid-1953.[46]

Conclusion

Both the fight over decentralization to avoid nuclear attack and that over Defense Manpower Policy Number Four reflected the geography, the rhetoric, and much of the substance of the later Sunbelt-Frostbelt controversy. Both parties had come to recognize the potential role of military spending in influencing the growth of the Sunbelt and the Northeast-Midwest corridor. They were already converting warfare into welfare, a transformation obvious in the Sunbelt debate of recent years. Although the rhetoric of each side relied on the concept of national defense, each was more anxious to protect the interests of certain cities and their parent regions than to defend the United States from the Soviets. Moreover, other issues, such as unemployment compensation, fair labor standards, federal spending on dams, price supports, shipbuilding subsidies, merchant marine subsidies, tax policies, transportation rates, general industrial decentralization, and the distribution of scientific research monies, were viewed from the same sectional perspectives. Obviously, arguments over military spending were part of a much larger sectional debate about the realignment of American culture.

From the above, it is clear that the Northeast and Midwest became interested in defense spending long before the economic troubles of the 1970s. The move of industry to the Sunbelt was already well underway by the 1950s, and the Northeast and Midwest were acutely aware of its threatening potential. The resulting debate over deindustrialization broke out as early as the 1950s, not in the 1970s. Also, like its later counterpart, this earlier controversy demonstrated the difficulty of attaining Rust Belt sectional unity. Just as today the Northeast-Midwest coalition struggles against internal disunity as often as against external competition, so it did in the 1950s. It lost the fights over both dispersal and DMP No. 4 due to its own lack of solidarity.

This article suggests the need for several future lines of inquiry into defense spending, city building, and the origins of the Sunbelt-Frostbelt struggle. The general question we must ask is, what happened to this urban-led sectionalism so clearly articulated in the 1950s? Did it die out or increase during the Vietnam War and the defense boom of the sixties? Did the open struggle over military resources continue through the fifties and sixties, or did other regional issues overshadow this conflict? If the Northeast and Midwest lost the struggle over defense spending, what were the exact circumstances of this defeat, and how did they set the stage for the Sunbelt controversy of the seventies?

Although the shift of American power and wealth to the South and West has been of momentous importance, American historians writing of the 1950s have often, if not usually, slighted or ignored it.[47] This article should encourage scholars to end this neglect; at the same time, it should remind contemporary commentators that the origins of the Sunbelt struggle go back at least to the urban rivalry of the early 1950s.

Notes

1. John Hekman and Alan Smith, "Behind the Sunbelt's Growth: Industrial Decentralization," *Economic Review* (Federal Reserve Bank of Atlanta) 67 (Mar. 1982): 4–13; Carl Abbott, *The New Urban America: Growth and Politics in Sunbelt Cities* (Chapel Hill: Univ. of North Carolina Press, 1981), 1–13; Richard M. Bernard and Bradley R. Rice, eds., *Sunbelt Cities: Politics and Growth since World War II* (Austin: Univ. of Texas Press, 1981), 1–30; Clyde E. Browning and Wil Gesler, "Sunbelt–Snow Belt: A Case of Sloppy Regionalizing," *Professional Geographer* 31 (Feb. 1979): 66–74. For purposes of this paper, my definition of the Sunbelt is that it is a term used to indicate the general shift of resources within the United States from the Northeast and Midwest to the South and West. *South* refers to the states of the Confederacy, and *West* refers to that portion of the United States west of the first tier of trans-Mississippi states.

2. Hekman and Smith, "Behind the Sunbelt's Growth," 4–13; Alfred J. Watkins, "'Good Business Climates': The Second War between the States," *Dissent* (Fall 1980): 476–85; Edward Ullman, "Amenities as a Factor in Regional Growth," *Geographical Review* 44 (Jan. 1954): 119–32; Horace Sutton, "Sunbelt vs. Frostbelt: A Second Civil War?" *Saturday Review* (15 Apr. 1978): 28–37; Joel Havemann, Neal R. Peirce, and Rochelle L. Stanfield, "Federal Spending: The North's Loss Is the Sunbelt's Gain," *National Journal* (26 June 1976): 878–91; Havemann and Stanfield, "'Neutral' Federal Policies Are Reducing Frostbelt-Sunbelt Spending Imbalances," *National Journal* (7 Feb. 1981); "A New Milestone in the Shift to the Sunbelt," *Nation's Business* 65 (May 1977): 69; Gurney Breckenfeld, "Business Loves the Sunbelt (and Vice Versa)," *Fortune* 95 (June 1977): 132–146; Bob Gottlieb, "The Phoenix

Growth Machine," *The Nation* (29 Dec. 1979): 675–88; "The Second War between the States," *Business Week* (17 May 1976): 92–123; "The Sun Belt Today—Still a Land of Opportunity, But . . . ," *Changing Times* 35 (Sept. 1981): 25–30.

3. Bernard and Rice, eds., *Sunbelt Cities*; Abbott, *New Urban America*.

4. Robert A. Hart, *The Great White Fleet: Its Voyage around the World, 1907–09* (Boston: Little, Brown, 1965), 162–78.

5. Roger W. Lotchin, "The City and the Sword: San Francisco and the Rise of the Metropolitan-Military Complex, 1919–1941," *Journal of American History* 65 (Mar. 1979): 996–1020; idem., "The Metropolitan-Military Complex in Comparative Perspective: San Francisco, Los Angeles, and San Diego, 1919–1941," *Journal of the West* 18 (July 1979): 19–30; idem., "The City and the Sword in Metropolitan California," *Urbanism Past and Present* 7 (Summer-Fall 1982): 1–16.

6. Fletcher Bowron to Vierling Kersey, 9 May 1945, Bowron Collection, Huntington Library.

7. "Statement of W. C. Mullendore," quoted in extension of the remarks of Representative John M. Costello, 78th Cong., 2d sess., 22 Nov. 1944, *Congressional Record* 90, pt. 11:A4503–05; "Address of Senator Pat McCarran to the California Legislature, June 9, 1944," quoted in extension of the remarks of Senator Joseph C. O'Mahoney, 78th Cong., 2d sess., 21 June 1944, *Congressional Record* 90, pt. 10:A3213–16.

8. Remarks of Representative Ralph E. Church on "National Defense and the Aviation Industry," 76th Cong., 1st sess., 27 June 1939, *Congressional Record* 84, pt. 7:79991–93.

9. John B. Rae, *Climb to Greatness: The American Aircraft Industry, 1920–1960* (Cambridge, Mass.: MIT Press, 1968), 119–72.

10. Neil P. Hurley, "The Role of Accelerated Tax Amortization in the National Industrial Dispersion Program" (Ph.D. diss., Fordham University, 1956), 50–51.

11. Jack Gorrie, "America's Security Resources," quoted in extension of the remarks of Senator Warren Magnuson, 83d Cong., 1st sess., 16 June 1952, *Congressional Record* 98, pt. 10:3733–35.

12. Remarks of Senator Harry P. Cain on "The Industrial Dispersal Program," 82d Cong., 1st sess., 14 Aug. 1951, *Congressional Record* 97, pt. 4:11043.

13. Edward T. Dickinson (Vice Chairman of the National Security Resources Board) to Senator Thomas H. Kuchel, 20 Feb. 1953, Modern Military Records Division, Central Files, 1949–1953, Records of the Office of Civil Defense Mobilization, Record Group 304, National Archives.

14. William J. Platt, "Industrial Defense: A Community Approach," *Bulletin of the Atomic Scientists* 9 (Sept. 1953): 261–64.

15. National Security Resources Board, Press Release for Friday, 6 June 1952, Central Files, 1949–1953, Record Group 304, National Archives, 1–2. According to Neil Hurley, the government exaggerated the degree of dispersal. Hurley, "Role of Accelerated Tax Amortization," 70.

16. Ibid.

17. Remarks of various representatives on the Rains Amendment to H.R.

3871, 82d Cong., 1st sess., 11 July 1951, *Congressional Record* 97, pt. 6:7978–88.

18. Ibid.
19. Ibid.
20. Harry S. Truman, "Statement by the President," 23 Aug. 1951, Processed Documents File, Record Group 304, National Archives.
21. Henry Parkman, "Nonmilitary Measures of National Defense," *Bulletin of the Atomic Scientists* 9 (Sept. 1953): 259–60; Ralph E. Lapp, "Eight Years Later," *Bulletin of the Atomic Scientists* 9 (Sept. 1953): 324–36. Much of this issue is devoted to dispersal and related issues of civil defense.
22. For the Senate debate on decentralization see various senators speaking on H.R. 9852, 48th Cong., 2d sess., June 1956, *Congressional Record* 102, pt. 8:10825–57.
23. Senator Carl Mundt speaking on H.R. 9852, 48th Cong., 2d sess., 22 June 1956, *Congressional Record* 102, pt. 8:10825–54. The debate runs from pp. 10825 to 10857.
24. Various representatives speaking on H.R. 2486, 84th Cong., 2d sess., 28 June 1956, *Congressional Record* 102, pt. 8:11283–94; remarks of various senators on dispersal, 84th Cong., 2d sess., 22 June 1956, *Congressional Record* 102, pt. 8:10825–57.
25. Ibid.
26. For the Senate vote see *Congressional Record* 102, pt. 8:10855; for the House vote, ibid., 11293–94.
27. Ibid.
28. Remarks of Representative Thomas Lane on the "Textile Industry in New England," 84th Cong., 1st sess., 26 Mar. 1953, *Congressional Record* 98, pt. 3:2982–84.
29. Remarks of senators Blair Moody and Burnett Maybank on "Supplementary Unemployment Compensation Benefits to Certain Unemployed Workers," 83d Cong., 2d sess., 23 Jan. 1953, *Congressional Record* 98, pt. 1:420–25.
30. Remarks of Representative Thomas Lane on "Textile Unemployment in New England," 83d Cong., 2d sess., *Congressional Record* 98, pt. 5:5699–6400.
31. "Statement of Seymour Harris, Chairman of the Committee on the New England Textile Industry," in extension of the remarks of Representative Edith N. Rogers, 83d Cong., 2d sess., 31 Mar. 1952, *Congressional Record* 98, pt. 9:A2040–43.
32. "Statement of William F. Sullivan, President of the National Association of Cotton Manufacturers," quoted in extension of the remarks of Representative Edith N. Rogers, 83d Cong., 2d sess., 20 Mar. 1952, *Congressional Record* 98, pt. 9:A2006–09.
33. "Statement of Solomon Barkin, Textile Workers Union of America," quoted in extension of the remarks of Representative Thomas J. Lane, 83d Cong., 1st sess., 24 Mar. 1952, *Congressional Record* 98, pt. 9:2019–21.
34. Extension of the remarks of Representative John F. Kennedy on "Condi-

tions in the Textile Industry," 82d Cong., 2d sess., 1 Apr. 1952. *Congressional Record* 98, pt. 9:A2080–81.

35. John F. Kennedy, "New England and the South: The Struggle for Industry," *Atlantic Monthly* 193 (Apr. 1954): 32–36.
36. Extension of the remarks of Representative Herbert C. Bonner on "Application of Defense Manpower Policy No. 4 to the Textile Industry," 82d Cong., 2d sess., 28 Mar. 1952, *Congressional Record* 98, pt. 9:A1988–89.
37. Extension of the remarks of Representative Thurmond Chatham on "The Distribution of Government Business," 82d Cong., 2d sess., 11 Feb. 1952, *Congressional Record* 98, pt. 8:A765.
38. Editorial from the *Raleigh News and Observer*, quoted in extension of the remarks of Representative Carl T. Durham, 82d Cong., 2d sess., 26 Mar. 1952, *Congressional Record* 98, pt. 8:A1899.
39. Debate over Defense Manpower Policy No. 4, 82d Cong., 2d sess., 20 June 1952, *Congressional Record* 98, pt. 6: 7720–30.
40. Ibid.
41. Ibid.
42. Remarks of Representative Mendel Rivers on H.R. 5969, 83d Cong., 1st sess., 29 July 1953, *Congressional Record* 99, pt. 8:10345.
43. Remarks of Representative John Shelley on "Manpower Policy," 83d Cong., 1st sess., 17 June 1953, *Congressional Record* 99, pt. 6:7422–23.
44. Remarks of Representative John Shelley speaking on Defense Manpower Policy No. 4, 83d Cong., 1st sess., 26 June 1953, *Congressional Record* 99, pt. 6:8180–82.
45. Remarks of Senator William Knowland speaking on H.R. 5969, 83d Cong., 1st sess., 22 July 1953, *Congressional Record* 99, pt. 7:9504.
46. Remarks of Representative Carl Perkins speaking on H.R. 5969, 83d Cong., 1st sess., 22 July 1953, *Congressional Record* 99, pt. 7:10342.
47. Eric F. Goldman, *The Crucial Decade and After: America, 1945-1960* (New York: Vintage, 1960); Robert J. Donovan, *Conflict and Crisis: the Presidency of Harry S. Truman, 1945-1948* (New York: Norton, 1977); Godfrey Hodgson, *America in Our Time: From World War II to Nixon—What Happened and Why* (New York: Doubleday, 1976); Norman L. Rosenberg and Emily S. Rosenberg, *In Our Times* (Englewood Cliffs: Prentice-Hall, 1982); Paul A. Carter, *Another Part of the Fifties* (New York: Columbia Univ. Press, 1977); Howard Zinn, *Postwar America: 1945–1971* (Indianapolis: Bobbs-Merrill, 1973); James Gilbert, *Another Chance: Postwar America, 1945–1968* (Philadelphia: Temple Univ. Press, 1981); William E. Leuchtenburg, *A Troubled Feast: American Society since 1945* (Boston: Little, Brown, 1983). Gilbert is one of the few historians of the postwar era to even list the term *Sunbelt* in his index.

5 Metropolitan Politics
in the American Sunbelt

Richard M. Bernard

In separate forums, Morton Sosna and Gerald Nash have argued that the South and the West, respectively, underwent greater changes during the Second World War than at any other time in their histories.[1] Considering the Civil War, Sosna's point seems at least debatable. Yet by setting aside the comparison with old times not forgotten, one can easily accept the central argument that World War II marked a major turning point for both regions. Few observers would dispute the claim that the presumably unswerving South has undergone a greater alteration in course in the last half-century than any other section of the country, and that major changes have overtaken the rapidly expanding West as well. By the 1970s political change had even come to one of the last strongholds of traditional power in those regions, local municipal government. In fact, from the perspective of the mid-1980s, one can now define four rather clear stages of postwar Sunbelt political development.

On the eve of World War II, cities of the South and Southwest were safely in the hands of an Old Guard of senior politicians who, although skilled in the ways of the ballot box, were relatively ill-prepared for an era of rapid growth and change. In most municipalities below the 37th parallel a "commercial-civic elite," to use Blaine A. Brownell's term, guided the ship of state. In Dallas, it was the Citizens' Charter Association; in Houston, the 8-F Club (a reference to a meeting room at the Lamar Hotel); in Atlanta, William Hartsfield and his chamber of commerce–based colleagues. In the machine-run cities of Memphis and New Orleans, the aging Crump and Choctaw Club organizations guided officeholders.[2]

Using the tools of prestige, money, and media control, the Old Guard businessmen who guided the destinies of most southern and southwestern municipalities controlled their hometowns as firmly as bosses Ed Crump and Robert Maestri managed both ends of the Mississippi Delta. In fact, in some cities, such as Hartsfield's Atlanta, Stanley Draper's Oklahoma City, and William Gunter's Montgomery, the line between civic leadership and machine politics was a thin one. Throughout the urban Sunbelt, Old Guardsmen, whether civic leaders or machine politicians, governed almost unchallenged, enjoying deferential support from the rest of the population.

To a certain extent, such deference was an extension of a three-hundred-year tradition in the Old South and the Southwest that not only endorsed the right of one's "betters" to rule but also accepted their goals as appropriate for the community. In the Spanish imperial Southwest, commercial expansion was the objective of both the rulers and the ruled. In the South, deference predates even the founding of Jamestown, where the London Company was simultaneously government and sole employer. The presence of black minorities in the South, and of American Indian and, after Anglo takeover, Hispanic minorities in the Southwest, did not disrupt the doctrine of headlong growth, but it did give rise to a corollary. Expansion, yes, but not at the price of social change.

"Growth without social change," or in David Goldfield's phrase, "progress and tradition," thus became the watchwords of the two regions.[3] Always the goal of southwesterners, this seemingly contradictory proposition won wide acceptance in the South after the Civil War. The elite's effective use of the media helped to solidify public opinion. A stream of newspaper articles and editorials led average citizens to conclude that their personal quests for prosperity were tied to the elite's promotion of local business and industry. By the 1920s, "growth without social change" had become, again in Brownell's terminology, an "urban ethos."[4]

Events during and after the Second World War, however, conspired to undermine the power of the Old Guard. Among these, three factors stand out: population growth and change, the civil rights movement, and the increased involvement of the federal government in local affairs.

Wartime expansion of southern and southwestern defense cities and continued employment opportunities in the metropolitan Sunbelt brought to these areas many new voters who were not steeped in the traditions of deference. The sheer numbers of the in-migrants made difficult their enlistment in local political parties and organizations. So too did their social characteristics.

Two types of newcomers demonstrate this growing independence from the old politics. Along the outskirts of major cities stand the "carported" and overpriced homes of the Sunbelt's young urban professionals (yuppies), whose higher educational achievements and intense career commitments leave them with little time or interest in local politics. Few of these newcomers, from the high-tech workers of Raleigh-Durham to the Zenith executives of Phoenix, have personal connections to the old and powerful elite of their new, and often temporary, hometowns. Relatively few have developed the sort of strong local attachments that override career aspirations and link personal futures to particular cities. Although these in-migrants are sympathetic to the goals of local businesses, their commitments to particular Old Guard leaders are weak at best.

The other notable group of new voters are nonwhites. In the South, this group includes upwardly mobile black urban professionals, or "buppies," but it is still more reflective of television's workingman Fred Sanford than of TV physician Heathcliff Huxtable. The civil rights movement substantially increased the power of this urban electorate, giving force to the desires of a segment of the population little considered in earlier resource allocations. The movements for black and (in South Florida and the Southwest) Hispanic rights trained a generation of independent leaders, some of whom, including Atlanta's Andrew Young and Washington's Marion Berry, have attained considerable power.

In a more general sense, federal involvement has greatly altered the Old Guard's commercial and industrial plans, forcing city fathers to adjust municipal priorities to meet the needs of noncommercial urban groups and suburban governments. Beginning in the 1960s, several national programs offered Sunbelt cities their first large-scale federal funding, and with it, apparent autonomy from state legislatures. This independence proved incomplete, however, for those same initiatives—such as Lyndon Johnson's Community Action Program, and the Urban Development Action Grants of the years since Watergate—required considerable consultation with and sometimes the approval of groups outside city hall.

These three factors—population growth and change, the civil rights movement, and increased federal involvement with cities—affected the politics of both the municipalities themselves and their metropolitan regions. Mainly because of these factors, there arose between the 1940s and the mid-1980s four major challenges to the traditional power of the municipal Old Guard. Three of these battles were fought, and continue to be fought, within city boundaries. The fourth represents the external attack of the suburbs against central-city dominance.

The intraurban phase of the fighting began in the late 1940s, when a great many ambitious young veterans returned home from the war. These ex-servicemen, and the related reformer groups that followed them, generated the most modest of mutinies designed not to alter the chosen course but simply to put new people in command.

In a number of cases the returnees found overly cautious leaders overwhelmed by citizen demands. During the war military personnel and defense workers and their families flooded the cities of the Southern rim, inundating the Old Guard with cries for expanded services. John Dos Passos wrote of Mobile, for example, as "trampled and battered like a city that's been taken by storm. Sidewalks are crowded. Gutters are stacked with litter that drifts back and forth in the brisk spring wind. Garbage cans are overflowing. Frame houses on tree shaded streets bulge with men in shirtsleeves who spill out onto the porches and trample grass plots and stand in knots at the street corners."[6]

Vice control alone could exhaust city budgets. As the war neared its midpoint, some seven hundred cities had functioning red light districts, and the nation reported a hundred thousand more cases of syphilis than ever before registered in a single year. In New Orleans, "transient servicemen raised the level of vice to new highs and reinforced the local reputation for immoral diversions." In Norfolk, "V-Girls" became "V-D Girls" during imprudent efforts to raise military morale.[7] Less colorful but equally vexing were requests for schools, roads, utilities, and law enforcement that continued to mount with postwar in-migration. These amenities could only come through the New Deal tax-and-spend pattern still foreign to the South and Southwest.

Clearly, the times demanded the sort of bold advances that the Old Guard found too adventurous. Reluctant to endorse governmental activism, they looked unfavorably on most costly service demands. As residents of the older, more established sections of their communities, they often thought it unfair or unnecessary to tax their neighbors in order to extend services to newer areas. Moreover, when they did tax (or borrow) and spend, the old elite often let contracts to supporters. The resulting services generally failed to meet citizen expectations.

With expanding, nondeferential populations in real need and their demands shunned by the Old Guard as the siren songs of fiscal disaster, new political leaders sailed into action. Moving rapidly into all realms of statecraft, the veterans won more than their share of the offices contested in the decade after V-J Day. Younger businessmen, their political apprenticeships cut short by war, now formed a new generation of commercial-civic leadership. Even in the machine cities of Memphis and New Orleans priorities shifted to a pursuit of "growth without social change."

Archetypical of the GI revolt was the election of deLesseps S. "Chep" Morrison in New Orleans. In 1946 the handsome, 34-year-old scion of an eighteenth-century Creole family upset Mayor Maestri, a longtime ally of the Long family. *Time* labeled Morrison a "symbol of the bright new day which has come to the city of charming ruins," and the U.S. Junior Chamber of Commerce voted him one of the country's ten outstanding young men of 1947, an honor he shared with Congressman Richard Nixon. Morrison pledged to build a new New Orleans, erasing the city's image as a haven for sinful tourists and basing a modern economy on Pan-American trade.[8]

Veterans such as Morrison inspired other reformers so similar to and interlocked with the GIs that they did not constitute a clearly separate type. These reform organizations, such as Jacksonville's Citizens for Better Government, Oklahoma City's Association for Responsible Government, and the Charter Government Committee of Phoenix, were modern versions of the champions of efficiency who had come and gone in American cities since the early 1800s.

Although many GIs just wanted to replace the Old Guard in city hall, their reformer cousins sought to redirect local government. In reformer minds, a good government promoted business expansion while remaining fiscally conservative, honest, and efficient. A good government favored business subsidies, but treated human subsidies as wasteful expenditures and counterproductive threats to personal initiative. Little concerned with redistributing the benefits of growth, reformer groups sponsored slates of well-known businessmen who shared these views and who would hold office out of a sense of public duty.

Between 1945 and 1955, reformers succeeded in obtaining new charters for Houston, Dallas, San Antonio, and Phoenix. In Baton Rouge (1947), Nashville (1962), Jacksonville (1967), and Oklahoma City (1959–63) they championed successful city-county consolidation and annexation movements. In Memphis they gradually ousted the remnants of the Crump machine, concluding their efforts in 1968 with a change to a strong mayoral form of government. In New Orleans, Mayor Moon Landrieu picked up where Morrison had left off, leading the city government into biracialism by appointing blacks to official positions.[9]

The chief factor supporting the rise of both the veterans and the modern reformers was the growth of urban Sunbelt populations. Returning servicemen, wartime in-migrants, and other new residents expanded Sunbelt electorates, forcing old politicians to campaign heavily, many for the first time. The settlement of these newcomers on the fringes of major cities caused the development of social circles (and thus political influence groups) beyond the traditional bounds of the Old Guard. Older leaders held power bases in the businesses, civic clubs, churches, and schools of the prestigious neighborhoods near downtown. Newcomers within and outside the city boundaries tended to work for newer, smaller businesses (or in the suburban branches of older businesses); to join the outlying Lions, Kiwanis, or Rotary clubs; to belong to younger and peppier (and sometimes also preppier) churches; and to send their children to hastily constructed, wet-paint schools. The Old Guard did not know these people, and the newcomers knew the Old Guard only as names in the newspaper.[10]

This physical and social distance, coupled with the Old Guard's lack of enthusiasm for partisan campaigning and its reluctance to tax old neighborhoods for the development of new service areas, proved fatal to the political careers of many previously unchallenged incumbents. Those whom the reformers could not replace faded from the scene as fatigue and age took their toll.

By the 1960s, when a new set of captains was ready for a turn at the wheel, the Old Guard's power survived mainly only in local legend. The young businessmen of the GI and reformer movements were now in charge. And it was lucky for the Sunbelt that these younger leaders were in place, for the rise of minorities soon tested the political flexibility of urban leadership.

In the past, southern and southwestern municipal leaders had resolved political issues privately. In most cities, election campaigns had been considered an improper forum for the airing of political differences. Elections were shows of municipal solidarity. Conflict resolution was left to boardroom conferences at the chamber of commerce and luncheon dates at exclusive clubs. The political appearance of minorities in the 1960s and 1970s changed all that. First it was the nonviolent, direct action technique of the civil rights movement that forced cities to remap priorities. Later it was the election process itself that brought to the surface resentments and desires that had previously run silent but deep. Urban Sunbelt decision making has not been the same since.

The key events in this challenge, beyond the marches and demonstrations of the movement itself, were the 1965 passage of the Voting Rights Act and its subsequent repassage and strengthening. The original act, clearly the most important legislation for southern blacks since Reconstruction, strengthened federal protections for minority registration and voting. It also included a preclearance provision blocking officials in the states of the old Confederacy from making structural changes in their political systems without advance approval of the U.S. Department of Justice. An amendment in 1975 extended some coverage beyond the South and added Hispanics and several smaller minorities to the protected list. The 1982 version of the law, a remarkably liberal document considering the prevailing political winds, extended the provisions for preclearance and protection to non-English-speaking Americans. It also overturned an intervening court decision in Mobile that had obligated plaintiffs to prove discriminatory intent as well as effect.[11]

Backed by these protections and bolstered by the net influx of minority members into central cities, black and (more recent) Hispanic voters have registered in great numbers. Their strength at the polls is now apparent. The list of major Sunbelt or near-Sunbelt cities with recent or current black or Hispanic chief executives now includes Atlanta, Baltimore, Birmingham, Charlotte, Denver, Miami, New Orleans, Richmond, San Antonio, and Washington, D.C. In many more cities, blacks and Hispanics now have a voice on city councils, due in part to successful lawsuits against political units with at-large elections.

The most surprising of these minority victories came in Birmingham in 1979 when Dr. Richard Arrington, a zoologist, became the first black mayor of a city most known for its racial violence. Only sixteen years earlier, a Sunday morning bomb blast at a black Baptist church in Birmingham, and the brutality of Police Commissioner Eugene "Bull" Connor toward civil rights demonstrators, had galvanized President John Kennedy into action on civil rights. Although Arrington's power has not been total (for example, the council and mayor struggled for a year over the latter's selection of a police chief), his tenure signifies a major shift in power away from the conservative leadership of the past. Symbolic of the change was the pairing in Arrington's reelection campaign in 1983: both candidates were liberal academics, the opponent having earned his doctorate at Harvard.[12]

One of the newest of the minority mayors is Xavier Suarez of Miami, who defeated Raul Masvidal in a November 1985 runoff that determined who would be the city's first Cuban mayor. Incumbent mayor Maurice Ferre, a Puerto Rican, ran third in the primary. Suarez portrayed himself in the campaign as the Cuban candidate, as he had in three earlier losing efforts; Masvidal, endorsed by the major English-language newspapers (two white and one black), carried the banner of downtown business interests and won the support of non-Cuban Anglos and blacks.[13]

Whereas GIs and reformers brought personnel changes and greater efficiency in the pursuit of growth without social change, minority leaders have emphasized a different sort of personnel turnover (i.e., the disproportionate hiring of minority members) and the equitable distribution of public benefits. In the minority-controlled cities of the Sunbelt, growth is still a goal, but it is often second in importance after spoils. Although there is a continued emphasis on growth, there is an equal and sometimes stronger emphasis on sharing the benefits of that growth with the city's minorities.

Atlanta's handling of its gigantic airport expansion demonstrates the change. In the Georgia capital, Mayor Maynard Jackson accepted the commercial goal of airport redevelopment, but he redistributed the benefits of the new construction by diverting many of the lucrative public contracts to minority firms. The reformer goal of efficiency was also served when the contracted firms completed their work on time and under budget. Building on this success, Jackson insisted that white developers undertake public projects in tandem with minority contracting firms. When he took office, less than 1 percent of the city's business went to black companies. Jackson's successor, Andrew Young, who continued this program, recently claimed that 378 minority businesses hold some 30 percent of the city's contracts, worth about $106 million per year. As late as 1961, Atlanta's hiring of a black meter maid made front-page news in local papers. Today some 65 percent of all city hall workers are black.[14]

Related to the minority challenge, but sufficiently different to merit special labeling, is the threat posed by neighborhood protectionists. Since the late 1960s these most provincial of local interest groups have become the "sea dogs" of municipal politics. Theirs is a genuine, if somewhat elusive and undermanned, counterattack on the municipal consensus.[15]

What distinguishes the protectionists is their disavowal of the goal of growth. Often drawn together by race, ethnicity, or social class, the members of these groups have as their primary concern the preservation of their neighborhoods against the dredging operations of urban renewal, the scattering effects of school busing, and the deterioration allowed by governmental neglect. From Tampa's Cuban community of Ybor City, to the Mexican soutwest side of San Antonio, to the elite Emory University neighborhood of Atlanta, groups have formed to protest a variety of expansion projects that threaten community destruction, uncontrolled river flooding, and the building of freeways (including one running to the Jimmy Carter Presidential Library).[16]

Growth, civil rights, and federal activity have all contributed to the audacity of these urban raiders. Demographic and economic growth have had the negative effect of alerting neighborhoods to the need to fight for preservation. Expanding populations, not to mention expanding economies, need land and services. And, as inner-city victims of urban renewal and redevelopment have learned, land and the tax monies for services often come from the inner-city neighborhoods least benefited by city growth. The civil rights movement, meanwhile, taught minority leaders how to block this redistribution of wealth from poor neighborhoods to contractors and businesses. The federal government supported their underdog efforts and, through a series of programs such as the Community Action Program (CAP) trained indigenous leaders and expanded the powers of minority and nonminority neighborhoods to block undesired projects.

Because by definition neighborhood groups are in the minority, the voting booth has proved a less-favorable staging area for their protective strikes than have pressrooms, courtrooms, and the chambers of administrative panels. In these areas, neighborhood efforts have been much aided by the Environmental Protection Agency (EPA) requirement of an environmental impact statement for federally financed improvements. Originally intended to protect the natural world from ill-considered human destruction, EPA orders have had substantial impact in urban areas. The destruction of a neighborhood, and its psychological and sociological effects on the community and the residents, are now grounds for the suspension of construction projects. The most immediate threats posed by this ruling are to expanding cities that require substantial construction of highways and utilities to support their mushrooming growth. The never simple process of land condemnation and redevelopment in these cities now entails lengthy battles in the media and in the halls of government.

This sort of struggle was at the forefront of San Antonio's politics in the mid-1970s. Voters in the city's Mexican-American neighborhoods delayed north-side, Anglo development until the city council agreed to move against the flooding that had long troubled Mexican areas on the southwest side. Under the leadership of a social action group called Communities Organized for Public Service (COPS), the protectionists won a governmental infusion of $200 million into poor Hispanic areas.[17]

In the larger story of postwar urban Sunbelt politics, neighborhood advocates thus far have played only a small role. However, the protectionists' attacks have attracted great attention, and they have appeared to constitute a serious threat to the commonly perceived good. And, more and more, there is substance to this threat.

Even in electoral politics the impact of aroused neighborhoods cannot be discounted. In scattered contests from Raleigh, Durham, and

Chapel Hill, North Carolina, to Austin, Albuquerque, and Phoenix in the Southwest, controlled-growth advocates have captured city offices. In the 1970s much of this electoral activity was aimed at residential expansion, but by the mid-1980s expanding wholesaling and retailing establishments were the targets. As David Dowall, director of the Institute of Urban and Regional Development at the University of California at Berkeley put it, "What we're seeing in some places is a revitalization of the growth-control movement . . . but this time it is being applied to commercial development."[18]

In other cities, such as Houston, protectionists unable to capture city governments on their own provide crucial support for coalition administrations. In that southwestern metropolis, accountant Kathy Whitmire has won four mayoral elections with the support of black, yuppie, and gay neighborhoods. Black areas have been especially important. After the November 1985 election, the *Houston Chronicle* surveyed 84 key precincts and reported that Whitmire had lost all white and Hispanic areas (regardless of income level), but had captured 95 percent of the vote in black neighborhoods.[19]

In that campaign, Whitmire promised a moderate approach to growth management, while her opponent, former mayor (1964–74) and chamber of commerce president (1974–1985) Louie Welch, pledged to return the city to the unchecked growth policies of his earlier administration. The election, however, was not a clear-cut referendum on growth policy. Welch and some of his followers called the "straight slate," muddied the significance of the outcome by focusing attention on Whitmire's support from homosexuals and on an alleged AIDS threat to the community. Welch's offhand suggestion into a live microphone that officials should "shoot the queers" probably contributed to his downfall. To the extent that Whitmire in Houston and protectionists elsewhere have been successful, the urban ethos of growth without change breaks apart and an urban pathos for nondeveloping, nonadvancing inner-city peoples rises.

Faced with such serious internal revolts, city officials might be forgiven for taking too lightly the last challenge, that posed by the suburbs.[20] There are several reasons why the suburban threat might have seemed less troublesome. Chief among them is the fact that the leaders of Sunbelt cities and suburbs intermingle. Many of the newer urban commercial-civic elites live in the suburbs and see no conflict between urban and suburban interests. Moreover, in the geographically large cities of the region, the locus of major economic power has remained within city borders. In most areas, central cities still control regional planning and the distribution of new developments.

Like the veterans before them, suburban leaders seek only a share of developmental riches. There is no dispute over the central objective of expansion. Conflicts arise only as to the best methods for attracting businesses and the distribution of growth-generated services. In discussing industrial recruitment, suburbs often promote highway construction and oppose the building of metropolitan transit systems. The former helps suburban industrial recruitment, but the latter encourages low-income nonwhites to seek jobs in the predominantly white suburbs. Once an industry has relocated in the area, cities and suburbs compete to gain new junior colleges and to avoid new sewage treatment centers, both by-products of business relocation.

Thus, in some metropolitan areas, intergovernmental harmony is already a thing of the past. Some suburbs have begun both defensive maneuvers to prevent annexation, and offensive efforts to lure private and public development dollars away from central cities. Although this movement is far more advanced outside the Sunbelt, it is occurring around Miami, Tampa, Atlanta, Oklahoma City, and elsewhere.

The annexation battle between Edmond, Oklahoma, and Oklahoma City demonstrates the ability that some suburbs already have to alter central city priorities. In the early 1960s regionally powerful Oklahoma City snapped up hundreds of acres of unincorporated land outside its boundaries. Before it was through, the Sooner metropolis became America's geographically largest city (aside from those consolidated with other units of government). Fearful of being surrounded, the northeastern suburb of Edmond, a college town of some 10,000 whites and virtually no blacks, struck a unique deal with Arcadia, an unincorporated black community located some ten miles to the east. Allegedly promising to protect tiny Arcadia High School and its powerful basketball team from school consolidation, Edmondites annexed their neighboring community and the thin corridor of land along the state highway connecting the two locales. This action sealed off further Oklahoma City expansion on the northeast and stopped the momentum of its annexation drive. By 1986, independent Edmond's 40,000 residents had the highest per capita income in the state, and its Oak Tree Country Club was set to host the PGA Championship Golf tournament. Meanwhile, Oklahoma City school officials, unrestricted by city boundaries, have folded Arcadia High School into a neighboring school district.

As in this case, skirmishes between the business-minded leaders of central cities and those of the suburbs often take place in the offices of regional planning agencies. City and suburban officeholders both want their metropolitan areas to prosper, and both contribute to the planning effort, though cities are generally more energetic in industrial recruitment. Cooperation, however, goes only so far. Regardless of the city's political leadership (whether commercial-civic elite, minority, or coalition), its officials want to harbor as much development as possible within city boundaries. Suburban leaders, meanwhile, want to steal away clean industry and wholesale, retail, and service establishments for their own locales. Everyone wants high-tech growth.

This suburban challenge is, of course, largely the result of the in-migration of many young families seeking split-level comfort amidst eroded canyons and idle cotton fields outlined by rows of Civilian Conservation Corps trees. But the federal government has also played a role, and not one limited to encouraging population movements through mortgage guarantees and superhighway construction. Until 1965, city and suburban leaders went their separate ways, each seeking advancement for their own territories. There was little intergovernmental communication. In that year, however, federal planners intervened, making metropolitan regional organizations eligible for housing subsidies and requiring suburban consultation for model-cities grants. At the time there were only nine metropolitan councils of governments (COGs) in the whole country. The number of these mini–United Nations, which operate on the one-city, one-vote principle as planning agencies and debating societies, quickly swelled into the hundreds, and they expanded into rural areas as well. Great Society legislation gave them power, some of which they have retained through the years of federal disengagement. The prime tool of the COGs is their ability to collect and manage the data necessary for orderly planning. As the dispensers of information, they receive the support and attention of local governments, large and small. Although still underdeveloped sources of strength for suburban leaders, COGs nonetheless have aided those financially limited officials by contributing data and grant money to their efforts to break up the regional dominance of central cities.[21]

More discord lies ahead. As the suburbs grow in population and wealth, their own separate leaderships will grow too in economic and political influence. Regardless of strength, however, the suburbs pose no threat to the concept of growth without social change. In fact, with central cities increasingly given over to an urban pathos of internal concerns, the suburbs may shift the focus of the older growth ethos to the metropolitan level.

In many ways, Atlanta is the once and future flagship of Sunbelt metropolitan development. Guided for decades by a handful of business leaders, the younger ones coming from the postwar years of revolt and reform, the central city's government now has black hands at the tiller. As difficult a change as that was for the old leadership of the capital city of the South, it would have been much more traumatic if the black-controlled municipal government had not proven willing to accept growth as an important goal. Convinced that an improved quality of life for all Atlantans depended on continued expansion, the Jackson and Young administrations have kept communications open with the city's economic power brokers. In effect, a black city government now works hand-in-hand with a white commercial elite to encourage growth with social change—that is, growth with at least a modest redistribution of its benefits.

Beyond the city, however, white suburban power is unchallenged. Indeed, the government of Atlanta's neighboring DeKalb County, with a population larger than that of Atlanta proper, directly affects the lives of more people than does the Young administration in the central city. With strong local governments controlled by urban blacks and suburban whites, Atlanta's modern commercial-civic elite must bargain and compromise in a way that William Hartsfield and company never did. The net effect is a blend of the new metropolitan ethos for growth without social change with the new urban pathos for a fair distribution of the benefits of that growth. It is a metropolitan symbiosis based on growth and political change that should provide more enjoyable, if not smoother, sailing for the people of Atlanta and the Sunbelt as a whole.

Notes

1. Morton Sosna, "More Important Than the Civil War: The Social Impact of World War II on the South" (Paper presented at the annual meeting of the Southern Historical Association, Memphis, Nov. 1982); Gerald D. Nash, *The American West Transformed: The Impact of the Second World War* (Bloomington: Indiana Univ. Press, 1985. As used here, the Sunbelt refers to the states below the 37th parallel, running roughly across the tops of the states of North Carolina, Tennessee, Arkansas, Oklahoma, New Mexico, and Arizona. Elsewhere the author has included Southern California in this area, but this work neglects that region.

2. Blaine A. Brownell, *The Urban Ethos in the South, 1920–1930* (Baton Rouge: Louisiana State Univ. Press, 1975). Brownell used the term only in regard to southern cities, but it had wide applicability in the West as well. See Richard M. Bernard and Bradley R. Rice, eds., *Sunbelt Cities: Politics and Growth since World War II* (Austin: Univ. of Texas Press, 1983); Bradford Luckingham, *The Urban Southwest: A Profile History of Albuquerque, El Paso, Phoenix, and Tucson* (El Paso: Texas Western, 1982); David R. Johnson, John A. Booth, and Richard J. Harris, eds., *The Politics of San Antonio: Community, Progress, and Power* (Lincoln: Univ. of Nebraska Press, 1983): David M. Tucker, *Memphis since Crump: Bossism, Blacks, and Civic Reformers, 1948–1968* (Knoxville: Univ. of Tennessee Press, 1980); Edward F. Haas, *DeLesseps S. Morrison and the Image of Reform: New Orleans Politics, 1948–1961* (Baton Rouge: Louisiana State Univ. Press, 1974). In his survey of *The Deep South States of America: People, Politics, and Power in the Seven States of the Deep South* (New York: Norton, 1974), 467, journalist Neal R. Peirce argues that high population mobility prevented Miami from developing an "encrusted power structure." But as noted later, even here the "urban ethos" prevailed.

   For a dissenting view of urban political power in the New South, see Carl V. Harris, *Political Power in Birmingham, 1871–1921* (Knoxville: Univ. of Tennessee Press, 1977). According to Harris, elites controlled elections, but actual decision making was shared by many groups. If corroborated, Harris's views would bring Southern urban history more in line with national trends toward bureaucratic control over cities, as described in Jon C. Teaford, *The Unheralded Triumph: City Government in America, 1870–1900* (Baltimore: Johns Hopkins Univ. Press, 1984), and Kenneth Fox, *Metropolitan America: Urban Life and Urban Policy in the United States, 1940–1980* (Jackson: Univ. of Mississippi Press, 1986).
3. Goldfield, *Cotton Fields and Skyscrapers: Southern City and Region, 1607–1980* (Baton Rouge: Louisiana State Univ. Press, 1982). See also Lawrence H. Larsen, *The Rise of the Urban South* Lexington: Univ. of Kentucky Press, 1985); James C. Cobb, *Industrialization and Southern Society, 1877–1984* (Lexington: Univ. of Kentucky Press, 1985); idem, *The Selling of the South: The Southern Crusade for Industrial Development, 1936–1980* (Baton Rouge: Louisiana State Univ. Press, 1982).
4. Brownell, *Urban Ethos in the South*, xix–xx. John Mollenkopf, in *The Contested City* (Princeton: Princeton Univ. Press, 1983), argues that nationally the Democratic party has formed a urban progrowth coalition that has served well the party's political purposes. See also Jon C. Teaford, *The Twentieth-Century City: Problem, Promise, and Reality* (Baltimore: Johns Hopkins Univ. Press, 1986); Carl Abbott, *Urban America in the Modern Age, 1920 to the Present* (Arlington Heights, Ill.: Harlan Davidson, 1986); and Steven C. Ballard and Thomas E. James, eds., *The Future of the Sunbelt: Managing Growth and Change* (New York: Praeger, 1983).
5. This analysis builds on Carl Abbott, *The New Urban America: Growth and Politics in Sunbelt Cities* (Chapel Hill: Univ. of North Carolina Press,

1981), but it differs from his work in the identification of the GI reformer and minority challenges to Old Guard politics.

6. Quoted in Richard J. Lingeman, *Don't You Know That There is a War On? The American Homefront, 1941–1945* (New York: Perigee Books, 1970), 75.

7. Ibid., 88. Philip Funigiello, in *The Challenge to Urban Liberalism: Federal-City Relations during World War II* (Knoxville: Univ. of Tennessee Press, 1978), 144–150, tells of federal efforts to control venereal disease led by the untouchable Elliot Ness and his ironically named assistant, Raymond Clapp. In addition to Funigiello's work, the best overall treatment of the effects of the federal government on cities during and after World War II is Mark I. Gelfand, *A Nation of Cities: The Federal Government and Urban America, 1933–1965* (New York: Oxford Univ. Press, 1975). See also Peter K. Eisinger, "The Search for a National Urban Policy, 1968–1980," *Journal of Urban History* 12 (Nov. 1985): 3–24. For a broader view of urban-military relations, see Roger W. Lotchin, ed., *The Martial Metropolis: U.S. Cities in War and Peace* (New York: Praeger, 1984).

8. Haas, *DeLesseps S. Morrison.*

9. Richard M. Bernard, "Oklahoma City: Booming Sooner," 213–234; Arnold Hirsch, "New Orleans: Sunbelt in the Swamp," 100–137; and Bradford Luckingham, "Phoenix: The Desert Metropolis," 309–327; all in Bernard and Rice, eds., *Sunbelt Cities.* Amy Bridges, "Municipal Reform in the Southwest" (Paper presented at "The Sunbelt: A Region and Regionalism in the Making," Miami, 6 Nov. 1985); John C. Bollens and Henry J. Schmandt, *The Metropolis: Its People, Politics, and Economic Life* (New York: Harper and Row, 1975), 250–257; James C. Cobb, "Politics in a New South City: Augusta, Georgia, 1946–1971" (Ph.D. diss., University of Georgia, 1975); Floyd Hunter, *Community Power Structure: A Study of Decision Makers* (Chapel Hill: Univ. of North Carolina, 1953); Luckingham, *Urban Southwest,* 95–129; Peirce, *Deep South States,* 481–82; Tucker, *Memphis since Crump; New York Times,* 17 Jan. 1970.

10. For an example of the potential importance of this old inner neighborhood elite-outer area newcomer conflict, see J. Mills Thornton III, "Challenge and Response in the Montgomery Bus Boycott of 1955–1956," *The Alabama Review* 33 (July 1980): 163–235.

11. Armand Derfner, "Vote Dilution and the Voting Rights Act Amendments of 1982," in Chandler Davidson, ed., *Minority Vote Dilution* (Washington, D.C.: Howard Univ. Press, 1984), 145–163.

12. *New York Times,* 31 Oct. 1979, 13 Oct. 1983.

13. *Miami Herald,* 6 Nov. 1985; *Miami News,* 6 Nov. 1985; *New York Times,* 13 Nov., 14 Nov. 1985.

14. Bradley R. Rice, "If Dixie Were Atlanta," in Bernard and Rice, eds., *Sunbelt Cities,* 31–57; *New York Times,* 6 May 1985; Charles S. Bullock III and Bruce A. Campbell, "Racist or Racial Voting in the 1981 Atlanta Municipal Election," *Urban Affairs Quarterly* 20 (Dec. 1984): 149–164.

15. For comparisons with non-Sunbelt cities see Abbott, *New Urban America,* 211–240; Peter R. Gluck and Richard J. Meister, *Cities in Transition:*

Social Changes and Institutional Responses in Urban Development (New York: New Viewpoints, 1979), 179–204.

16. Gary R. Mormino, "Tampa: From Hellhole to the Good Life," in Bernard and Rice, eds., *Sunbelt Cities*, 138–161; Johnson, Booth, and Harris, eds., *Politics of San Antonio; New York Times*, 5 Sept. 1985.

17. Johnson, Booth, and Harris, eds., *Politics of San Antonio; Time* (13 Apr. 1981): 59; Paul Burka, "Rule, Hispania," *Texas Monthly* (Apr. 1981): 164–168.

18. *New York Times*, 2 Dec. 1985.

19. UPI release, 9 Nov. 1983; *New York Times*, 20 Oct. 1985; *Washington Post*, 21 Oct. 1985; *Houston Chronicle*, 30 July, 6 Nov. and 7 Nov. 1985. Ironically, it took a Mexican-American mayor to restore momentum to the cause of growth in San Antonio. In 1981 Henry Cisneros, a growth advocate, captured the mayor's office against a major progrowth Anglo leader. Mexican-Americans who had endorsed the restrained growth policies of COPS faced a limited choice. In order to support a Mexican-American candidate, they had to accept his progrowth policies.

20. Kenneth Jackson's *Crabgrass Frontier: The Suburbanization of the United States* (New York: Oxford Univ. Press, 1985) is the definitive work on the rise of suburbs and their challenge to central city governments. See also Jon. C. Teaford, *City and Suburb: The Political Fragmentation of Metropolitan America, 1850–1970* (Baltimore: Johns Hopkins Univ. Press, 1979). Although both works are excellent, Teaford gives short shrift to the post–World War II era, and neither covers suburbs in the South and Southwest in more than passing comparisons. See also Peter O. Muller, *Contemporary Suburban America* (Englewood Cliffs, N.J.: Prentice-Hall, 1981).

21. Bollens and Schmandt, *Metropolis*, 303–309.

6   Politics and Growth
in Sunbelt Cities

Amy Bridges

For all the recent attention to Sunbelt cities, we know remarkably little about their distinctive style of politics and government. The lack of scholarly work on Sunbelt cities leaves three deficits in understanding urban history and politics. First, our understanding of city politics is almost wholly informed by knowledge of the Northeast and Midwest. Indeed, in the not-too-distant past the student of city politics was likely to read only about New York, New Haven, and Chicago, and perhaps Floyd Hunter's Regional City. Although the regional bias in the study of city politics is no longer so complete, we are still without an account of urban political development in the Sunbelt, much less a rethinking of urban politics that includes such an account. Second, lack of attention to the Sunbelt has meant lack of attention to reform government. Concentrating on the Northeast and Midwest, political scientists and historians have closely documented the municipal reform movement campaigning against bosses, patronage, and corruption but have provided only partial accounts of its triumphs. Third, the lack of historical studies has encouraged scholars to understand the Sunbelt as one vast region reaching from coast to coast, despite the very great differences between the states that were once the Confederacy and the states of the Southwest. Whatever the cities of the southern half of the United States have had in common for the last ten or fifteen years, their differences over the course of the twentieth century suggest that it is sensible to distinguish between the cities of the Old South and the cities of the Southwest. I consider only the latter to be Sunbelt cities.

Just as the big cities of the Northeast and Midwest have commonly been governed by political machines, and the cities of the South by Bourbon coalitions, the cities of the Southwest have boasted a distinctive style of local politics. It is in the Southwest that the municipal reform movement had its greatest triumphs in the Progressive Era. Since that time citywide elections, nonpartisanship, and commission and council manager governments have been the rule not only for small cities (as in other regions) but also for big city politics. If, elsewhere, municipal reformers were either confined to smaller cities or condemned to valiant but futile opposition, in the urban Southwest good government advocates have ruled for generations.

The course of reform governance in Sunbelt cities may be broken into three periods: from the turn of the century to World War II, from World War II to 1975, and from 1975 to the present. It is fair to say that the cities of the Southwest were politically founded in the Progressive Era. Between the turn of the century and the First World War, Houston, Fort Worth, Austin, Dallas, Oklahoma City, Tulsa, Phoenix, San Diego, San Jose, and Albuquerque first incorporated, enacted new city charters, or were given new city charters by their state legislatures. Like Galveston, Texas, the best-known case of municipal reform, nearly all these cities adopted commission and later city manager charters (or some combination of the two). Reform government, however, was more a *de jure* than a *de facto* reality in these early years.

The cities of the Southwest were refounded in the years immediately following the Second World War. Between 1945 and 1955 San Antonio, Oklahoma City, Houston, Albuquerque, San Jose, Phoenix, and Dallas adopted new reform charters or witnessed other significant political changes. These changes created regimes that, collectively, served as the basis for most textbook accounts of municipal reform.

Both the structure and the priorities of those governments provoked opposition. In 1976, under federal pressure, San Antonio—and many other cities in its wake—chose to create a district system of representation. That change ushered in the third era of politics in the Sunbelt, one of greater representation of people of color, and changed governmental priorities.

Across these three stages growth has been the dominant theme of local politics. In the Progressive Era the small but ambitious and capital-starved towns of the Southwest sent out emissaries seeking trade, and solicited railroads and utilities in the nation's investment centers. Nourished by 1940s defense spending, the fledgling towns grew to metropolitan industrial status. The more tightly integrated economy of the postwar years, and the intercity competition it has generated, mean that growth and redevelopment—though now contentious and much debated—remain at center stage in local politics. Another persistent theme in Sunbelt cities has been the prominence of organized business groups in local politics. This essay describes the three eras in the political development of the urban Southwest, tracing the course of reform governance, growth strategy, and business activism. A concluding section discusses alternative explanations for the trajectory of urban political development in the Southwest.

Boss Tweed and V. O. Key Head West

The businessmen who organized reform government, the citizens who supported it, and the intellectuals who propagandized for it shared a vision of what reform governance should look like. In this vision, the abolition of ward representation and parties broke the link between particularistic citizen demands and municipal government. In their place citywide elections and nonpartisanship would ensure the election of men committed to the interests of the city as a whole. Reducing the mayor to a ceremonial role—if the office continued to exist at all—would do away with opportunities for demagoguery. City managers, appointed rather than elected, would be "removed as far as possible from the immediate effects of public opinion."[1] Municipal employees would be hired on merit rather than according to political persuasion. City councils were to be the architects of broad policies, while city managers were to plan coherently, administer professionally, provide the council with a range of options for realizing their policies, and be consistently frugal. Confident that the adoption of new city charters would bring all else to pass, reformers campaigned for new charters, saw them enacted, and retired from politics.

The elimination of a strong mayor and the move to nonpartisanship did, as reformers intended, make the construction of a centralized and dominating political machine virtually impossible. Nonpartisanship created an environment in which unity among politicians was very difficult to achieve; in both the commission form and later, under city manager charters, the tendency toward disorganization and factionalism was extremely strong. The most common pattern of local politics under reform charters, then, was not at all what reformers intended. Across the Southwest a profusion of transient alliances, factions, and "rings" governed with little consistency and few notable politicians. In Phoenix, "a curious combination of big city bossism and Old West frontierism" characterized city government for decades.[2] In San Diego, "each election was a free-for-all, with independent candidates enlisting as much personal support as possible."[3] In Albuquerque, the early years of the city manager plan were "engulfed" by "the uproar and confusion of factionalism."[4]

In important respects, politics in these towns followed the pattern V. O. Key described in *Southern Politics*. Key looked at politics in the states of the former Confederacy, tracing the consequences of monolithic adherence to the Democratic party. "Technically," Key argued, "the description of the politics of the [one-party] south amounts to the problem of analyzing the political struggle under a system of nonpartisan elections," which is of course the case for the cities examined here.[5] Both in the southern states and in Sunbelt cities political competition was factionalized and disorganized. That made it difficult for voters to identify candidates with policies, and nearly impossible to throw the rascals out. Worse, in the absence of party competition candidates tended toward demagoguery, and although their rhetoric was often populistic, the reality is that in the absence of parties public policy tends to be conservative.

Although reform charters for the most part had disorganizing effects on politicians, some politicians were able to see and take the opportunities provided by reform arrangements. The commission form of government was subject to quite straightforward politicization.[6] In the pure commission form, citizens elected the heads of city departments. Citizens in Austin, for example, elected five commissioners, to head the departments of parks, streets, police, finance, and public affairs (this last commissioner was also the mayor). Commissioners inevitably became closely associated with their service-providing bureaucracies. Services provided won friends among citizens and among the firms most closely concerned with departmental work. Employment opportunities provided the materials for the construction of personal machines. This was the situation in Dallas, for example, which had nonpartisan commission government from 1907 to 1931. In the genteel language of a proreform observer, "It was common practice for [each commissioner] to depend for political support on his departmental subordinates." Similarly, the commissioner was bound to court the favor of "those pressure groups that had a direct interest, usually a selfish one, in his work."[7] Commission government, then, failed to halt the collusion of city officials and interest groups, the courting of constituent interests, or patronage employment. Worse, commission government made no provision for centralization. Only rarely did commissioners create a "ring" that governed coherently; more often they simply competed with one another for resources.

Despite the formidable barriers to centralization, a few Sunbelt politicians had long and successful careers of municipal leadership. Albuquerque's Clyde Tingley, Oscar Holcombe of Houston, and Tom Miller in Austin each governed his city for the better part of three decades. These Sunbelt centralizers had important shared characteristics. Like New York's Boss Tweed, they formed strong alliances with other politicians, put government employees to good organizational use, and styled themselves the benefactors of laboring men and people of color. They ensured their dominance of city politics by pursuing growth strategies that courted not only the kind of small businessman always dependent on city government (like tavern owners) but also the sort of farseeing (and wealthier) businessman whose economic stake was in planning, real estate, and growth. Each centralizer dominated his city by organizing massive popular support and leading administrations efficient enough to stave off, for at least a generation, another round of reforming zeal.

Tingley and Miller capitalized on their low status origins. Tingley was a member of Albuquerque's commission government from 1923 until 1955, except for the years 1934–38, when he was governor. From 1923 until 1946 he was in firm control of Albuquerque's government. Tingley was a barely literate machinist who carried his union card well into his old age (despite the fact that his marriage made him a wealthy man). As alderman, as "mayor," and during four years as governor of New Mexico, Tingley was solicitous of organized labor and disadvantaged citizens. He also styled himself "Albuquerque's number one city builder," claiming credit for utilities and an infrastructure that kept pace with a growing population, and for a park system, a zoo, an expanded school system, a beach, a civic auditorium, and an airport.[8]

Similarly, Tom Miller campaigned as a friend of union labor and of Austin's black citizens. He served as mayor of Austin from 1933 until 1949, and again from 1955 until 1961. Although under the city charter the mayor has "no regular administrative duties," Miller was the center and driving force of Austin's government. Miller's long tenure, his good relationship with the city manager, and the excellent rating of Austin's bonds all were symptomatic of his ability to reconcile the demands of reform tenets, economic growth, and popular support.[9]

If Tingley and Miller were men of the people, Oscar Holcombe was the "old gray fox"—a gentleman Democrat and master politician of the first order. Holcombe first served as mayor in 1921 and left that office for the last time in 1957, having served for 22 of the intervening 36 years. Holcombe had strong ties to organized labor and to the black community, and on at least one occasion won the endorsement of the city's Spanish press.[10] He was also a skillful booster of Houston, traveling to St. Louis and to Rocky Mountain cities to promote Houston's virtue as a port. More, Holcombe was a pioneer in appointing a planning commission for Houston as early as the 1920s. His campaigns consistently stressed public improvements to accommodate growth.[11]

Outside the Southwest, Sunbelt centralizers had a contemporary counterpart in Kansas City's Tom Pendergast. Pendergast constructed a formidable machine despite Kansas City's city manager charter. In 1938, when would-be reformers met as the Houston Charter Commission to draft charter changes (which were not successful), Pendergast was the subject of some discussion. One member of the commission had this to say:

> I respect a good politician. I respect Tom Pendergast. I would accept his word as quickly as I would accept the word of anyone . . . This is the part they played. They control the popular vote . . . Mr. Pendergast is wise enough that he and his organization will retain their power. They must give Kansas City good government . . . It is a pleasure to read of the structures which have been built. . . . That has come from the city manager form of government.[12]

If that reformer was right, Pendergast governed because he and his colleagues accepted a division of labor between themselves and the city manager. The politicians organized consent, while the city manager saw to it that the city's infrastructure kept pace with growth. Not incidentally, this modus vivendi was facilitated by the resources made available to Tingley, Holcombe, and Miller by the Roosevelt administration in Washington. Equally important, Tingley, Holcombe, and Miller—unlike Pendergast or Tweed—were not corrupt. So they were able to satisfy both ordinary voters and supporters of municipal reform. For many Sunbelt business leaders, however, the political styles of the 1920s and 1930s seemed inadequate to the challenges anticipated for the postwar era. So the cities of the Southwest required refounding.

Good Government in the Golden Age of Reform

In the decade following the Second World War, the cities of the Southwest were refounded. In Houston, Austin, San Antonio, and Phoenix, municipal reformers organized another round of charter revisions. In Phoenix and San Antonio, advocates of reorganization also formed committees and campaigned to take over city government; this happened in Albuquerque and San Jose as well. In Oklahoma City a reenergized chamber of commerce selected and funded candidates in whom they could have confidence.[13]

Unlike their Progressive forebears, these reformers did not retire from politics after an intitial burst of zeal. In Phoenix, for example, nearly every city council member elected between 1949 and 1975 was a nominee of the Charter Government Committee.[14] In Albuquerque the Citizens' Committee controlled city government from 1954 to 1966.[15] In San Antonio, Good Government League nominees won 77 of 81 council races between 1955 and 1971.[16] In Houston the 8-F crowd, in Fort Worth the Seventh Street Gang, and in San Jose the Book of the Month Club, while not openly sponsoring candidates, set the agenda for local government.[17] The Good Government League and its counterparts in other cities created regimes that served as the basis for most textbook accounts of municipal reform. The common product was government that was small, efficient, and largely concerned with orderly growth.

Reformers in Phoenix may well have been the most self-conscious about their mission and accomplishments. In the spring of 1949 the president of the Arizona Young Democrats and his Republican counterpart decided to form an organization to slate candidates for the fall municipal election in Phoenix. At the same time, an older (and wealthier) group had been organized with similar goals. In July twenty-nine men and women met to form the Charter Government Committee (CGC). The CGC's platform promised to bring the new city manager charter to life by appointing a professional city manager, end the rule of "political bosses" at city hall, and "insure efficient and economical government." Not surprisingly, the self-description of this group and its philosophy were immensely self-serving. Here the CGC describes its philosophy:

> The philosophy of the Charter Government Councils has been simple. Those who contribute to the election of Charter candidates do so to insure sound and efficient government. Out of Good Government comes pride and community self-respect and these in turn result in continued steady economic growth from which all citizens benefit, including those who have made contributions in time, effort, and money.

The government they favored was of course limited government. As Jack Williams, who served as mayor of Phoenix, explained, "All government is by nature dictatorial. . . . The less of it the better."[18]

Both the Phoenix City Council and the CGC offered publications celebrating the successes of reform. In 1960 population growth and annexation headed the list. A $70 million bond issue was devoted to sewers, streets, water systems, parks, the airport, and a municipal building. *A Decade of City-Manager Government in Phoenix* boasted of administrative accomplishments, streamlined purchasing and other procedures, and improved fiscal management.[19] Seven years later the city council's pamphlet contrasted "35 years of confusion" prior to 1950 with the "council manager plan reform" since 1950. Tax rates had been reduced 23 percent since 1949; the tax rate was cut in 1950, 1951, and 1955, and remained constant at $1.75 after 1955. Although Moody's rated the city's bonds "Baa" in 1950, the bonds had by 1967 achieved an A rating. Since 1960 an additional $30 million bond issue had been approved by the electorate. Again, infrastructure improvements were many, as the city worked to pave, light, water, and drain its expanding area. Again too, annexation was a priority, and the council was at pains to explain the pitfalls of a failure to continue to incorporate its sprawling surroundings. Also planned were a convention center, airport improvements, an art museum and little theater, and parks and libraries. By 1967 there were also antipoverty efforts. Despite participation in federal programs, however, social services were not a part of the council's list of accomplishments.[20]

Alongside the council's achievements were the efforts of the chamber of commerce to recruit new industry to Phoenix.[21] Before seeking those new investors, the Chamber devised a political agenda meant to improve Phoenix as an environment for business. Among other changes, the chamber sought to alter the tax base, and encouraged the passage of urban development bond issues. In 1979, in fact, the *Wall Street Journal* congratulated Phoenix on "its willingness to limit government and free the private sector." Chamber representatives and their booster organization, the Thunderbirds, invited prospective investors to visit at the chamber's expense, escorted them about town, and presented them with dossiers of Phoenix's attractions as a site for industrial location. Moreover, the general manager of the chamber "made all of the authorizations regarding what concessions *the city* would be willing to make in order to attract a given industry." All of this courting and conceding worked: having targeted the electronic industries, Phoenix counted among its new employers Motorola, AiResearch, General Electric, Goodyear Aircraft, Kaiser, and Sperry Phoenix.[22]

Elsewhere, too, the agenda of municipal government was annexation and pursuit of growth. The story of Sunbelt annexations has already been well told: however contentious annexation may have seemed in the Southwest, there was hardly a city that was not the envy of every mayor in the Northeast and Midwest for its ability to gobble up its own sprawling suburbs. Strategies for economic growth varied. In Houston, as late as 1963, the ship channel and related businesses accounted for 11 percent of the city's workforce, and the oil industry has remained central to the city's economy.[23] But Houston also accomplished the great coup of attracting the NASA Space Center, and built up a corridor of research hospitals. Austin never strayed from its white-collar strategy of the Progressive years. Albuquerque, like Phoenix, recruited high-technology and electronics industries.[24]

Small wonder that these governments were popular with middle-class and affluent voters. The very success of growth strategies increased the stream of reform supporters. Changes in Albuquerque make the point well. When Clyde Tingley was the city's most prominent politician, its largest employer was the Santa Fe Railroad yards. By 1946 the state's largest employer was the Sandia Corporation, a laboratory founded by researchers from the Los Alamos laboratory, which conducted basic research for development of the atomic bomb.[25]

In addition to middle-class support, these governments were protected by legal barriers to participation. Texas, for example, retained the poll tax until 1966, and required annual registration (in January!) for some years after that. Early registration and literacy testing were both required in Arizona.[26] Even when those obstacles were overcome, poor prospects for victory in citywide elections and the absence of party competition depressed turnout. In Phoenix the percentage of eligible voters who cast ballots dropped steadily from 53 percent in 1949 (the first year of the Charter Government Commission) to 32 percent in 1957, "a trend," a reform supporter reported, "which probably indicates satisfaction with the status quo."[27] Nor did reform groups make great efforts to solicit minority supporters. The Albuquerque Citizens' Committee, for example, only once nominated a Hispanic on its slate. Taken together, then, nonpartisanship, citywide elections, and, exclusionary rules minimized the participation and representation of potential constituents and kept their dissatisfactions from becoming effective political demands.

Whatever satisfaction there may have been with the status quo, by the 1960s there were also reasons for dissatisfaction and conflict. Downtown areas were showing signs of deterioration, and there was division about the urban renewal strategy for redevelopment. Annexation kept a dispersed population within city boundaries, but could not check the dispersal of retail and commercial space to other nuclei. "Second" downtowns appeared in San Antonio, Phoenix, and Albuquerque, dividing the business community against itself.[28] At the same time, the partnership of municipal government and the business community sometimes strayed from joint concern for the public good to conspiracy for private gain. Even in the absence of outright corruption, the circle consulted on policy and planning was very small.[29] Citizens who were unrepresented were increasingly vocal about their discontent. For all of these reasons the cities' erstwhile respectable leaderships came to be portrayed as the villains of local politics. By 1966 the Albuquerque Citizens' Committee was denounced as a "small, exclusive, power-hungry group of men operating a Tammany Hall machine to perpetuate their control of city government."[30] Changing this system would take tremendous effort and also help from a higher authority.

Rebellion and Reorganization

Good government advocates in the Southwest created regimes that encouraged "a quiescent, acquiescent citizenry, where only the business community and the property-owning middle class need to be politicized." Here government was "a somnambulistic institution," ordering growth in the midst of political consensus.[31] Challenge to that consensus came from three places. First, growth produced diversification and thence division within the business community. This meant there was debate and uncertainty about growth strategy, particularly concerning downtown areas. Second, growth itself produced opposition. This sentiment was reflected in the airport sign reading "Leaving San Diego? Take a friend." Third, the political consensus of good government was founded on exclusion, and rebellion against exclusion was persistent.

Pursuit of growth brought both division among business leaders and division between growth advocates and popular groups. First, deteriorating central cities and satellite downtowns divided the business community against itself. At issue was whether municipal government's growth strategy should remain focused on the "old" downtown or shift its attention to a satellite. Just this sort of division undermined the solidarity of the Good Government League (GGL) in San Antonio and the Albuquerque Citizens' Committee.[32] Second, although good government always insisted it was small and efficient, the reality was that rapid growth required sizable public financing for infrastructure, water, public buildings, and fancier projects such as sports arenas. That spending raised issues of absolute willingness to spend money and issues of equity among residents. Bond issue defeats became more and more common across the Southwest as taxpayers questioned the benefits (either for their own pocketbooks or for the public good) of continued aggressive growth strategies. There were other costs of growth as well, for example, traffic congestion or stress on public services like the school system. Antigrowth sentiment, then, involved a broad spectrum of issues from equity to economic rationality to quality of life.[33] We will never know whether good government regimes could have forged a new consensus or compromise between growth and antigrowth sentiment, because the challenge to exclusionary rules forced a reorganization of political life.

In retrospect it seems inevitable that civil rights issues eventually overwhelmed good government. Nevertheless, the very efficacy of exclusionary rules made changing the political order from within impossible. In the first place, the exclusive tendency of good government groups can hardly be doubted. For example, in San Antonio the city's wealthiest census tract was home to eight of the thirty-six persons who served on the city council between 1965 and 1971; only 22 of 77 GGL candidates were Hispanic or black, although even in 1955 the city was 46.5 percent people of color. When, in the mid-1960s, Hispanic leaders supported independent candidates as alternatives to the GGL, GGL fundraising letters warned, "Somehow we've got to awaken more San Antonioans to the dangers of radical racism and brown power which Torres, Pena, and the barrio gangs preach."[34]

There were, in addition, the legal barriers to voting cited earlier. Once the white primary, literacy testing, and similar barriers were abandoned, the efficacy of the rules of political life at excluding diversity became apparent. Houston, for example, had a system of elections that became known elsewhere as the "black beater." City council members had to be nominated in their home districts, and were required to win elections citywide. The system beat blacks because those militant enough to win nomination in their own districts were offensive to the citywide electorate. Between 1959 and 1979, nine black or Mexican-American candidates in Houston won their districts but lost the general election to the city council.[35] Elsewhere, intermittent efforts to organize citywide slates to compete with good government groups generally met with defeat. Much of the good government political order conspired toward that outcome: low participation in city politics, the costs of mounting citywide campaigns, the difficulties of voter choice in nonpartisan systems, and the higher turnout of social groups with whom good government remained popular.

Good-government supporters had an additional strategy. As minority populations threatened to become majority populations, suburban annexation offered the opportunity to replenish the ranks of Anglo voters. In Dallas and Houston citizen groups brought suit against the city government, claiming that annexation had this discriminatory result.[36] In 1973 the at-large electoral system in Dallas was found unconstitutional because it "operates to limit minority access to the election process or . . . dilutes or minimizes their vote."[37] In the same year a Houston group brought suit, but four years later, the court ruled on behalf of the city. For Houston and San Antonio, Justice Department intervention awaited enactment of the preclearance provisions of the Voting Rights Act of 1975. Under those provisions both cities were required either to forgo annexation or to change to a district system of municipal elections (in Houston, a mixed system).[38] Perhaps in anticipation of such contentious reorganization, Albuquerque in 1974, and Phoenix in 1982, voted changes to district elections for city council.[39]

The political maneuvering to bring Justice Department rulings to life was complicated and not without ironies. In Houston, minority leaders proposed a city council of sixteen district seats and four at-large seats. Business leaders proposed a four-four plan. City government eventually proposed a 9-5 plan, arguing that it would provide adequate minority representation and, moreover, that it was the smallest city council the Justice Department was likely to allow. In the public debate over this plan, minority leaders opposed it and business leaders, although initially in opposition, became its strong proponents. When this charter revision, which dramatically increased the representation of people of color, was passed by a two-to-one margin, analysis of the vote showed that 72 percent of Mexican-Americans and 87 percent of black voters opposed the change.[40] In San Antonio, conservatives opposed district elections to the last, though charter revisions there passed — on the strength of greatly increased turnout among people of color — by fewer than 1,700 votes out of 61, 387 cast.[41]

The immediate effects on representation were dramatic. The first election after charter revision in San Antonio produced a city council of five Hispanics, one black, and four Anglos. The first election after charter revision in Houston sent three blacks and one Hispanic to the city council.[42]

The returns are not yet in, however, on what increased representation will mean for the style and content of southwestern city politics. On one hand, Barry Kaplan has argued that Houston's minority politicians will be easily accommodated by its business leadership. Administrations succeeding the adoption of the 9-5 plan showed little if any divergence from Houston's tradition of conservative local government. Businesses have continued to take the lead in proposing solutions to Houston's growth problems. Like the majority community, moreover, the minority community vests leadership in its business owners. Thus, although minority participation and representation have increased, the direction of city government seems unchanged.[43]

On the other hand, at a minimum, increased participation and representation will alter the distribution of municipal goods and services. In Houston the election of Ben Reyes to represent the city's Mexican-American community brought a series of rewards to his district, ranging from paving and parks to libraries. More broadly, capital improvement funds have been "spent evenly at about ten percent per district."[44] In San Antonio the change in municipal priorities and the gains of the Mexican-American community have been more dramatic, encompassing both a change in redevelopment priorities and a redistribution of municipal services. This has been evident in the influence and successes of Communities Organized for Public Service (COPS), an Alinsky-style federation in the city's Hispanic community. It is important to note that now, as in the past, apparent increases in systemic largesse are paid for by the federal government. Thus "[COPS's policy] influence on the city council is most clearly evident in the distribution of federal funds [e.g., UDAG and CDBG monies] for neighborhood improvements."[45]

In addition to redistributing monies and services, increased participation and representation posed challenges to the growth strategies of good government. As an example, in San Antonio COPS insisted on low-income housing as a component of redevelopment sites originally planned for commercial uses.[46] We may expect, moreover, that there and elsewhere, difficult questions will be raised about the nonprofessional job opportunities that will be provided by various investment strategies. Henry Cisneros, intent on a high-status, high-tech corridor for San Antonio, could not promise that it would deliver much to his core consistuency.[47]

The challenges of what Charles Hamilton called the "new normalcy" of national politics are likely to affect local politics in the Southwest. Hamilton argued that the enfranchisement of people of color by the civil rights acts was likely to bring in its wake demands for collective benefits requiring increased governmental activism. On the national scene, one result has been the platform of Jesse Jackson's presidential campaigns. In local politics, demands for housing, nonprofessional employment opportunities, employment and training, drug treatment, and other services are bound to appear as a result of increased access, participation, and representation. At the local level, as at the national level, the "new normalcy" may require "a much more coherent, coordinated look at public policies and private activities."[48]

Those demands will raise other issues of governance, both larger and smaller. In examining San Antonio before its latest refounding, a number of authors noted that the standard practices of city government underserved poor communities. Poor communities tended not to have curbed streets, because curbing and other improvements were provided to those who paid special assessments that poor people could not pay. Poor communities also did not have swept streets, because street-sweeping equipment required curbs in order to work. Changing the distribution of municipal goods and services, even if newly participating groups do not succeed in changing municipal priorities, requires changes in the usual procedures and practices of local government. It remains to be seen whether the many can put to their own uses a government designed to serve the interests of the few. The alternative is for southwestern cities to create something new under the sun.

Discussion

How can this pattern of urban political development be understood? In part, the changes in the local political agenda follow from growth alone. Annexation issues, competing nuclei of retail and office space, and no-growth initiatives have been the common lot of expanding cities. The distinctive political history of the urban Southwest, however, requires some more elaborate explanation. For the most part, political scientists have argued that a conservative political culture accounted for both the embrace of municipal reform and the public policies of reform governments in the Southwest. Yet much of what is known about political culture in the Southwest does not reflect that supposed conservatism. In the decades spanning the turn of the century, for example, Texas and Oklahoma were fertile grounds for socialism and populism. New Mexico, Arizona, and Southern California were all scenes of IWW activism and very militant labor struggles. Municipal reform itself was seriously contested, both in the Progressive Era and during the refoundings of later years. Labor leaders in Houston in the 1940s, for example, cari-

catured the proposed city manager as a Hitler who would undermine
democratic rights at home even as American GIs fought for them over-
seas. Thus, if the city governments of the Southwest were conservative,
growth oriented, business dominated, and populated by municipal reformers, this was not because reform was the natural product of local
political culture. Rather, the puzzle is to explain how reformers, businessmen, and conservatives came to dominate local political culture.

I cannot completely solve that puzzle here. I suggest, however, that
to understand those processes we need to look at the strategic location
of the Southwest in American political development. The reason is that
cities are not autonomous polities in charge of their own destiny. As
Lynn H. Lees has said, we must look at what happens *to* cities as well
as what happens *in* cities. In addition, social groups within cities seek
assistance from higher governments and outside sources. As they find
allies elsewhere, the legal, political, and economic environment of the
city affects its development. For the cities of the Southwest, two elements of what I am calling strategic location had profound effects. First,
the Southwest was capital-poor. Second, the Southwest was, relative to
other regions, a latecomer to the party system.

It was the lack of capital that caused the small but ambitious cities
of the Southwest to organize to campaign for, seek out, solicit, and in-
duce investment of every sort: railroads, utilities, federal military spending. In the early period, moreover, southwestern cities were very vulnerable to the financial manipulation and service withdrawal of utilities
and mass transit companies owned by out-of-state companies. The presence of those companies was a prominent feature of municipal politics,
as it was for state politics. Politicians were accused of being creatures
of the utilities; government ownership was debated as a cure to the
utilities' arbitrary behavior. Utilities and transit companies were targets
of repeated labor conflicts. In addition, investor pressure may well have
induced the adoption of reform charters. Students of city politics have
tended to associate business prominence and power with company towns:
Coca-Cola in Atlanta, or, for that matter, Hewlett-Packard in San Jose.[49]
This survey of the Southwest suggests, instead, the *lack* of local capital
as an inducement to collective strategizing by local businesses. Much
of the character of local politics followed from this organization. Lotchin,
for example, has shown how politics and culture in San Diego, San Francisco, and Los Angeles were informed by their efforts to win the status
of home port for the (then largely imaginary) Pacific Fleet at the end
of World War I.[50] Since the Second World War, the substance of inter-

urban competition has changed, and local sources of wealth have grown. If anything, however, this has meant a greater need for urban business organization in the Northeast and Midwest, not less in the Southwest.

In the meantime, the tradition of aggressively planning growth, and the consequent prominence of business in local politics, are well established southwestern traditions. What one observer said of the Tulsa Chamber of Commerce might well be generalized to its counterparts elsewhere: "The Chamber's attitude towards local affairs may be described as a blend of philanthropy and commercial prudence." The philanthropy "made plutocratic influence in city affairs seem wholesome and legitimate."[51] To the extent that the efforts of organized business, or business and government together, seemed, like the moon, to move the tide that lifts all boats, that too made plutocratic influence wholesome and legitimate.

Strategic location is also a way to understand the political choices of the Southwest. As Martin Shefter has argued, the West was less attached to the "system of '96" than was the Northeast or the Old South. As a result, the West had a greater "regional receptivity to reform."[52] More simply, municipal reformers here faced only the barest beginnings of party organization, rather than the entrenched organizations of the Northeast and Midwest (much less the one-party fervor of the South). Moreover, early reformers had allies in state government who, for their own reasons, supported nonpartisanship and voting restrictions. In the Progressive Era, then, a variety of regional characteristics (quite independent of political culture in the cities themselves) benefited municipal reformers.

If business organization and the absence of attachment to the party system facilitated the creation of reform regimes, the rules reformers created in turn assured their continued dominance. As we have seen, the system created by municipal reformers became, in the 1960s, an unbeatable one. Thus, a third factor in the political development of southwestern cities is the institutional arrangements that shape local political life. The presence or absence of such things as parties and citywide or district elections affects who gets what and the pattern of public policy. The reason citizens fight over the rules of political life is that the rules play an important part in determining the outcome of political activities.

In the urban Sunbelt of the 1960s and 1970s, rebellion and dissatisfaction were understandable. However, just as the early trajectory of political development was not simply an outgrowth of local forces, so the reorganization of the urban Southwest in the past decade has been in large part the result of forces external to Sunbelt cities themselves. If in 1900 or 1915 the Southwest was not closely bound to the national party system, or its cities directly affected by federal policies, by 1975 this was no longer so. The Southwest has become more partisan over the course of the century, and the federal government more interventionist. The activities of the federal government are a fourth element determining the political development of the urban Southwest. Although the particulars may be different, the federal presence has been continuous. All the Sunbelt centralizers of the early period benefited from the Democratic largesse of the New Deal administrations; all the citybuilders of the Southwest have sought defense spending; water resource development, though not discussed here, has been a prerequisite for growth, and federal assistance has been vital. In each of these eras, those who had allies at the federal level—whether they were allies who spent money or allies who issued court decisions—were advantaged over those who did not.

In this essay I have provided a sketch of the political life of Sunbelt cities since their "foundings" at the turn of the century. Politics in southwestern cities is best understood when connections are made between local politics and the larger patterns of American political life. Moreover, in each era the rules of the political order are important in determining who got what from politics. Politics in southwestern cities, then, is a product of both endogenous elements (for example, the social groups in cities and their political goals, political rules) and exogenous forces (for example, national political parties, the federal government). In my further work on southwestern cities, I hope to better specify in what ways rules matter, to offer more precise explanations of how rules change, and to elaborate the ways in which the fortunes of southwestern cities have been connected with American political development more broadly.

The political development of the urban Southwest is distinctive, and it presents an opportunity to look closely at reform regimes. In the years preceding World War II local political life was often characterized by factionalism and disorder, although a few cities enjoyed governance by gifted centralizers. The three decades immediately following the war were the heyday of municipal reform, with reform regimes providing efficient administration and promoting rapid growth. More recently, local governments have been reorganized to provide greater representation of diverse populations. This may result in more equitable service delivery and altered policy priorities. Alongside those changes much of the reform legacy endures. If reformers were "just morning glories" in the Northeast, they have been hardy perennials in the Southwest.

Notes

1. Philip Trounstine and Terry Christensen, *Movers and Shakers: The Study of Community Power* (New York: St. Martins, 1982), 83.
2. Leonard E. Goodall, "Phoenix: Reformers at Work," in Leonard E. Goodall, ed., *Urban Politics in the Southwest* (Tempe: Arizona State Univ. Press, 1967), 114.
3. Harold A. Stone, Don K. Price, and Kathryn Stone, *City Manager Government in Nine Cities* (Chicago: Public Administration Service, 1950), 143.
4. Dorothy I. Cline, *Albuquerque and the City Manager Plan, 1917–1948* (Albuquerque: Univ. of New Mexico Press, 1951), 12.
5. V. O. Key, Jr., *Southern Politics* (New York: Vintage, 1949), 16.
6. An excellent survey of the commission government experience is provided by Bradley Rice, *Progressive Cities: The Commission Government Movement in America* (Austin: Univ. of Texas Press, 1977).
7. Stone, Price, and Stone, *City Manager Government*, 414.
8. For an account of Tingley's career, see Toby Smith, "Remembering Clyde," *Impact* 6 (4 Jan. 1983): 10–13; Michael J. Schingle, "Albuquerque Urban Politics, 1891–1955: Aldermanic vs. Commission-Manager Governments" (Senior thesis, University of New Mexico, 1976). The University of New Mexico Library has the very useful manuscript of Edna Ferguson's biography of Tingley; her papers and correspondence are also useful.
9. For politics in Austin in the early period, see Stone, Price, and Stone, *City Manager Government*; and Floylee Hunter Hamphill, "Mayor Tom Miller and the First Year of the New Deal in Austin, Texas" (M.A. thesis, University of Texas at Austin, 1976).
10. For union endorsements, see Holcombe Papers, Box 1, Folders 1 and 2, Houston Municipal Research Library. The endorsement is in *La Tribuna*, 13 Nov. 1924.
11. Holcombe's campaign speeches are in the Holcombe Papers at the Houston Municipal Research Library. The Political Campaign Collection there is also very useful. Holcombe's career is also discussed in David G. McComb, *Houston: The Bayou City* (Austin: Univ. of Texas Press, 1969).
12. Houston Charter Commission Papers, Houston Municipal Research Library, Box 2, Minutes for 20 June 1938.
13. The most accessible general sources for southwestern cities in the postwar era are Goodall, ed., *Urban Politics in the Southwest*; and Richard M. Bernard and Bradley R. Rice, eds., *Sunbelt Cities: Politics and Growth since World War II* (Austin: Univ. of Texas Press, 1983). In addition, for San Jose, see Trounstine and Christensen, *Movers and Shakers*; for San Antonio, see David R. Johnson, John A. Booth, and Richard J. Harris, eds.,

The Politics of San Antonio: Community, Progress, and Power (Lincoln: Univ. of Nebraska Press, 1983).

14. Bradford Luckingham, "Phoenix: The Desert Metropolis," in Bernard and Rice, eds., *Sunbelt Cities*, 319.

15. Dorothy I. Cline, "Albuquerque: The End of the Reform Era," in Goodall, ed., *Urban Politics in the Southwest*.

16. David R. Johnson, "San Antonio: The Vicissitudes of Boosterism," in Bernard and Rice, eds., *Sunbelt Cities*, 240.

17. For the 8F crowd, see Barry J. Kaplan, "Houston: The Golden Buckle of the Sunbelt," in Bernard and Rice, eds., *Sunbelt Cities*, 203–204. For San Jose, see Trounstine and Christensen, *Movers and Shakers*, 96–97. For Fort Worth, see Martin V. Melosi, "Dallas-Fort Worth: Marketing the Metroplex," in Bernard and Rice, eds., *Sunbelt Cities*, 182.

18. Brent Whiting Brown, "An Analysis of the Phoenix Charter Government Committee as a Political Entity" (M.A. thesis, Arizona State University, 1968), chap. 2; the Charter Government Committee platform, ibid., 46; its "philosophy," ibid., 40; Williams quote, ibid., 42.

19. Paul Kelso, *A Decade of Council-Manager Government in Phoenix, Arizona* (Phoenix: Phoenix City Council, 1960).

20. City of Phoenix, "The Phoenix Story of Municipal Government 1950–1967" (Mimeo, Sept. 1967).

21. Michael Francis Konig, "Toward Metropolitan Status: Charter Government and the Rise of Phoenix, Arizona, 1945–1960" (Ph.D. diss., Arizona State University, 1983), chap. 6.

22. The *Journal* quote is from Konig, "Metropolitan Status," 204; for the city's concession, ibid., 201 (emphasis added); for recruitment successes, ibid., 205–16.

23. McComb, *Bayou City*, 177, 203–204.

24. Robert Turner Wood, "The Transformation of Albuquerque, 1945–1972" (Ph.D. diss., University of New Mexico, 1980), chap. 3, section 3 discusses recruitment of industry.

25. Ibid., 97.

26. For restrictions on voting, see Bryan D. Jones and Delbert A. Taebel, "Urban Politics in Texas," in Robert D. Wrinkle, ed., *Politics in the Urban Southwest* (Albuquerque: University of New Mexico Institute for Social Research and Development, Pub. No. 81, Sept. 1971), 12; John E. Crow, "City Politics in Arizona," ibid., 29.

27. Kelso, *Decade of Council-Manager Government*, 11.

28. For Albuquerque, see Wood, "Transformation," 226–244; for Phoenix, see Konig, "Metropolitan Status," chap. 4; for San Antonio, see Johnson, Booth, and Harris, eds., *Politics of San Antonio*, 245.

29. For the corruption example, see Richard M. Bernard, "Oklahoma City: Booming Sooner," in Bernard and Rice, eds., *Sunbelt Cities*; for the small-circle characterization of San Jose and Albuquerque, see Heywood T. Sanders, "Beyond Machine and Reform: The Politics of Postwar Development in Sunbelt Cities" (Paper delivered at meeting of American Political Science Association, 6 Sept. 1984).

30. Cline, *Albuquerque and the City Manager Plan*, 19.

31. Charles Cotrell and R. Michael Stevens, "The 1975 Voting Rights Act and San Antonio, Texas," *Publius* 8 (Winter 1978): 79–99.

32. John A. Booth, "Political Change in San Antonio: Toward Decay or Democracy?" in Johnson, Booth, and Harris, eds., *Politics of San Antonio*, 194; and Cline, "Albuquerque."

33. For discussions of antigrowth sentiment, see Trounstine and Christensen, *Movers and Shakers*, 99–105; Rabinowitz, "Albuquerque: City at the Crossroads," in Bernard and Rice, eds., *Sunbelt Cities*, 262; and Anthony W. Corso, "San Diego: The Anti-City," ibid., 338–339.

34. Juanita C. Hernandez, "Chicano Political Mobilization in San Antonio City Politics, 1973–1981" (Senior thesis, Harvard University, 1982), 19–20.

35. Jaime Davila, "Houston City Politics: The 1979 Change from At-Large to Single-Member Council Districts and Its Effect on Mexican-Americans (Senior thesis, Harvard University, 1982), chap. 2, 15–17. The term "black beater" is from Cleveland; see Lee Sloan, "Good Government and the Politics of Race," *Social Problems* 17 (Fall 1969): 161–174.

36. Davila, "Houston City Politics"; Kaplan, "Houston."

37. Davila, "Houston City Politics," chap. 3, 3.

38. For Houston, see Davila, "Houston City Politics," chap. 3, 1–11; for San Antonio, see Cotrell and Stevens, "Voting Rights Act."

39. Luckingham, "Phoenix," 320; Rabinowitz, "Albuquerque," 262.

40. Davila, "Houston City Politics," chap. 3, 14–35.

41. Hernandez, "Chicano Political Mobilization," 77.

42. Ibid., 79; Kaplan, "Houston," 207.

43. Kaplan, "Houston," 206-208.

44. Davila, "Houston City Politics," chap. 4, 1–9.

45. Joseph D. Sekul, "Communities Organized for Public Service: Citizen Power and Public Policy in San Antonio," in Johnson, Booth, and Harris, eds., *Politics of San Antonio*.

46. Ibid., 181–182.

47. Ken Anderberg, "Henry Cisneros: For Now, He's San Antonio's," *American City and County* 100 (Jan. 1985): 24–36.

48. Charles Hamilton, "Political Access, Minority Participation, and the New Normalcy," in Leslie W. Dunbar, ed., *Minority Report* (New York: Pantheon, 1984), 3–25.

49. For example, see Edward C. Banfield and James Q. Wilson, *City Politics* (New York: Vintage, 1966), chap. 18, especially 263–64.

50. Roger W. Lotchin, "The Metropolitan-Military Complex in Comparative Perspective: San Francisco, Los Angeles, and San Diego, 1919–1941," *Journal of the West* 18 (July 1979): 19–30.

51. Bertil L. Hanson, "Tulsa: The Oil Folks at Home," in Goodall, ed., *Urban Politics in the Southwest*, 210.

52. Martin Shefter, "Regional Receptivity to Reform: The Legacy of the Progressive Era," *Political Science Quarterly* 98 (Fall 1983): 459–83.

Models of Ethnic and Racial Politics
     in the Urban Sunbelt South

Ronald H. Bayor

The southern portion of the Sunbelt has experienced significant change since the end of World War II. In the growth of its cities,
its population increase (especially from northern migration), its economic vitality, and its political importance, the region can now be called
the New South, a term long used by southerners but only recently a reality. It is also these very factors that define the *Sunbelt* label. One of the
most crucial areas in which the South has seen change is its pattern of
ethnic and race relations. Since 1945 black-white contact has undergone
major shifts, and since 1960, with the Cuban migration, and 1965, with
the immigration act of that year, the South has become the destination
point for large numbers of immigrants.[1] For the first time southern cities, like their northern counterparts in the nineteenth and twentieth
centuries, are experiencing large-scale foreign immigration.

This essay addresses these racial and ethnic changes in four cities (Atlanta, Miami, San Antonio, and Houston) and analyzes their implications for present and future intergroup relations in regard to the political
process. These four cities were chosen because they illustrate various
sections of the region and contain large black and/or Hispanic populations. Although not representative of all Southern cities, they do ex-
emplify the Sunbelt urban South—cities showing population and economic growth, a concern with maintaining that growth, and a legacy
of civil rights activities.

One way to understand what has happened is to consider a thesis developed by Nathan Glazer and Daniel Moynihan suggesting a northern
and a southern model of intergroup relations. In the northern model,
they saw many competing groups differing "in wealth, power, occupa-
tion, values, but in effect an open society prevail[ing] for individuals and
for groups. Over time a substantial and rough equalization of wealth
and power can be hoped for even if not attained. . . . There is competition between groups . . . but it is muted, and groups compete not through
violence but through effectiveness in organization and achievement."

The northern model therefore stressed conflict resolution, and accommodation eventually was secured, whatever the initial intensity of conflict. Each group "was able to find a place in the American economy, society, and polity." However, in the southern model, " society is divided into two segments, black and white. The line between them is rigidly drawn. Other groups must choose to which segments they belong. . . . Violence is the keynote of relations between the groups." The stress, then, was on "the sharp division between two groups, and only two groups, and the significance of law in defining the rights and privileges of each group." Based as it was on separatism, violence, and the black-white split in society, the southern model did not provide for negotiation and compromise to meet group demands, as did the northern model.[2]

Exceptions, of course, can be made to these models. In the North, violence was sometimes evident between groups and conflict or competition was not always muted when groups felt threatened. However, a resolution of the conflict was usually achieved, and each group was able to secure some piece, however meager, of the American pie. There was a tendency for groups, after initial resistance, to make room for others, to accept an adjustment of the ethnic power structure.[3] This does not mean that equality was achieved in the North but only that other groups were understood to be legitimate competitors and were owed some recognition. There was eventually some sharing of the political spoils.

The history of the urban South well into the twentieth century fit the pattern of the southern model. With rare exceptions, there was little effort to acknowledge black demands or in any way to see blacks as a legitimate competing group. For the most part, blacks received little political recognition until at least the World War II period.[4] And, beginning in the 1890s, how whites and blacks acted toward each other was carefully determined by law. A caste system therefore developed in the South, with blacks treated as inferiors. They were denied voting rights and access to public accommodations, city services, and educational funds, and were constantly harassed with violence. Segregation in all phases of white-black contact was the law.[5]

The other ethnics in the South—for example, Jews, Italians, and Chinese—were viewed as part of either the white or black group. If considered part of the black caste, as were the Chinese, they were similarly treated as inferior. But even those groups somewhat accepted into the white majority were never considered true equals. The violence against Italians in New Orleans in 1891, and the lynching of Leo Frank in 1915, as well as Ku Klux Klan attacks and general discrimination against both Italians and Jews, indicated their limited acceptance. There was simply little room for differences in the southern model, and therefore stronger pressure to assimilate totally into the favored white Protestant majority. By assimilating, or by at least muting their differences, these white ethnics tried to find acceptance in the white majority. But these groups were never a major concern in the South, because the white-black split held primacy. There was little awareness of America, let alone the South, as a multiethnic society.[6]

In the immediate post–World War II period the northern model began, on a limited scale, to appear in the South. In the 1880s and 1890s, in an effort to deny blacks any political power, a white primary was initiated. Whoever won the primary won the general election, so blacks were in effect disfranchised. In some cases, blacks were able to retain some degree of political power through their ability to vote in general elections. This usually meant little in terms of political office or state and city elections, but it did play a role in votes on bond issues. In Atlanta, for example, black support for the passage of bonds was sought and resulted in trade-off benefits in terms of funding for black schools. A 1921 bond vote resulted in the building of the first high school for blacks in the city.[7] However, blacks mostly were ignored politically, although they fully understood the importance of the vote. As the *Atlanta Daily World* (a black newspaper) noted in 1932 in urging blacks to vote, "With [the vote] they have something with which to bargain. A people with nothing with which to bargain cannot be surprised reasonably when economic and industrial opportunities pass on by their doors."[8] This situation prevailed until the mid-1940s, when the U.S. Supreme Court ruled against the white-only primary in the South and blacks were allowed to vote in primary elections. The white politicians now had to deal with blacks as a legitimate group with some power, and in race relations, "power considerations lay beneath all minority relationships."[9] This was the beginning of the end of the caste system and the repercussions were felt very quickly. For example, Mayor William Hartsfield of Atlanta, who had not before considered black demands, now began to respond.

The efforts of the All-Citizens Registration Committee, beginning in 1946, to register blacks (black registration tripled in Fulton County in three weeks), and the efforts of the Atlanta Negro Voters League after 1948 to present a united front of black Democrats and Republicans, convinced Hartsfield and other white politicians that some black demands had to be met. Within a few years black police had been hired in the city, housing needs were considered, and, most important, black leaders now had access to city hall to present their grievances.[10] The race-related problems were far from being solved. Although a black was elected to the Atlanta Board of Education in 1953, not until the mid-1960s were blacks elected to the state senate or the city council. School segregation remained, many black Atlantans continued to live in slums, and access to public accommodations came slowly and mainly through the efforts of the federal government. Yet in the 1940s blacks were starting, although still from a weak position, to "compete, bargain, and come to agreements in a style familiar . . . from Northern urban politics."[11]

A political coalition eventually developed in Atlanta linking blacks and the white business and economic elite. From the early 1950s through the 1960s, mayoral contests were decided by these two groups. Whites elected to office were often beholden to their black supporters. In an effort to maintain the economic growth of the city, and cognizant of the economic repercussions of racial conflict in other southern cities, the white business group, although slowly and sometimes reluctantly, gave in to many black demands. Particularly during the civil rights movement, the white leadership was faced with a choice between economic growth and the racial status quo. Economic needs, as in many southern cities, finally took precedence over racial concerns. As Ivan Allen, two-term mayor in the 1960s, commented, "I wasn't so all-fired liberal when I first moved into City Hall, but when I saw what the race-baiters were doing or could do to hold back the orderly growth of Atlanta, it . . . swung me to the extreme end opposite them." With the recognition that traditional southern handling of the race issue could destroy Atlanta, and with the black-white contacts and coalitions formed in the political arena, other related problems — public school desegregation, public transportation desegregation, and similar situations — could be solved through negotiation and compromise.[12]

The same process of change occurred in a number of other southern cities, although not always with the same speed. In Miami it was not until the mid- to late 1960s that blacks secured some power in metropolitan and city politics. In Houston and San Antonio, as in Miami, progress was slowed due to at-large council or commission voting, long after the white primary was eliminated. In the Texas cities, annexation also played a role in weakening black and other minority voting strengths.[13] Change was coming slowly even with the Voting Rights Act of 1965 and the civil rights movement, but there was now some room for negotiation and an initial adjustment of the racial power structure. It became clear to many white business and political leaders in the South that economic and political stability could be achieved only with racial harmony and some political accommodation. However, there was little desire for extensive change. The end of the caste system and the emergence of northern-style ethnic or racial politics is an ongoing process, still evident in the South today.

The development of a competitive, conflict-resolving race-relations system based on the northern model is only part of the change in the South. Because of large-scale Hispanic and Asian settlement and the recognition of the ability and right of these groups to compete for power, the South has also experienced the beginnings of a pluralistic intergroup pattern and the comprehension that the region is defined in more than black-white terms. It is no longer necessary to fit into white or black categories, since there is now a sense of other groups and a new awareness of coalition politics. In Georgia, for example, although only about 1.1 percent of the state's population is Hispanic and 0.5 percent Asian, these groups are heavily concentrated in the Atlanta area. Over 75,000 Hispanics of various nationalities resided in metropolitan Atlanta in 1987, an increase from 13,000 in 1970 and 50,000 in 1979. Significant numbers of Koreans, Chinese, Indians, and Vietnamese also live in the area. Many of these people are middle class, educated, upwardly mobile, and concerned with securing and protecting their rights.[14]

Atlanta politicians, both black and white, have turned their attention to these new groups. Indications of a growing awareness of Atlanta's Hispanic population were evident in the 1970s, as revealed by a report prepared for the Atlanta Regional Commission in 1979 noting the location and needs of this group within the Atlanta metropolitan area. City officials had already responded to some of the recommendations made in the study about easing Hispanic adjustment to the city. For example, in the early 1970s the Atlanta Community Relations Commission had secured the translation of all city documents into Spanish. There has been an ongoing effort to hire Hispanic police officers and more recently, as Mayor Andrew Young stated in 1986, to "see that Hispanics get a fair share of the [city] contracts." There is also a Mayor's Task Force on Hispanics in Atlanta, and a Hispanic Advisory Council meets once a month with the police department to deal with this community's problems. Furthermore, the city administration has developed plans to begin cultural-awareness training for the police so that an understanding of the Hispanic community can be achieved.[15] Asians, too, have received attention from Atlanta's political leaders. The Young administration has sought to bring Asians into the police department.[16]

Both black and white politicians who earlier saw the South only in biracial terms have had to come to terms with pluralism. Blacks, who spent many years fighting for equality and recognition, have become leaders in cities such as Atlanta just at a time when it is necessary to deal with recognition of other groups. This is not always easy. Hispanics and Asians are recognized as distinct groups with whom accommodation must be reached, but, as elsewhere in the Sunbelt, there is some tension.[17] Other groups have also taken note of the new situation in the city. The Atlanta-area Jewish community, which has increased sixfold since 1945, mainly because of northern migrations, has attempted to form coalitions with these other ethnics, Asians as well as Hispanics, in an effort to organize conflict-resolution committees. And there has been close cooperation between black and Jewish political, business, and religious leaders in the Atlanta Black–Jewish Coalition, formed in 1982 under the auspices of the local chapter of the American Jewish Committee to mobilize support for an extension of the Voting Rights Act.[18] The coalition has made an effort to discuss issues pertinent to the two communities and to strengthen ties, and exemplifies the desire to forge working relationships across ethnic-racial lines in the South.

The coalition efforts in Atlanta and the attempts to incorporate new groups into the political spectrum have proceeded relatively smoothly in this city, as compared to Miami. The Miami area illustrates the intense pluralistic political competition over interests and values between non-Latin whites, blacks, and Hispanics that can also define the New South Sunbelt city. Disagreement over the issue of official bilingualism is one symbol of this conflict. The Dade County Commission voted in 1973 to make the county officially bilingual. By 1980 an opposition had developed in the form of the Citizens for Dade United, which secured enough petition signatures to put the issue of bilingualism on the ballot. The proposal called for the elimination of funding for the 1973 bilingual resolution by forbidding the use of county money for the purposes of promoting "any language other than English or for the promotion of 'any culture other than that of the United States.' " The measure was inspired by resentment against growing Cuban economic and political power. A poll taken at the time of the vote indicated that among various groups, Jews gave the antibilingual resolution the strongest support. The leader of the petition drive, a post–World War II immigrant from Russia, asked, "How come the Cubans get everything?" and expressed her desire to bring Miami back to "the way it used to be." The resolution passed, with 71 percent of non-Latin whites supporting it and blacks and Cubans voting against it. The black opposition was based on the view that the measure was discriminatory. Although the Cubans saw in this vote the possible formation of a black-Hispanic coalition, there were tensions between these two groups over jobs, politics, services, and government funds.[19]

Blacks had been largely barred from participating in Miami politics by the poll tax (abolished in 1937), by the white primary, and after that by the procedure of at-large city commission elections. Thus blacks had to wait until the 1960s before they began to see the end of the caste system and were able to compete with whites. There was therefore natural resentment toward the Cubans, a third group with whom to share political power.[20] In Miami in 1981, blacks were the major group responsible for the defeat of the Cuban candidate for mayor, Manolo Reboso, and the reelection of Maurice Ferre (of Puerto Rican background), who was also supported by non-Latin whites. Latins made up 36 percent of the voters; blacks, 30 percent; and non-Hispanic whites, 34 percent.[21] The Miami area, which represents one of the most ethnically diverse parts of the Sunbelt, exemplifies the northern model of ethnic competition-conflict, ethnic bloc voting, coalition formation, and resistance-accommodation. There is no caste system or simple black-white split here, but rather a number of competing groups (including occasional intragroup Hispanic rivalries), an awareness of a multiethnic society, and an effort to compete through nonviolent means.

This competition will continue as the Hispanic population increases and as Hispanic political power grows in the city and county. The first Cuban on the Miami City Commission was elected in 1973, and the first Cuban member of the Dade County Commission in 1982. By 1985 Cubans, with 40 percent of the registered voters in Miami, had a majority on the Miami City Commission. In addition, a Cuban had been appointed metropolitan county manager by the Dade County Commission, indicating growing Hispanic strength outside the city of Miami. One black, Miller Dawkins, also sat on the Miami City Commission. Defeating a Cuban opponent, Victor DeYurre, in 1985 in a campaign in which one issue was whether Dawkins represented only black interests, Dawkins won a majority of the black and non-Latin white vote and DeYurre captured the Latin vote.[22]

Furthermore, in 1985 a Cuban, Xavier Suarez, was elected mayor over another Cuban candidate, Raul Masvidal, in a runoff election. Maurice

Ferre, Miami's six-term incumbent, had lost in the earlier vote due to his alienation of black voters—he had previously supported the ouster of Howard Gary, Miami's city manager and the "highest ranking black official in the areas." Ferre had received 96 percent of the black vote in 1983 but secured only 10 percent in 1985. In the runoff the black vote became the battleground between the two Cuban candidates.[23] With the two top contenders for the mayoral position Cuban, and the city commission secured by Cubans, it is clear who is winning Miami's ethnic political battles. However, the three groups are still competing for political power and positions.

Even within this ongoing competitive struggle there have been attempts to develop new coalitions. As in Atlanta, the American Jewish Committee in Miami is involved in an effort to develop ethnic understanding. The boards of the committee and the Cuban National Planning Council in Miami meet twice a year to work out "joint approaches . . . on local issues," and cooperate on such concerns as immigration and bilingual education.[24]

The appearance of a northern model and a fundamental change in urban politics is also evident in other parts of the urban Sunbelt South. In San Antonio whites (those of Anglo, German, and French backgrounds) had controlled the city politically since antebellum days. Blacks, indicating the legacy of the caste system and the southern model, had little political power, although they were occasionally manipulated by the local political machine. Subsequently, while they secured some favors, blacks were often ignored with respect to housing, jobs, and other group needs. As in Atlanta, blacks retained the vote in general elections and were at times solicited by the white power structure to support certain candidates, but they had little real power because of the white primary. Nonetheless, blacks organized and fought for their political rights through such organizations as the Bexar County Educational League, formed in 1939, the San Antonio Negro Voters' League, and local chapters of the National Negro Congress and the NAACP, which, among other goals, sought to end the white primary system.[25]

Mexican-Americans, always a large segment of the population (about 38 percent in the 1930s), fared somewhat better because they were recognized as part of a multiethnic machine coalition as early as the late 1800s. But this was, like the blacks, a group whose political power was regulated by non-Latin whites. Also, with the large Anglo and German migrations into the city at the turn of the century, the increasing political and economic influence of these groups, and the emergence of new machines and various reform movements in the twentieth century, the Chicanos received less attention from the political leaders. Chicanos were provided only token political power until the 1970s, and received even less attention in terms of city services. The recent shift in the racial-ethnic intergroup pattern was partly the result of outside forces. The end of the white primary, the civil rights movement, the Voting Rights Act of 1965 and its 1975 amendments, and other federal government reforms hastened the needed change and inspired other reforms.[26]

Blacks and Mexican-Americans temporarily united in 1948 to elect the first black, George J. Sutton, to the school board, but the real victories came later. A black was first elected to the city council in 1965. San Antonio led the South in abolishing segregated lunch counters in 1960, a decision that was a by-product of the white elite's increasing willingness to see blacks as a group worthy of more recognition. Mexican-Americans also saw their political emergence as a result of the outside impetus toward change, coupled with community activism. Organization of the Mexican-American community had occurred as early as 1921 in the effort to secure full political, economic, and social rights. La Orden de Hijos de America, founded in that year in San Antonio, worked for these goals. It was an assimilationist, middle-class group, and its members wanted to be considered good American citizens. Various Mexican-American organizations appeared later with the same general thrust. The League of United Latin American Citizens (LULAC) was founded in 1929 to encourage Americanization, to support a political role for the Chicano community, and to fight discrimination, particularly in the schools; the American GI Forum was begun in 1947 to push for veterans' rights and political involvement. Increasing attention to the need for political action is indicated by these groups as well as by those organized in the 1960s—Mexican-Americans for Political Action, and the Viva Kennedy clubs.[27]

San Antonio Chicanos started a new, neighborhood-based, grassroots group called Communities Organized for Public Service (COPS) in 1974; its goal was to "gain recognition as an equal in the bargaining process." Recognition was to be achieved through massive voter registration efforts, and by putting pressure on city hall for the delivery of more services to the Mexican-American areas of the city. Another group involved in registration work was the San Antonio–based Southwest Voter Registration Education Project, established in 1974 to increase Mexican-American political involvement in Texas. In 1976 the Atlanta-based Voter Education Project (VEP), which had been concerned primarily with black registration, joined with the San Antonio group to foster all minority voting in Texas. Although blacks and Mexican-Americans usually had not seen themselves as allies, their fight for political rights produced some unity at times. The announcement of the joint cooperative effort noted that "we are working to show that a minority political coalition, composed of blacks and Mexican-Americans who have, until recently, been denied access to the political process, can have a positive impact for all the citizens of Texas." According to John Lewis, executive director of VEP, the objective was "to foster a sense of cooperation and unity between these two minority groups which have historically followed separate paths of development." Both organizations demanded full minority access to all social, political, and economic arenas. Also active was the Mexican-American Legal Defense and Educational Fund (MALDEF), which challenged at-large district elections in San Antonio and worked to secure and enforce the 1975 Voting Rights Act.[28]

The combined effort of Mexican-American and coalition groups proved to be very effective in increasing the number of registered voters and in changing the ethnic makeup of the city government. The Southwest Voter Registration Education Project dramatically increased the number of Hispanic registered voters in the Southwest during the late 1970s. During a three-week period in 1984, COPS registered 16,000 Chicanos in San Antonio. With registration, Mexican-Americans have secured more political power and influence in states such as Texas. Spurred by an end to the poll tax in 1966, state provision for Spanish-language registration and voting forms as of 1975, and federal action, changes came quickly.[29]

City council elctions in San Antonio were the first indication of the ethnic shift. Traditionally, council members were elected by an at-large vote that weakened the strength of the Mexican-Americans concentrated on the south and west sides of the city. Fearing a growth in the Mexican-American voting population in San Antonio, the city leaders in 1972 annexed surrounding Anglo-dominated areas in an attempt to dilute further the Chicano vote. Under the Voting Rights Act of 1975, the Justice Department threatened to retroactively nullify the annexation unless a new single-member council district plan was developed. The vote in 1977 on whether to change to single-member council districts split along ethnic lines, with Chicanos carrying the vote for the new plan. In that year's elections Mexican-Americans, who previously had never secured more than three seats on the nine-member council, were able, along with blacks, to take a majority of the positions on the new eleven-member council. A coalition of blacks and Chicanos thus wrested control of the council from the non-Latin whites. Temporarily losing control in 1979, the minorities regained their majority on the council in 1981. After a series of confrontations between the Anglo establishment and the minorities, an accommodation was worked out, based on the realization that little could be accomplished in the city without Anglo-minority collaboration. According to political scientist Thomas A. Baylis, San Antonio after 1977 began to see some cooperation among several influential groups: "moderate Anglo businessmen, city officials and council members on the one side, and COPS members and several minority councilmen on the other." The unifying factor was the importance of maintaining economic development in the city, and that began to pull the factions together. The burgeoning cooperation was exemplified by the creation in 1980 of United San Antonio—an organization that brought together the city's various racial, ethnic, and other elements to strive for economic growth.[30]

A growing cooperation between the competing groups was also realized in the mayoral elections, where ethnic political alliances have been formed. "Through 1979, no candidate who relied predominantly on the Mexican-American vote had won." Henry Cisneros, a Mexican-American councilman, was elected mayor in 1981 with 90 percent of the vote on the city's Mexican-American west side, but he also won a number of Anglo votes. He had previously worked with the Anglo leadership through the Good Government League, described in a *Texas Monthly* article on San Antonio's politics as the "political arm of the downtown establishment." Having ties with both COPS and the Anglo establishment, Cisneros was the perfect choice to secure a resolution of the ethnic-based political battles. Cisneros saw himself as a coalition candidate and campaigned on a consensus platform; he was successful in bringing the various groups together behind him. He won in 1981 with 62 percent of the total vote, and was easily reelected in 1983, drawing support from all segments of the city. Cisneros became a strong supporter of economic growth as well as minority rights, and thereby became the embodiment of the perfect Sunbelt coalition of interests. As one student of San Antonio politics noted, by 1981, "San Antonio had apparently passed from an Anglo elite-dominated machine system to a coalition system in which no single class or ethnic group held complete power over political decisions." A pluralistic political system had developed in which power was shared by competing groups.[31]

The city of Houston represents a similar story. Both Mexican-Americans and blacks were neglected groups with relatively little political power. As elsewhere, blacks had been largely disfranchised by the imposition of the white primary. Nonetheless, this group was organized politically through the Progressive Voters League and the Independent Voters League, both of which worked for black political rights. To support Mexican rights, particularly in regard to the police, the Mexican-American community organized La Asamblea Mexicana in 1924, and was successful in securing the hiring of Mexican-American policemen to patrol Chicano neighborhoods. At times the Mexican-American and black communities formed coalitions, as they did during the 1920s to fight Klan activity in the city.[32]

Political organization for the Mexicans came during the 1930s. In 1935, the Latin American Club was formed in Houston to register eligible Mexican-American voters and to represent group interests before city leaders. This club eventually became a chapter in LULAC and continued to work for Mexican-American rights. After World War II, LULAC and the American GI Forum, as in San Antonio, fought for "social, political, and economic equality and the opportunity to practice and enjoy that equality." Further political interest and activism was evident with the formation of Viva Kennedy clubs, the Political Association of Spanish-Speaking Organizations (PASSO), and the La Raza Unida party.[33]

As elsewhere, the white primary, the poll tax, at-large council voting, and annexation prevented blacks and Hispanics in Houston from competing equally with whites for political positions. The end of the white primary in 1944 and the abolition of the poll tax in 1966 brought the minorities into full political competition. The number of black and Mexican-American registered voters increased every year after the poll tax was eliminated. In 1944 blacks had been "20 percent of the voting age population [but] made up only 5 percent of the electorate." With the founding of the Harris County Council of Organizations in the late 1940s to register and mobilize the black vote, the situation changed. By 1967 blacks represented almost 17 percent of the registered voters, and as with the Atlanta Negro Voters League, white candidates eventually sought endorsements from this organization.[34] The growing strength of the minorities began to be noticed in a number of ways. An initial indication of this was the appointment of a black policeman in 1947. In 1958 the first black was elected to the school board in Harris County, the first black to win any public office since Reconstruction. The first black administrator in the Houston school system was appointed in 1963, and in 1969 the Houston Teachers Association had its first black president. The police department appointed its first Hispanic captain in 1980.[35]

The election and appointment of blacks to various poisitions, and black registration activity, encouraged a try for higher office in 1969. The first black mayoral candidate, Curtis Graves, although capturing only 32 percent of the vote in 1969 and losing to the incumbent Louis Welch, did well in black and Mexican-American neighborhoods. His candidacy awakened the white leadership more fully to the emerging minorities. Mayor Welch, who received less than 6 percent of the black vote and faced the possibility of opposing Graves again in two years, began to cultivate black voters. As he said, "I have heard this vote and I sympathize with it. It is my sincere hope that during the next two years I will be able to let these people know that their problems represent the problems of the entire community." The mayor then stated that he would ask the city council to pass a minimum housing code to improve slum housing. The strong vote Graves received, according to Welch, represented the black desire for a more active voice in government, and he pledged to support that active voice.[36]

By 1970 blacks were 25.7 percent, and Mexican-Americans 15.1 percent, of Houston's population; together they made up about 35 percent of the registered voters by 1971. Once again these communities played an important role in the mayoral election. In 1971, Welch opposed Fred Hofheinz, who received significant black and Chicano support due to his pledge to set up a police review board. The contest was thrown into a runoff election that Welch won, but only after the campaign had been racially polarized. Although Welch said he would try to win more black votes in the runoff, his supporters called for a white turnout to stop the minority bloc vote. Hofheinz did well in minority areas and set the stage for his future victory.

More significant were the actual minority victories in 1971. In the school board election a black and a Mexican-American won positions; in the city council vote, Judson Robinson, Jr., became the first black elected to the council, and Mexican-American Leonel Castillo was elected city controller. Hofheinz accurately noted after the election that it "showed that no future Mayor could be elected unless he listened to the needs of 'all of Houston.'" He was right. In 1973 and again in 1975 Hofheinz was elected mayor with strong support from the black and Mexican-American communities, and they have figured prominently in campaigns since then.[37]

In the Houston city council, however, minorities still had little power.

This elective body was chosen on an at-large basis. By 1979 only one black (and no Mexican-Americans) had won a seat on that board. The Justice Department rectified this situation when it suspended city elections in 1979 in order to study compliance with the Voting Rights Act. Houston had annexed six mainly white areas in 1977. The issue, as in San Antonio, was whether that annexation had diluted the minority vote. In response to Justice Department pressure, the city developed a new plan to elect the council. Five of the fourteen seats were to be elected at-large, and the others on a single district basis. The 1979 council vote elected three blacks and one Mexican-American. The minorities now were in an effective position to compete, negotiate, and secure concessions in a way similar to northern ethnic politics. The business elite in Houston was willing to accept some division of power with the minorities in an effort to prevent potential conflict that would limit economic growth.[38]

These four cities—Atlanta, Miami, San Antonio, and Houston— represent the political alterations brought about as a result of the civil rights movement, federal intervention, immigration, and political organization within the minority communities. White flight has also played a role, as indicated by the efforts in San Antonio, Houston, and (as early as the 1950s) Atlanta to annex surrounding white areas in an attempt to dilute the burgeoning minority vote. Nonetheless, in these cities of the Sunbelt South a northern model of ethnic and race relations has emerged and urban politics has been fundamentally changed. The different cities represent variations of that change, but all are far removed from the rigid, violent, and politically noncompromising caste system of earlier years. From the intense competition for power in Miami, to the accommodations worked out in Atlanta, San Antonio, and Houston, to the coalition building and recognition of a multiethnic society found in all these cities, a New South is evident. This is not to say that all southern cities have shifted to a northern model. During the civil rights movement, those cities with "little or no population or economic growth in the postwar period . . . typically experienced considerable racial turmoil" and resistance to change, as compared to cities that had both population and economic growth and that successfully sought new industry and migrants.[39]

Cities with burgeoning postwar economies and populations, where business and political leaders understood the connection between racial or ethnic accommodation and stability, were those that saw the northern model emerge. The functioning and economic development of these cities had become dependent on the cooperation of the various ethnic or racial communities (Hispanic, black, white, Asian). The establishment of single-district rather than at-large council voting in a number of Sunbelt cities indicates by itself the greater importance of neighborhoods and racial-ethnic coalitions to the future of this region. As in northern cities, civic renaissance and economic growth will ultimately depend on the ability of many interest groups to work together. Certainly this has already been realized in Atlanta, San Antonio, and Houston, with Miami likely to follow in the near future. As one social scientist has noted, "Situations most conducive to the growth of new understandings and realistic adjustments will be those in which highly important outcomes are unavoidably dependent upon long-continued cooperation among individuals [and groups], no one of whom has overwhelming power."[40] The importance placed by Sunbelt cities on civic and economic improvement, the continued immigration of Hispanics and Asians, and the willingness of all groups to work together to enhance their city will result in the northern model becoming firmly entrenched in the urban Sunbelt South. Whether the sharing of political power leads to equality, the end of neighborhood segregation, and the opening up of job opportunities is a question for the future. Certainly northern cities still have not reached that point. What we see is an ongoing process whose resolution is still being worked out—but a process based on the acceptance of pluralism and conflict resolution.

More research needs to be done on particular cities to understand all the local variations. The impact of political shifts on other aspects of intergroup relations also needs study. Comparisons between contemporary Sunbelt cities and northern cities during their large-scale racial and ethnic migrations would add much to an understanding of social-group dynamics and urban growth and adjustment during times of stress. Useful historical as well as regional comparisons can be made. For example, differences between 1840s Boston and 1960s Miami, or between postwar Atlanta and Los Angeles (both of which elected their first black mayors in 1973), are some of the important research topics that will require study as the intergroup situation evolves.

Notes

1. Franklin J. James, Betty L. McCummings, and Eileen A. Tynan, *Minorities in the Sunbelt* (New Brunswick, N.J.: Center for Urban Policy Research, 1984), 4–5.

2. Nathan Glazer and Daniel Moynihan, *Beyond the Melting Pot,* 2d ed. (Cambridge, Mass.: M.I.T. Press, 1970), xxiii–xxiv; Nathan Glazer, "Ethnicity—North, South, West," *Commentary* (May 1982): 73–74, 78; Nathan Glazer, "Politics of a Multiethnic Society," in Lance Liebman, ed., *Ethnic Relations in America* (Englewood Cliffs, N.J.: Prentice-Hall, 1982), 128–149. Glazer and Moynihan suggested that the northern model was moving south, particularly evident in Atlanta, and that the southern model could be seen in the North. However, Glazer in his later works suggested that a third model—a western model—developed out of the southern and has been extended to all other parts of the country. The western model grew out of government efforts to regulate intergroup relations through laws and to mandate equality among a number of groups by specifically providing special benefits and protection to certain minority groups. I would argue that the northern model, rather than the southern (or its variation, the western model), became the norm in intergroup relations.

3. See, for example, Ronald H. Bayor, *Neighbors in Conflict: The Irish, Germans, Jews and Italians of New York City, 1929–1941,* 2d ed. (Urbana: Univ. of Illinois Press, 1988).

4. Blaine A. Brownell, "The Urban South Comes of Age, 1900–1940," in Blaine A. Brownell and David R. Goldfield, eds., *The City in Southern History: The Growth of Urban Civilization in the South* (Port Washington, N.Y.: Kennikat, 1977), 153; Don H. Doyle, *Nashville since the 1920s* (Knoxville: Univ. of Tennessee Press, 1985), 225.

5. Howard N. Rabinowitz, *Race Relations in the Urban South, 1865–1890* (New York: Oxford Univ. Press, 1978).

6. Robert Seto Quam, in collaboration with Julian B. Roebuck, *Lotus Among the Magnolias: The Mississippi Chinese* (Jackson: Univ. Press of Mississippi, 1982), 45–51; Leonard Dinnerstein, *The Leo Frank Case* (New York: Columbia Univ. Press, 1970); Richard Gambino, *Vendetta* (New York: Doubleday, 1977); Kenneth T. Jackson, *The Ku Klux Klan in the City, 1915–1930* (New York: Oxford Univ. Press, 1967), 52; David M. Chalmers, *Hooded Americanism: The History of the Ku Klux Klan* (Chicago: Quadrangle Books, 1968), 71, 78, 110.

7. E. Bernard West, "Black Atlanta—Struggle for Development, 1915–1925" (M.A. thesis, Atlanta University, 1976), 15, 17–24.

8. *Atlanta Daily World,* 21 Mar. 1932.

9. Hubert M. Blalock, Jr., *Black-White Relations in the 1980s* (New York: Praeger, 1979), 156.

10. *Atlanta Journal,* 25 Apr. 1956; Atlanta Negro Voters League to voters, 2 Sept. 1949, William B. Hartsfield Papers, Box 10, Emory University Special Collections; John H. Calhoun, interview, 7 Aug. 1985. Calhoun was active in the founding of the Registration Committee and the Voters League. He was also cochair of the Georgia Voters League and executive director of the Atlanta chapter of the NAACP in the 1960s.

11. Glazer and Moynihan, *Beyond the Melting Pot,* xxiv.

12. Ivan Allen, Jr., with Paul Hemphill, *Mayor: Notes on the Sixties* (New York: Simon and Schuster, 1971), 87, 219; Ivan Allen, Jr., interview, 29

July 1985; Ronald H. Bayor, "A City Too Busy to Hate: Atlanta's Business Community and Civil Rights," in Harold Sharlin, ed., *Business and Its Environment* (Westport, Conn.: Greenwood, 1983). For a discussion of the economic factor's impact on racial change in various southern cities, see Edward F. Haas, "The Southern Metropolis, 1940–1976," in Brownell and Goldfield, eds., *City in Southern History*, 171, 181–183; and Elizabeth Jacoway and David R. Colburn, eds., *Southern Businessmen and Desegregation* (Baton Rouge: Louisiana State Univ. Press, 1982), 6–7; as well as essays on southern cities such as Atlanta, for example, by Alton Hornsby, Jr., ibid., 120–136.

13. Raymond A. Mohl, "Miami: The Ethnic Cauldron," in Richard M. Bernard and Bradley R. Rice, eds., *Sunbelt Cities: Politics and Growth since World War II* (Austin: Univ. of Texas Press, 1983), 82–83; Barry J. Kaplan, "Houston: The Golden Buckle of the Sunbelt," ibid., 205–206; Robert Brischetto, Charles L. Cotrell, and R. Michael Stevens, "Conflict and Change in the Political Culture of San Antonio in the 1970s," in David R. Johnson, John A. Booth, and Richard J. Harris, eds., *The Politics of San Antonio: Community, Progress, and Power* (Lincoln: Univ. of Nebraska Press, 1983), 76, 78, 86–87, 90; John A. Booth, "Political Change in San Antonio, 1970–82: Toward Decay or Democracy?" ibid., 195.

14. *Atlanta Constitution*, 18 June 1987, 26 Feb. 1984, 15 Feb. 1979; Atlanta Regional Commission, "The Assessment of Special Service Needs Among the Hispanic Population of the Atlanta Area" (Atlanta: Georgia State University Center for Urban Research and Service, 1979), 3.

15. Atlanta Regional Commission, "Assessment of Special Service Needs," xiv–xv; Mayor Andrew Young, interview, 13 Feb. 1986; *Atlanta Constitution*, 14 and 15 Feb. 1979, 18 June 1987.

16. Mayor Young, interview.

17. Ron Arias, "In Search of El Dorado," *Atlanta Weekly* (4 Dec. 1983): 28; *Atlanta Journal and Constitution*, 24 Aug. 1985, 25 Jan. 1986, 18 June 1987.

18. Atlanta Jewish Federation, *Metropolitan Atlanta Jewish Population Study: Summary of Findings* (Atlanta, 1985), 2–3; "The Black-Jewish Coalition: A Brief History, 1982–1987" (Atlanta, 1987), mimeographed, in author's possession.

19. *New York Times*, 17 Sept. 1980, 2 and 9 Nov. 1980. See also Hall Tennis and Dewey W. Knight, Jr., "Minorities and Justice in Greater Miami: A View from the Metro Courthouse," *Urban Resources* 2 (Spring 1985): 14, 22, 24.

20. *Washington Post*, 23 May 1980; Raymond A. Mohl, "Race, Ethnicity, and Urban Politics in the Miami Metropolitan Area," *Florida Environmental and Urban Issues* 9 (Apr. 1982): 6, 23–24; *New York Times*, 28 Apr. 1980, 23 May 1980.

21. *New York Times*, 11 Nov. 1981, 4 Nov. 1985.

22. Ibid., 11 Nov. 1981, 7 Nov. 1985; Mohl, "Miami: Ethnic Cauldron," 84; Raymond A. Mohl, "Ethnic Politics in Miami, 1960–1986," in Randall M. Miller and George E. Pozzetta, eds., *Shades of the Sunbelt: Essays on Ethnicity, Race, and the Urban South* (Westport, Conn.: Greenwood, 1988), 149; *Miami Herald*, 6 Nov. 1985.

23. *New York Times,* 31 Jan. 1985, 4, 7, and 12 Nov. 1985; *Atlanta Journal and Constitution,* 13 Nov. 1985.

24. Edwin Black, "Hispanics and Jews: A Hopeful New Alliance," *B'nai B'rith International Jewish Monthly* 100 (May 1986): 16.

25. John A. Booth and David R. Johnson, "Community, Progress, and Power in San Antonio," in Johnson, Booth, and Harris, eds., *Politics of San Antonio,* ix–x; John A. Booth and David R. Johnson, "Power and Progress in San Antonio Politics, 1836–1970," ibid., 9–10, 15–16, 23, 25–27; Ralph J. Bunche, *The Political Status of the Negro in the Age of FDR,* ed. by Dewey W. Grantham (Chicago: Univ. of Chicago Press, 1973), 70, 73–74, 131, 464–65; Judith Kaaz Doyle, "Maury Maverick and Racial Politics in San Antonio, Texas, 1938–1941," *Journal of Southern History* 53 (May 1987): 198–201, 203, 206, 209–11, 214–15; Robert A. Goldberg, "Racial Change on the Southern Periphery: The Case of San Antonio, Texas, 1960–1965," *Journal of Southern History* 49 (Aug. 1983): 351, 354; Darlene Clark Hine, *Black Victory: The Rise and Fall of the White Primary in Texas* (Millwood, N.Y.: KTO, 1979), 115–16, 152.

26. Booth and Johnson, "Community, Progress, and Power in San Antonio," ix–x; Booth and Johnson, "Power and Progress in San Antonio Politics," 9–10, 15–16, 23, 25–27; David Montejano, *Anglos and Mexicans in the Making of Texas, 1836–1986* (Austin: Univ. of Texas Press, 1987), 279–281, 293; Goldberg, "Racial Change," 352; Doyle, "Maury Maverick," 199.

27. Brischetto, Cotrell, and Stevens, "Conflict and Change," 76; Doyle, "Maury Maverick," 222; Goldberg, "Racial Change," 350, 353, 371–72; Montejano, *Anglos and Mexicans,* 280–81; Ralph C. Guzman, *The Political Socialization of the Mexican American People* (New York: Arno, 1976), 133; Rodolfo Acuña, *Occupied America: The Chicano Struggle Toward Liberation* (San Francisco: Canfield, 1972), 189–90; Matt S. Meier and Feliciano Rivera, *The Chicanos: A History of Mexican Americans* (New York: Hill and Wang, 1972), 240–48.

28. Brischetto, Cotrell, and Stevens, "Conflict and Change," 85; Carl Abbott, *The New Urban America: Growth and Politics in Sunbelt Cities* (Chapel Hill: Univ. of North Carolina Press, 1981), 232–33; Voter Education Project press release, 12 July 1976, Clarence Bacote Papers, Woodruff Library, Special Collections, Atlanta University; Goldberg, "Racial Change," 362; F. Chris Garcia and Rudolpho O. de la Garza, *The Chicano Political Experience: Three Perspectives* (North Scituate, Mass.: Duxburg, 1977), 180–83.

29. Brischetto, Cotrell, and Stevens, "Conflict and Change," 78, 86–87; William Dunn, "The Growing Political Power of Blacks and Hispanics," *American Demographics* 6 (Sept. 1984): 26, 29; "A Surge of Hispanic Power," *Macleans* 97 (14 May 1984), 32–33; *Atlanta Journal and Constitution,* 20 Dec. 1987.

30. *New York Times,* 17 Jan. 1977, 4 Apr. 1977, 29 Mar. 1981, 6 Apr. 1981; Brischetto, Cotrell, and Stevens, "Conflict and Change," 75, 87, 90; Booth, "Political Change in San Antonio," 195, 197–98; Thomas Baylis, "Leadership Change in Contemporary San Antonio," in Johnson, Booth, and Har-

ris, eds., *Politics of San Antonio,* 102–4; Montejano, *Anglos and Mexicans,* 280–81.

31. Tucker Gibson, "Mayoralty Politics in San Antonio, 1955–1979," in Johnson, Booth, and Harris, eds., *Politics of San Antonio,* 127; Nicholas Lemann, "First Hispanic," *Esquire* 102 (Dec. 1984): 480, 484; Paul Burka, "Henry B. and Henry C.," *Texas Monthly* 14 (Jan. 1986): 222, 224, 226; *New York Times,* 6 Apr. 1981; "Hispanic Power," *Macleans,* 33; Brischetto, Cotrell, and Stevens, "Conflict and Change," 92–93; Booth, "Political Change in San Antonio," 194.

32. F. Arturo Rosales, "Mexicans in Houston: The Struggle to Survive, 1908–1975," *Houston Review* 3 (Summer 1981): 228–30, 237, 239; Charles Davidson, *Biracial Politics: Conflict and Coalition in the Metropolitan South* (Baton Rouge: Louisiana State Univ. Press, 1972), 15–16; Bunche, *The Political Status of the Negro,* 553, 567; Hine, *Black Victory,* 58, 115–16.

33. Rosales, "Mexicans in Houston," 241–44, 247.

34. Davidson, *Biracial Politics,* 41–43, 55–57, 84–85; Kaplan, "Houston," 205.

35. Davidson, *Biracial Politics,* 85, 121; David G. McComb, *Houston: A History* (Austin: Univ. of Texas Press, 1981), 171–72.

36. *New York Times,* 22 Nov. 1971, 9, 16, 17 Nov. 1969.

37. Ibid., 14 and 22 Nov. 1971, 9 Dec. 1971, 5 Dec. 1973, 3 Dec. 1975, 23 Nov. 1977, 21 Nov. 1979, 16 Nov. 1981; Davidson, *Biracial Politics,* 18; Bureau of the Census, *1970, Characteristics of the Population* 1, pt. 45, *Texas* (Washington, D.C.: Government Printing Office, 1971).

38. *New York Times,* 28 Mar. 1979, 21 and 24 Nov. 1979; Kaplan, "Houston," 205–7. Before a 1955 charter revision, five of the eight city council members were elected by ward. After 1955 all were elected at large. See Davidson, *Biracial Politics,* 60.

39. Jacoway and Colburn, *Southern Businessmen and Desegregation,* 11.

40. Robin M. Williams, Jr., *Strangers Next Door: Ethnic Relations in American Communities* (Englewood Cliffs, N.J.: Prentice-Hall, 1964), 351.

8   New Origins, New Homeland, New Region

American Immigration and the
Emergence of the Sunbelt, 1955–1985

Elliott Barkan

Sociologists and economists, demographers and historians, public policy makers and union officials, small manufacturers and directors of major corporations have, during the past two decades, focused increasing attention on the Sunbelt region of the United States. The wave of the future has been said to lie in the warmer climates. Northerners have been relocating to warmer places, ranging from Miami to San Diego to Honolulu. Growth rates in several southern and southwestern states have been very impressive. Indeed, rapid urbanization and population growth in these regions have reflected changes in traditional residential and lifestyle patterns.

More specifically, appealing living conditions and new economic opportunities have been drawing greater numbers of Americans to Florida, Alabama, Louisiana, Texas, Arizona, California, and Hawaii. But do these states have the same magnetism for foreigners migrating to the United States? Has there been a similar southerly shift in immigrant settlement patterns? If so, to what can it be attributed? And if not, why not?

This essay offers a brief historical inquiry, albeit into rather recent data. The purpose is not to attempt demographic projections but to initiate an exploration into the links between a definable Sunbelt region and American immigration patterns. Although the historical background can be traced to 1929, this essay concentrates on the 1970s and early 1980s because the Immigration and Naturalization Service (INS) only began computerizing its records in 1972. Specifically, this essay focuses on key southern, southwestern, and western states and their principal ports of entry. It is not limited to the mainland, for it includes Hawaii. Honolulu is often overlooked as a Sunbelt city, yet its recent economic, political, and demographic patterns, as well as its climate and environment, are quite consistent with the Sunbelt criteria discussed elsewhere in this volume.

This analysis concentrates on Miami, New Orleans, El Paso, Phoenix,

Los Angeles, and Honolulu—the principal urban ports of entry (together with San Ysidro and the other key entry centers on the Mexican border) along this nation's broad Miami-to-Honolulu axis. That axis encompasses nine states: Florida, Alabama, Mississippi, Louisiana, Texas, New Mexico, Arizona, California, and Hawaii. The data for these key cities and states may reveal important evidence linking recent immigration patterns to the emergence of the Sunbelt.

The Pacific and Caribbean Rims Come of Age

The shifting importance of certain immigration ports and destinations has been determined by their proximity to the recent sources of American-bound newcomers. The southerly chain of cities is relatively closer to the center of powerful—and frequently convulsive—international political, economic, and demographic changes. The past several decades have witnessed revolutionary upheavals and devastating wars, American and Soviet military intervention abroad, and horrific civil wars of holocaust proportions. All of these events have set off unprecedented waves of desperate refugees. At the same time, profound economic, technological, and political alterations have occurred in many nations in the Caribbean, Central and South America, and especially Asia. This combination of human suffering and historic development on a global scale has taken place concurrently with the dramatic expansion of international trade and nonimmigrant travel; the worldwide dissemination of American culture and political influence; and dramatic revisions of U.S. immigration laws since 1945, revisions dismantling the discriminatory quotas that had preponderantly favored northern and western Europeans.

These events have triggered a complex, interrelated series of occurrences. Quite suddenly and unexpectedly, Caribbean and Pacific coast states, such as Florida, Texas, and California, have become decidedly more important centers of international trade and new gateways for immigrants and refugees. The economic renaissance of Florida's Dade County (Miami), for example, involved links throughout the Caribbean and South and Central America. Likewise, the movement of several Pacific nations to center stage in the world economy significantly enhanced California's already strong position in the nation's economy. In addition, the accompanying new tides of Asian and Pacific immigration overlapped the continuing flow of newcomers from Mexico. The rippling effects of these events created many new opportunities along the Miami-Honolulu axis, thus drawing native Americans and immigrants to the nation's southern rim.

This regional axis for entry and settlement has been particularly accessible to immigrants from many of the southern and tropical regions caught up in recent worldwide changes and disturbances. The immigrants and refugees from these areas have been disproportionately attracted to the Sunbelt region, principally for three reasons: its proximity to their homelands, its familiar climate, and the presence of existing colonies of the same or related ethnic groups. Obviously, refugee resettlement programs begun in the 1970s had an important impact. Equally significant were the economic opportunities many newcomers found in these places. Undoubtedly, the expanding economies along the axis facilitated the absorption of these new peoples. Many recent immigrants established new businesses catering to expanding ethnic communities or providing new outlets for products from their homelands. The very selective patterns of settlement within the Sunbelt region suggest that ethnic factors have actually had great weight in the selection of final destinations. To that extent, earlier migration patterns to specific Sunbelt cities took on vitally new importance, as conditions in various Latin, Asian, and Pacific nations compelled ever-greater numbers to seek new homelands. Thus, newcomers replicated the experiences of many earlier Caribbean, Mexican, Chinese, Japanese, and, to a lesser extent, European and Canadian immigrants in following established immigrant paths to these southern and western destinations.

The immigration data suggest that these trends were limited and involved certain port cities and states. However, those data, including alien registration records, cannot fully reveal the actual (that is, final or more permanent) destinations of the foreign-born population. In contrast to these important INS data sources, federal censuses indicate that the movement of foreigners into certain southern and western states during the 1970s significantly exceeded the number who had indicated those residential destinations on arrival or processing. Substantial relocation or secondary settlement appears to have occurred. Several southern and western states clearly have benefited from the extraordinary growth in U.S. immigrant and refugee populations since the late 1950s. Unquestionably, the shifting sources of immigrants and refugees during the past three decades is a key factor in understanding both the present geographic distribution of America's new immigrants and subsequent internal migration trends.

The Miami-Honolulu Axis

The shift in immigration sources from the Atlantic Rim to the Pacific Rim and the Carribean has been nothing short of revolutionary. Between 1951 and 1965, 53 percent of American immigrants came from Europe, and only 6.6 percent from Asia. During the next fifteen years, from 1966 to 1980, less than one-quarter had European origins, compared with 30 percent whose roots lay in the Asian, Pacific, and Middle Eastern regions. Well over one-third continued to come from North America, mainly Mexico, but that region's proportion had risen only 10 percent between the two periods. However, the statistics for this fifteen-year period somewhat obscure the profound changes actually underway during the 1970s and fully evident by the early 1980s. For the years 1981 through 1985, only 11.2 percent of new immigrants came from Europe—nearly an 80 percent decline in their porportion from the 1951–1965 period. Over 48 percent of newcomers between 1981 and 1985 were from Asia—far more than a sixfold leap from the pre–1965 era. In addition, North and Central America's share slipped to 18 percent for the 1981–1985 period, while only 6 percent were from South America. The other dramatic change involved Caribbean immigration, because legislative changes opened wide the nation's doors, especially for Cubans. From under 7 percent prior to 1965, the Caribbean share of total immigration jumped to nearly 18 percent during the 1970s and leveled off at 13 percent during the early 1980s.

The 1980 census also brought home quite forcefully both the recency of arrival and the extraordinary recasting of the foreign-born population during the 1970s. According to 1980 census statistics, nearly half of America's foreign-born had arrived before 1965, but there were vast regional disparities. Among Europeans, three-fourths of the foreign-born had arrived before 1965, but for Asians the proportion was less than one-fifth, and for North and Central Americans somewhat more than a third. More significantly, 47 percent of all Asian newcomers had entered the United States or obtained permanent resident status between 1975 and 1980, compared with one-fourth of all those from the Americas and just 8 percent of the Europeans.

Thus, the United States is currently experiencing a substantial redistribution among its foreign-born population. The single most relevant point concerning these new Americans is to be found less in the momentous socioeconomic changes within the United States than in that set of dual developments noted earlier: the momentous changes abroad that have profoundly altered the lives of millions of peoples and the changes in U.S. immigration law since 1945. These legislative changes culminated in the abandonment of the quota system in 1965 and the extensive commitment to refugee resettlement most fully embodied in the Refugee Act of 1980. In terms of the foreign-born, then, the growing importance of the Miami-Honolulu axis lies in this interplay of war, revolution, civil war, economic upheaval, refugee movements, immigration law reform, and the appealing environmental and social conditions found in the Sunbelt.

The impact of this course of events can be judged by focusing on immigration data for selected Sunbelt cities as ports of entry, the relative importance of their states as intended residences of newcomers, and the findings of the 1970 and 1980 censuses. To provide a context, consider that in the quarter-century following the onset of the Great Depression in 1929, only 6 percent of all immigrants arrived at Gulf and Pacific ports. Less than 3 percent went to Miami. About 8 percent came legally across the Mexican border into the Southwest, but nearly 20 percent entered from Canada. Most significantly, almost 60 percent of all newcomers arrived in New York City.

During the decade prior to the 1965 immigration reforms, only 1 percent of the three million new Americans entered at Gulf Coast ports, primarily New Orleans, which itself received a mere 25,500 immigrants. However, 15 percent of the newcomers came across the Mexican border—double the number in the previous period. Another harbinger of change was already visible between 1955 and 1965. Due to the Cuban revolution and exodus, well over 200,000 Cuban refugees entered through Miami. At the other end of the southern axis—in large part initially influenced by the great number of servicemen stationed abroad who married and returned with Asian spouses—substantially more than a quarter of a million newcomers came in through the Pacific Coast, including almost 118,000 via Honolulu and 83,000 through Los Angeles. In these eleven years Miami, Los Angeles, Honolulu, the Gulf Coast, and the Mexican border accounted for almost 30 percent of America's immigrant entries; New York City's share had dropped by one-fourth but still stood at 43 percent.

Although not entirely discernible, the important developments discussed above were indeed shifting the arenas of immigration activity in this country to the south and west, particularly toward the ends of the Miami-Honolulu axis. Between 1966 and 1979, over half a million newcomers, mostly Cuban refugees, arrived in Miami (nearly 9 percent of the national immigration total) and another half million or more arrived in Honolulu for processing. During this period, one in five newcomers landed in ports along the Pacific Rim. Los Angeles' share was still a modest 5 percent, although it was rising steadily and approaching 10 percent of the nation's total by 1979. In addition, the number of immigrants entering through the Gulf ports nearly tripled, increasing their share of all immigrants processed to about 3 percent. Furthermore, the average annual number of documented aliens entering via the Mexican border rose by 30 percent. During the fourteen years following the immigration reforms of 1965, more than 32 percent of all newcomers still landed in New York—America's traditional portal of portals—but now even more, almost 38 percent, came in through the Miami-Honolulu axis (see table 8.1).

Indeed, Miami has been to Cubans what Los Angeles and Honolulu became for different Asian groups. From 1960 through 1969, Miami was second only to New York City as a port of entry (with over 351,000 persons processed), primarily because most of the nearly one-quarter-million Cubans admitted or adjusted to permanent resident status during those years—99,300 in 1968 alone—came through the Miami area. Miami occupied second place again in 1977, when 66,900 Cubans were admitted or adjusted, almost two-thirds of them in Miami. The seventies, on the other hand, was clearly Honolulu's decade, as much as the sixties had been Miami's. Honolulu was the second immigration port in every year but 1977. More than 449,000 persons entered through Honolulu during the 1970s, over 70 percent of them Korean or Filipino.

The absence of any INS data for 1980–81 prevents a full assessment of what happened during those two years, but when the data became available for 1982–85, it was clear that Honolulu had fallen far behind Miami and Los Angeles, and even below Seattle and Chicago. One major cause for this shift appears to be changes in airline routing, including the introduction of nonstop flights between Seoul and Los Angeles. Nonetheless, it is probably significant that during the 1970s more than two of every five immigrants arriving in Honolulu identified California as their destination, and one-fourth of them specifically mentioned the Los Angeles area. The key role that southern California played in the

Table 8.1 A Comparison of the Principal Ports of Entry for Immigrants in the U.S.: 1929–1954, 1955–1965, 1966–1979, 1982–1985

	1929–54 % of Total	1955–65 % of Total	1966–79 % of Total	Summary 1955–79 % of Total	1982–85 % of Total
U.S. Totals	2,934,694	3,115,943	5,834,040	8,949,983	2,267,806
El Paso	—	3.18% (99,004)	1.90% (110,919)	2.35% (209,923)	1.96% (44,347)
Gulf Coast[a]	2.10% (61,670)	1.10% (34,376)	1.18% (68,895)	1.15% (103,271)	3.55% (80,563)
Honolulu	.38% (11,176)	3.77% (117,615)	9.42% (549,759)	7.46% (667,374)	3.61% (81,924)
Los Angeles	.52% (15,177)	2.67% (83,218)	4.66% (271,810)	3.97% (355,028)	13.72% (311,176)
Mexican Border[b]	7.55% (221,639)	15.02% (468,118)	13.38% (780,697)	13.95% (1,248,815)	11.30% (256,149)
Miami	2.90% (85,718)	6.75% (210,244)	8.84% (515,540)	8.11% (725,784)	6.76% (153,319)

New Orleans	1.72% (50,500)	.82% (25,550)	.53% (30,869)	.63% (56,419)	.87% (19,793)
Pacific Coast[c]	3.92% (114,909)	8.39% (261,357)	21.50% (1,254,716)	16.94% (1,516,073)	29.28% (664,078)
New York City	58.84% (1,726,774)	43.10% (1,342,971)	31.88% (1,859,892)	35.79% (3,202,863)	22.62% (512,940)

Sources: 1929–36: unpublished tables from INS; 1937–54: *Annual Reports* of the INS; 1955–79: *Annual Reports*, Tables 5 and 12; 1982: *Statistical Report* of the INS, Table IMM 5.1; 1983–85: unpublished tables from INS.

[a]Gulf Coast included Houston, New Orleans, San Antonio, and Tampa. While Dallas is not placed in any clear category, it did receive 31,806 immigrants between 1982 and 1985.

[b]Mexican Border included Brownsville, Calexico, Del Rio, Douglas (AR), Eagle Pass (TX), Hidalgo (TX), Laredo (TX), Nogales (AR), Roma (TX), San Luis (AR), and San Ysidro (CA). Other ports are not reported; the totals, therefore, are actually greater.

[c]Pacific Coast included Guam, Honolulu, Los Angeles, Portland, San Diego, San Francisco, Seattle, and Tacoma.

resettlement of refugees reflects the extraordinary degree to which Los Angeles has been the mecca for many Latinos and Asians. According to Linda Gordon, of the Office of Refugee Resettlement, by 1985 approximately 40 percent of all Southeast Asian refugees were living in California, three times the number in the second-ranked state, Texas. It is, therefore, not surprising that, as surely as the 1960s belonged to Miami and the 1970s to Honolulu, the 1980s appear to belong to Los Angeles. As a port of entry, Los Angeles may not have surpassed New York numerically but it has come closer than any other Sunbelt city to doing so, processing nearly 14 percent of the nation's total immigration between 1982 and 1985, compared to New York's much reduced 22.6 percent (see Table 8.1).

An Ellis Island in the Sunbelt?

During the years 1982 and 1985, the percentage of newcomers entering through Miami, Honolulu, and the Mexican border districts declined. However, the cumulative percentage for the Miami-Honolulu axis rose from over 37 percent to more than 43 percent of the total number of immigrants, in large part because of the increase in Central Americans, South Americans, and Asians entering through such cities as Los Angeles, New Orleans, El Paso, San Ysidro, and Miami.

Yet these rising percentages alone do not fully convey the extraordinary changes that have taken place over the past three decades. In terms of percentage of arrivals, Miami, New Orleans, Honolulu, and the Mexican border districts appear to be not much stronger as ports of entry in the 1980s than they had been in the eleven years prior to the immigration legislation of 1965. In fact, El Paso's share dropped quite noticeably. If, on the other hand, one looks at the average annual number of newcomers processed, the picture is rather different. For Miami and New Orleans the number of immigrants for the 1982–1985 period doubled that of 1955–1965, as was also true for Honolulu (although the latter figure was far below Honolulu's peak years in the late 1960s and 1970s). For the Mexican border, the average annual number admitted increased by half, and for El Paso, after lagging for a time, it rose by almost one-fourth. The Gulf ports witnessed a more than fivefold jump in the average number admitted in the early 1980s. If one includes all those admitted along the entire Pacific Coast Rim, the annual average leaped by 600 percent. Undoubtedly, the most astonishing transformation oc-

Table 8.2　　The Miami-Honolulu Axis: A Comparison of the Average Annual Number of Immigrants Processed in Selected Ports of Entry: F.Y. 1955–1979, and 1982–1985

Port of Entry	1955–65	1966–79	1982–85	
		% Change 1966–79 vs. 1955–65	% Change 1982–85 vs. 1955–65	% Change 1982–85 vs. 1966–79
1. U. S. Totals	283,268	409,406 +44.5%	566,937 +100.1%	+38.5%
2. Total for Miami–Honolulu Axis (Ports 3 – 9 Below)	94,374	163,403 +73.1%	236,868 151.0%	+44.9%
3. Miami	19,113	36,178 +89.3%	38,380 +100.8%	+6.1%
4. New Orleans	2,323	2,166 -6.7%	4,948 +113.0%	+128.4%
5. Gulf Coast	3,125	4,835 +54.7%	20,141 +544.5%	+316.6%
6. El Paso	9,000	7,784 -13.5%	11,087 +23.2%	+42.4%
7. Mexican Border	42,556	54,786 +28.7%	64,037 +50.5%	+16.9%
8. Los Angeles	7,565	19,074 +152.1%	77,794 +928.3%	+307.9%
9. Honolulu	10,692	38,580 +260.8%	20,481 +91.6%	-46.9%
10. Pacific Coast	23,760	88,050 +270.6%	166,022 +598.7%	+88.6%
11. New York	122,088	130,519 +6.9%	128,235 +5.0%	-1.7%

For sources and definitions see Table 8.1.

curred in Los Angeles. At a time when the national average only doubled, Los Angeles' proportion of the nation's immigrants processed soared more than nine times above the earlier figure (see table 8.2).

Consequently, Los Angeles has been touted as the new Ellis Island. But of course, in an exact sense, Los Angeles is not an Ellis Island any more than New York City was Ellis Island or San Francisco was Angel Island. In fact, downtown Miami actually came closest to the Ellis Island image in its handling of early Cuban refugees. Nevertheless, the whole screening process has been altered, most of it now being done in the immigrants' home countries. Los Angeles International Airport, although the main entry point, does not perform the functions that Ellis Island did at the turn of the twentieth century. More importantly, it cannot, given the ongoing role of San Francisco, San Ysidro, and Seattle, ever monopolize the admission of immigrants in the West or in the Sunbelt to the extent that New York has in the East (60 percent of all newcomers between 1820 and 1930 entered the United States through New York). However, Los Angeles is now the dominant port of entry in the Miami-Honolulu axis and for the entire West Coast. Nationally, it is second only to New York City as an immigrant port of entry.

New York, of course, has had a towering presence in American immigration history. Not only was New York City the gateway for millions, but it became home to a substantial proportion of those millions due to its superb geographic and economic position. During various periods in U.S. history between one-third and one-half of all immigrants entering at New York City remained in New York State, the majority of them in New York City. It is in that broader, dramatic sense that Ellis Island has been made synonymous with New York City and the label subsequently applied to Los Angeles by the media. There was a time during the twentieth century when Galveston and Honolulu each seemed to be emerging as Ellis Islands along the Miami-Honolulu axis. Nor can we overlook Miami's claim, with its ethnic dynamism and economic growth. Recent Latino immigrants have made that city once more a thriving metropolis, a trade center for much of Latin America and the Caribbean, and a destination for many newcomers from those same regions. Intrigued by these patterns, Newsweek's Tom Morganthau recently labeled Miami "America's Casablanca," with its "jazzy, hectic, almost lunatic concatenation of ethnicity, glitz, and restless energy," led by its first Cuban mayor, Xavier Suarez.

Nevertheless, it is Los Angeles—for geographical, economic, cultural, and historical reasons—that will surely come closest and for a far greater length of time, to most truly emulating the original Ellis Island on the Hudson. Geographically, Los Angeles possesses a vast sprawling size, metropolitan stature, ready access to a rich hinterland, and a very appealing climate. Economically, the city plays a powerful role in California's economy, serving as a vital trade center on the Pacific Rim with links to many Asian and Pacific nations, and offering dynamic growth and a wealth of opportunities. Culturally, Los Angeles has, for well over a century, been both a host to an ever-broadening range of ethnic communities and, since the early 1900s, the center of one of the largest mass media concentrations in the world. As a consequence, Los Angeles has acquired a polyglot image and cultural milieu akin to New York's as well as a mystique of being unconventional, receptive to newcomers, and a vanguard of cultural innovation. Historically and demographically, Los Angeles has in this century been the recipient of ever-deepening channels of particularly diverse migration streams. The new immigrants have etched themselves deeply not only into the character of this extraordinarily multicultural center but also into the minds of countless numbers who dream of migrating to this country. For all these reasons, it is quite apt to describe Los Angeles, as one scholar recently did, as "the eastern capital of the Pacific Rim."

Ethnic Diversity in the Sunbelt

The cities along the Miami-Honolulu axis have all participated in changes that suggest the emergence of a distinct region. In terms of immigration and the foreign-born, however, striking differences appear in terms of national backrgound, intended destination, and ultimate settlement. For example, during the period 1972–79, 47 percent of those admitted or adjusted in Miami were Cubans, and 14 percent were Colombians, Ecuadorians, and Peruvians. That trend has continued into the 1980s with the addition of more Central American and Caribbean peoples. Cubans were prominent among those in New Orleans, along with Hondurans, Guatemalans, and those from Belize, as well as over 6,200 Vietnamese in 1978. In the 1980s Southeast Asians, Koreans, and East Asian Indians have been far more visible. El Paso, not surprisingly, saw well over 90 percent of its new arrivals coming from Mexico, a trend that continued during the early 1980s. Phoenix had a similar profile, but its proportion of Mexican newcomers declined to two-thirds as more Canadians, Asians, and Central Americans began arriving in 1976. Honolulu was quite different. During the 1970s some 44 percent of immigrant arrivals were Filipino, and 29 percent were Korean. The volume of newcomers admitted in Honolulu dropped steeply during the 1980s, but Filipinos and Koreans still constitute the majority of those processed there, with Australians and various Pacific Islanders comprising another sizable proportion.

Once again, the most unusual contrast remains with Los Angeles. Whereas in each of the other five cities considered one or two groups clearly predominated, in Los Angeles the two leading groups in the 1970s, Mexicans and Cubans, each accounted for only 9 percent of the city's total number of immigrant arrivals. The Vietnamese made up 8 percent because 14,400 were adjusted in 1978–1979 (14 percent of the national total). In addition, 6 percent of the Los Angeles newcomers in the 1970s were Chinese, about 5 percent came from El Salvador, and Filipinos ranked sixth. The eclectic composition of Los Angeles' immigrant population has most closely paralleled that of New York. This has been even more true during the 1980s, for the city's diversity has included steadily growing numbers of Central Americans, Southeast Asians, Egyptians, Iranians, and Soviet Jews, as well as such earlier groups as Mexicans, Filipinos, Thais, East Asian Indians, Canadians, and Britons, to name but a few.

New Immigrant Settlement Patterns

By the 1970s important distinctions also emerged in the settlement patterns of the new immigrants. Half of El Paso's newcomers planned to remain in Texas. Some two-thirds of the immigrants to Miami, New Orleans, and Phoenix intended to remain in the states of Florida, Louisiana, and Arizona, respectively. The extreme instance of the gateway effect along the axis—newcomers passing though to other destinations—was Honolulu. Only 15 percent of the 383,500 who arrived there between 1972 and 1979 planned to remain in Hawaii; over two-fifths were on their way to California. Los Angeles was again singular in its pattern. Unlike all the other ports of entry along the axis between Miami and Honolulu, 174,343 people out of the 190,083 admitted or adjusted in Los Angeles between 1972 and 1979, or some 92 percent, indicated that California would be their state of residence; and, in fact, 38 percent of the total number specifically mentioned the Los Angeles area itself as their intended destination. Moreover, one-fourth of those processed in

El Paso, San Ysidro, and Honolulu were also bound for Los Angeles during the 1970s.

This varied gateway effect suggests the differential nature of the transformation of the Sunbelt region, whether it is seen as a single entity or as comprised of somewhat distinct subregions. The shift in the distribution of the foreign-born population to the states lying along the Miami-Honolulu axis, although not massive, has occured, strengthened by secondary settlement patterns, especially among some recent refugee groups. The primary, or intended, residential designations given by newcomers have notably increased for these states during the past three decades. This pattern has affected some states more than others, because of varying economic and educational opportunities, the appeal of climate, the effects of chain migration, and, in the case of refugees, deliberate resettlement programs. It is the cumulative picture of these patterns of residence as well as entry that confirms the emergence of the Sunbelt as a recognizable and distinct region, or, at the very least— given that all the states have not been equally affected by these developments—recognizable and distinct areas.

The picture, however, is curiously mixed. The actual numbers of foreign-born admitted rose significantly, and the ethnic background of the new arrivals underwent some alteration. The number of foreigners moving into the Sunbelt increased substantially during the twenty-five year period from 1955 to 1979. Yet, for the most part, only slight changes occurred, in overall percentage terms, in the states of intended residence listed by all immigrants upon arrival and during processing. For example, fairly uniformly across the two periods 1955–1965 and 1966–1979, albeit with some increases in the 1970s, 0.6 percent of the nation's immigrants said they were going to Louisiana, and 1 percent to Arizona; 6 percent indicated Texas; and 1.25 percent listed Hawaii. The percentage saying they were going to, or remaining in, Florida did rise from 4 percent to 6.7 percent after 1965. Moreover, during the entire period, more than one in five consistently specified California as a destination, a figure only slightly behind New York. Indeed, by 1976 the number citing California exceeded New York. Since then California has remained in the lead, with the gap widening tremendously by 1982 (163,000 versus 85,000) and closing only somewhat by 1985 (155,400 versus 104,700).

The annual alien registration forms from 1940 to 1980 largely corroborate the observations drawn from the immigration data. In terms of the aliens reporting in Florida, Louisiana, Arizona, and Hawaii, somewhat over 6 percent were recorded in Florida, about 0.7 percent in Loui-

Table 8.3 A Comparison of Immigration and Census Data on the Intended Destinations and Subsequent Resettlement Patterns of Foreign-Born Persons in Selected Sunbelt States, 1970–1980.

State	State's Foreign-Born 1970 & % of U.S.	No. Designating State 1970–79[a] & % of U.S.	1980 Census: Foreigners Citing Arrival 1970–80[b] & % of U.S.	State's Foreign-Born 1980 & % of U.S.	Foreign-Born Population Difference Between 1970–80 (Cols D/A)	Census Arrivals as a % of Foreign-Born in 1980 (Cols. C/D)	Foreign-Born Increase as a % of Designations (Cols. E/B)
	A	B	C	D	E	F	G
U.S. Totals	9,619,302	4,336,001	5,560,363	14,079,906	4,460,604 46.4%	39.5%	+2.9%
California	1,757,990 18.3%	957,021 22.1%	1,804,835 32.5%	3,580,033 25.4%	1,822,013 +103.6%	50.4%	+90.4%
Florida	540,284 5.6%	268,020 6.2%	326,306 5.9%	1,058,732 7.5%	518,448 +96.0%	30.8%	+93.4%
Hawaii	75,595 .8%	77,768 1.8%	69,938 1.3%	137,016 1.0%	63,421 +86.2%	51.0%	-18.4%
Louisiana	39,542 .4%	27,700 .6%	40,109 .7%	85,502 .6%	45,960 +116.2%	46.9%	+65.9%
Texas	309,772 3.2%	270,796 6.3%	446,715 8.0%	856,213 6.1%	546,441 +176.4%	52.2%	+101.8%

	A	B	C	D	E	F	G
Arizona	76,570	41,594	58,897	162,806	86,236	36.2%	+107.3%
	.8%	1.0%	1.1%	1.2%	+112.6%		
Six States Totals	2,799,753	1,642,899	2,746,800	5,880,302	3,082,549	46.7%	+87.6%
	29.1%	37.9%	49.4%	41.8%	110.0%		

Sources: Department of Justice, *Annual Reports of the Immigration and Naturalization Service, 1970–79*, Tables 5, 12, and 12A; Department of Commerce, *1970 Census of the United States. General Social and Economic Characteristics*, vs. 1, 4, 6, 11, 13, 20, 34, 45, Tables 140 & 141; *1980 Census of Population. U.S. Summary. General Social and Economic Characteristics* (PC80-1-C1), Tables 77, 99, 236, 246.

aData are for fiscal years 1970–79, that is July 1, 1970 through September 30, 1979. Data for October 1979–March 1980 were damaged by the INS.

bBecause the Census Bureau used estimates based on samples, the total figure exceeds the actual net increase shown in Column E. Other factors are clearly involved, too, not least of which was the large number of undocumented aliens counted in the 1980 census. In addition, our immigration data covers July 1, 1969 through September 30, 1979, whereas the census data cover 1970 through March 1980 and, therefore, some of the greater numbers in this total for arrivals could include those who came between October 1979 and March 1980, a greater number than probably came in the last half of 1969. The percentages reliably suggest the direction of the data even if they are not entirely precise, for two different sets of data are under review. In addition, approximately 157,300 more entered in F.Y. 1980 than in 1970. Many of the 266,000 refugees arriving between F.Y. 1979 and 1980 had not been adjusted to immigrant status by Sept. 30, 1980, and would not have appeared in the INS reports. There is also the issue of mortality and emigration rates, and finally the error margin for this data—based on the 15% sample size used—is the largest of all the summary tables.

siana, 1.3 percent in Arizona, and 1.4 percent in Hawaii. The figure for Texas fluctuated between 6 percent and 8.7 percent from 1960 to 1980. California was an exception, however, which suggests some of the limitations of relying exclusively on data about future state of residence and underscores a dynamic characteristic among a sizable number of the foreign-born population. Despite the fact that more people in every year prior to 1976 indicated that New York rather than California would be their destination, as early as 1960 the number of aliens actually registering in California (19.2 percent of the total) had surpassed that for New York (18.8 percent) and never again fell behind. By 1980, the last year of such registrations, almost 27 percent reported from California, versus only 14.9 percent from New York State. Alien data did not conclusively indicate the location of the foreign-born, because naturalized persons did not continue to register. The fact is, however, that in 1978, again in 1980, and in each year since 1983, more persons have become citizens in California than in New York State. Of all the states along the Miami-Honolulu axis, it appears that California is both drawing and holding greater numbers and percentages of foreigners than any other state. Moreover, Los Angeles itself has also drawn and retained, proportionally and numerically, more immigrants than any of the other principal cities in this study (and second only to New York).

U.S. census reports support the alien registration findings and go well beyond the immigration data in disclosing what has been happening among America's foreign-born. In doing so, they add an important dimension to the descriptions based on the immigration records. The 1970 and 1980 census data, for instance, show most definitely that many immigrants said one thing about their residential intentions and often subsequently did another. They reveal, too, that the development of a significant foreign-born pattern of settlement with respect to the Sunbelt has in fact been underway for at least three decades. The increases in the foreign-born population in the Sunbelt region, and in the specific states included here, far exceeded the national trends.

While the total foreign-born population rose 46.4 percent during the 1970s, it more than doubled in the South (120 percent) and nearly doubled in the West (98 percent), compared with only a 9.4 percent increase in the Northeast. Most of this increase occurred in the Sunbelt states proper. Indeed, some of the specific cities along the Miami-Honolulu axis registered quite noteworthy changes. In Miami, there was a 33 percent increase in foreigners during the 1970s (after even greater growth in the 1960s), while in New Orleans the increase totaled 20 percent. In Honolulu, despite the fact that more than eight out of ten newcomers said they were going elsewhere, the increase was 93 percent. In Los Angeles it reached 96 percent, and in El Paso and Phoenix it more than doubled.

Another factor highlights the complexity of foreign-born settlement patterns in the Sunbelt: the presence of sizable secondary migrations. Only 31 percent of the foreign-born in Florida, and 36 percent in Arizona, reported entering the United States during the 1970s, yet the percentage of foreigners in those two states had, by 1980, jumped 96 percent and 113 percent, respectively. Forty-seven percent of Louisiana's foreign-born population said they had arrived in the country during the 1970s, but the state's total number of foreign-born more than doubled. A majority of the foreign-born in Hawaii, Texas, and California reported the same, but Hawaii's foreign population went up 86 percent, California's doubled, and Texas's leaped 176 percent (see table 8.3).

Thus, for all of the Sunbelt states under analysis here, except Hawaii, the increase in the number of foreign-born reported in the 1980 census surpassed the number of newcomers who said they had arrived in the 1970s or the number who, on admission or processing, had indicated they intended to reside in those particular states. For example, the difference between the increase in foreign-born persons reported in the 1980 census and the number who had designated that particular state to the INS during the 1970s was 66 percent in Louisiana, 90 percent in California, 93 percent in Florida, 102 percent in Texas, and 107 percent in Arizona. Only in Hawaii was the census figure lower (18.4 percent), confirming—when compared with some of the other Sunbelt states— the more pronounced role of Honolulu as an intermediate port of entry than as a magnet for newcomers from abroad, notwithstanding the relative increase in its immigrant population (see table 8.3).

In sum, between 1970 and 1979, 1.83 million foreigners out of a national total of 4.34 million, or 42.23 percent, were admitted or adjusted to permanent status in the states along the Miami-Honolulu axis (including all ports of entry along the Mexican border). Some 38 percent of the newcomers designated the nine states in this study as their intended residence. Those states did, in fact, contain 42.6 percent of all the foreign-born in 1980. Overall, they also recorded over 3.1 million more immigrants in 1980 than in 1970, which amounted to 70 percent of the nation's total change in its foreign-born population (and well over 80 percent of the increase in the entire western and southern sections of the country).

This discussion of various migration and remigration patterns enables us to draw other meaningful conclusions from the 1980 census. Although it is beyond the scope of this chapter to analyze the census reports in greater detail, tables 8.4 and 8.5 reveal some of the major changes that occurred between 1960 and 1980. The tables echo the observations already made about trends during those decades. Although the total foreign-born population in the nation fell by 1 percent during the 1960s, it rose by 33 percent in the nine states along the Miami-Honolulu axis. In the 1970s the number of foreign-born increased by 46.4 percent; in those nine states it more than doubled. By the end of this twenty-year period the net foreign-born population in the nine-state Sunbelt had almost tripled. Moreover, two-fifths of the total foreign-born population in the United States in 1980 had arrived in the 1970s, but nearly 47 percent of those living in the southern and western arc of states had entered in that decade. Only Arizona and Florida had smaller percentages of 1970s immigrants than the national figure. In the case of Florida, more than one-third, mostly Cubans, had come in the 1960s, far above the proportion reported among all foreigners in 1970. In contrast to those two states, statistics for California, Hawaii, and Texas show that over half of their newcomers had entered during the 1970s. On the other hand, New York's foreign-born population fell by more than one-fourth between 1960 and 1980, and only a third of its 1980 population had entered in the 1970s.

Immigration along the Miami-Honolulu axis during the 1970s was especially pronounced among groups from particular regions of the world. The South American population more than doubled, the number of Central Americans and Asians more than tripled, and the increase in persons from the Caribbean (other than Cuba) was more than fivefold. Even the number of Europeans had risen over 5 percent, although falling 9.6 percent nationwide. Specific ethnic groups showed significant changes, too. A tripling of the Mexican foreign-born population was reported; Filipinos and East Asian Indians were 166 percent and 356 percent more numerous, respectively; and the Korean immigrant population jumped nearly sevenfold. At the same time, however, British, Italian, and Soviet foreign-born groups decreased in size across the nation (by 2.5 percent, 17.5 percent, and 12.4 percent, respectively). Other dramatic increases were reported in the number of Iranian, Vietnamese, and Chinese immigrants. Comparatively few Vietnamese had migrated to the United States before the fall of Saigon in 1975, and few Iranians before the Iranian revolution in 1979; during the first half of the 1980s both migrated or resettled disproportionately in the Sunbelt states, especially California.

Table 8.4   Growth of Foreign-Born Population in States along
Miami-Honolulu Axis, 1960–1980

State	1960 N	1970 N	1970[a] %	1980 N	1980[b] %	Total[c] %
Alabama	14,955	15,988	6.9	39,002	143.9	160.8
Arizona	70,318	76,570	8.9	162,806	112.6	131.5
California	1,343,710	1,757,990	30.8	3,580,033	103.6	166.4
Florida	272,161	540,284	98.5	1,058,732	96.0	289.0
Hawaii	68,900	75,595	9.7	137,016	81.3	98.9
Louisiana	30,557	39,542	29.4	85,502	116.2	179.8
Mississippi	8,058	8,125	0.8	23,527	189.6	192.0
New Mexico	21,408	22,510	5.2	52,405	132.8	144.8
Texas	298,791	309,772	3.7	856,213	176.4	186.6
Total Miami-Honolulu Axis	2,128,858	2,846,376	33.7	5,995,236	110.6	181.6
New York	2,289,314	2,109,776	-7.8	2,388,938	13.2	4.4
U.S. Totals	9,738,155	9,619,302	-1.2	14,079,906	46.4	44.6

Source: Bureau of the Census, *1980 Census of Population, Detailed Characteristics of Population*, PC80-1-D1, *United States Summary* (Washington, DC: U.S. Government Printing Office, 1984), table 254; and PC80-1-D2, state vols. 2, 4, 6, 10, 12, 19, 25, 32, 33, and 44, table 195.

[a]Percent change for 1960–1970; figure represents increase unless otherwise indicated.
[b]Percent increase for 1970–1980.
[c]Percent increase for 1960–1980.

It seems clear that new ethnic groups have been making their way to America's Sunbelt, following the patterns of earlier groups. The census data outlined above reinforce the patterns found in other sources. A majority of the newcomers recorded in the 1980 census along the Miami-Honolulu axis appear to have gone directly there, but many others resettled in that region after first residing elsewhere, or at least indicating that they planned to do so.

Table 8.5 1980 Composition of Foreign-Born Population in States along Miami-Honolulu Axis, by Period of Arrival

State	Pre-1960 N	%	1960–64 N	%	1965–69 N	%	1970–74 N	%	1975–80 N	%
Alabama	14,328	36.74	4,221	10.82	4,392	11.26	5,030	12.90	11,022	28.26
Arizona	67,550	41.49	17,924	11.01	18,435	11.32	25,063	15.39	33,834	20.78
California	959,460	26.80	358,277	10.01	457,461	12.78	681,042	19.02	1,123,793	31.39
Florida	375,687	35.48	162,282	15.89	188,457	17.80	153,756	14.52	172,570	16.30
Hawaii	38,555	27.94	9,764	7.07	18,759	13.59	29,253	21.20	40,685	29.48
Louisiana	24,910	29.13	9,767	11.42	10,716	12.53	10,541	12.33	29,568	34.58
Mississippi	7,913	33.63	2,631	11.18	2,730	11.60	3,185	13.54	7,068	30.04
New Mexico	17,214	32.85	5,632	11.75	6,059	11.56	9,009	17.19	14,401	27.48
Texas	236,660	27.64	73,764	8.62	99,074	11.57	162,802	19.01	283,913	33.16
Miami-Honolulu Axis Total	1,725,063	28.77	650,262	10.85	806,083	13.45	1,079,661	18.01	1,716,854	28.64
New York	997,187	41.77	209,968	8.79	348,379	14.58	391,333	16.38	444,471	18.61
U.S. Totals		38.24		9.43		12.84		15.79		23.66

Source: Bureau of the Census, *1980 Census of Population, Detailed Characteristics of Population*, PC80-1-D1, *United States Summary* (Washington, DC: U.S. Government Printing Office, 1984) table 254; and PC80-D2, state vols. 2, 4, 6, 10, 12, 19, 25, 32, 33, and 44, table 195.

The Emergence of a Sunbelt Region

The decisive fact underlying recent migration patterns has been the dramatic shift in immigrants' place of origin to areas closer to the southern and Pacific rims of the United States. Proximity to the homeland, a compatible climate, existing nuclei of ethnically kindred settlements, myriad economic oppotunities, and economic, social, and cultural linkages between America and native countries all have heightened the role of the Sunbelt axis in contemporary American immigration history. Moreover, the southern and western regions have been attracting increasing numbers of new arrivals and foreign-born persons who had not orignally entered or resided in the Miami-Honolulu axis.

California in particular stands out, and there is some validity to Los Angeles being labeled the new Ellis Island. Even if the metaphor is not quite an accurate one, historically speaking, the symbolism is. Los Angeles stands in a firm leadership position among the Sunbelt cities, still ready to receive unflagging numbers of newcomers from Asia, the Pacific, the Middle East, and Latin America. If not yet the new portal of portals, it is certainly the closest rival New York City has had in the last 150 years of immigration. And it is most significant that such a city is a key link along the Sunbelt axis.

Miami, New Orleans, San Ysidro, Los Angeles, and Honolulu (and to a lesser extent Dallas, Houston, El Paso, Phoenix, and Tucson) have played, and will continue to play, important roles as America's ports of entry. Consequently, the Sunbelt has indeed assumed a most significant place in contemporary American immigration history, paralleling its increasingly important position in the economic life of the nation and in the Pacific and Caribbean basins. The Sunbelt has no monopoly on immigration, or course, and cannot be treated monolithically. Yet, the cities situated along a sweeping southerly and westerly arc, linked together by comparable experiences, have emerged as undeniably important ports of entry as well as centers of new immigrant communities. As a result, the Sunbelt now stands as a recognizable and potent force in American immigration. Demographic projections, such as those by Leon Bouvier and Anthony Agresta, suggest that it will remain so for many decades, barring any extensive revisions in our system of admissions.

Hence the Sunbelt has become a reality in the lives of many of America's foreign-born. Newcomers are extensively involved in the important economic and demographic shifts underway in the region. The Sunbelt—diverse in its environments and heterogeneous in its peoples and subcultures—has emerged at the cutting edge of American immigration.[1]

Note

1. One other factor we have not mentioned but which surely contributed to the internal migration of some foreign-born toward the South, Southwest, and West during the 1970s was their retirement to these regions. It is not readily possible to determine the weight of this, but what can be noted from the 1980 census is:

   First, of the states studied here, only Arizona (23.88%) and Florida (19.62%) had significantly higher percentages of their population, aged five or more, who had resided in a different state in 1975 than the national figure of 9.68% (i.e., California's was only 8.54% and Texas 10.99%.).

   Second, only in Florida (68.3%) was the percentage among these particular people of persons with former residences in either the Northeast or North Central regions significantly greater than the national figure of 48% (Again, California's was only 49.3% and Texas' 39.46%; Arizona's was 51.25%.).

   Third, however, it is probably of some import that while, on the one hand, the foreign born population in both the Northeast and North Central regions did fall among nearly every European group shown, except Greeks, Portuguese, and Yugoslavians (the last in the Northeast), as well as among Canadians and Cubans, there was, on the other hand, an increase in every one of these foreign born groups in the South, except among Swedes and Scots. In the Western region there were more French, Germans, Greeks, Dutch, Portuguese, English, and Russians than in 1970. (Since I am discussing only Europeans here, I am not going into the changes among other North, Central and South Americans or Asians.)

   Fourth, although the various percentages of people who moved in between 1975 and 1980 may have been, for most of the states here, close to the national averages, that neither precludes significant movement between 1970 and 1974 nor the possibility that foreign born persons could have been a disproportionate part of even these average percentages. Therefore, the considerable drop in the number of European foreign born in the Northeast and North Central regions, accompanied by the considerable increases in the South, and to a lesser extent in the West (leaving aside the matter of mortality among them, which was likely to have been substantial given the length of time many had been here) may be part of the internal migration we have hypothesized to have occurred along with the considerable influx of new immigrants and may in part have been related to the retirement of a goodly number of them to the Sunbelt region.

Note on sources

Three principal sources of immigration data were used in preparing this paper. First, unpublished tables prepared and furnished to the author by the INS statistics section provided important data for the pre-1937 period. Second, for the period 1937–1978, see the Department of Justice's *Annual Report of the Immigration and Naturalization Service* (Washington, D.C.: U.S. Government Printing Office, 1937–1978), primarily tables 5, 6, 6B–D, 12, 12A, 12B, and 16 (table 19 contains ports-of-entry data prior to 1955); and for the period since 1979, the *INS Statistical Yearbook* (Washington, D.C.: U.S. Government Printing Office, 1979–1985), wherein the entry data is given in table IMM 5.1 (beginning in 1985, the latter table was limited to new arrivals only). Third, and most important, this paper is based on raw data from the public-use computer tapes available from the INS containing the immigration records for 1972 and 1985 (computer tapes for the 1980–1981 period, however, were damaged by the INS and thus data for these years were unattainable).

For the 1970 census data, see Bureau of the Census, *Census of Population: 1970, General Social and Economic Characteristics*, vols. 1, 4, 6, 11, 13, 20, 34, and 45 (Washington, D.C.: U.S. Government Printing Office, 1972), tables 49, 140, 141, and 144. For 1980, see Bureau of the Census, *1980 Census of Population, Characteristics of Population, General Social and Economic Characteristics*, PC80-1-C1, *United States Summary* (Washington, D.C.: U.S. Government Printing Office, 1983), tables 77, 99, 232, 236, and 246–50, and pt. C2, state vols. 2, 4, 6, 10, 12, 19, 25, 32, 33, and 44, tables 63 and 116; and *1980 Census of Population, Detailed Population Characteristics*, PC80-1-D1, *United States Summary* (Washington: D.C., U.S. Government Printing Office, 1984), table 254, and pt. D2, state vols. 2, 4, 6, 10, 12, 19, 25, 32, 33, and 44, table 195. The statistics and tables in this paper were adapted from these sources and prepared by the author.

Refugee and refugee adjustment data can be found in the *INS Annual Reports*, table 6B–D; in Linda W. Gordon, "Settlement Patterns of Indochinese Refugees in the U.S.," *I & N Reporter* (Spring 1980): 6–10; and in Gordon's later essay, cited below. Also useful are Bureau of the Census, *Statistical Abstract of the United States, 1985*, (Washington, D.C.: U.S. Government Printing Office, 1984), tables 127 and 128, and the *INS Statistical Yearbook, 1985*, table ref. 4.1.

A recent work of enormous value, both in terms of data and theoretical analysis, is James T. Fawcett and Benjamin V. Carino, eds., *Pacific Bridges: The New Immigration from Asia and the Pacific Islands* (New York: Center for Migration Studies, 1987). Among the many superb essays are Benjamin Carino, "Impact of Emigration on Sending Countries," 407–26; Linda Gordon, "Southeast Asian Refugee Migration to the United States," 153–74; Peter Xenos et al., "Asian Americans: Growth and Change in the 1970s," 249–84; Leon Bouvier and Anthony J. Agresta, "The Future Asian Population of the United States," 285–301; and James T. Fawcett and Fred Arnold, "Explaining Diversity: Asian and Pacific Immigration," 453–73.

In addition, see Michael C. LeMay, *From Open Door to Dutch Door: An Analysis of U.S. Immigration Policy Since 1820* (New York: Praeger, 1987); Ellen Percy Kraly, "U.S. Immigration Policy and the Immigrant Populations of New York," in Nancy Foner, ed., *New Immigrants in New York* (New York: Columbia Univ. Press, 1987), 35–78; Kurt Andersen, "The New Ellis Island," *Time* (13 June, 1983): 18–25; "Immigrants: The Changing Face of America," *Time* (special issue, 8 July 1985); Tom Morganthau, "Miami," *Newsweek* (25 Jan. 1988): 22–29; and the special issue of *Newsweek* devoted to the "The Pacific Century," 22 Feb. 1988. Additionally, Judith Lyons recently published an article that included a survey of motives for migrating among recent immigrants: "1 in 6 California Students Foreign Born," *Asianweek* (29 Jan. 1988): 14–55.

Finally, this author has written a number of other articles on recent immigration patterns and the roles of New York, Los Angeles, California, and Honolulu, data from which have been used for the comparative analysis in the present essay: Elliott R. Barkan, "Whom Shall We Integrate? A Comparative Analysis of Immigration and Naturalization Trends of Asians Before and After the 1965 Immigration Act," *Journal of American Ethnic History* 3 (Fall 1983): 29–56; idem., "Immigration through the Port of Los Angeles," in M. Mark Stolarik, ed., *Forgotten Doors: the Other Ports of Entry to the United States* (Philadelphia: Balch Institute, 1988), 161–91; idem., "New York City: Immigrant Depot, Immigrant City," in Gail Stern, ed., *Freedom's Doors: Immigrant Ports of Entry to the U.S.* (Philadelphia: Balch Institute for Ethnic Studies, 1986), 1–12; "Portal of Portals: Speaking of the United States 'as though it were New York'– and Vice Versa," in William Pencak and Randall Miller, eds., *Immigration to New York* (New York: New-York Historical Society, 1990); idem., "The Forgotten Port of Entry: Honolulu, America's Western Portal to the East" (Paper presented at the Pacific Coast Branch meeting of the American Historical Association, Honolulu, Aug. 1986); and idem., "Evermore the Golden Gate: Recent Immigration and Naturalization Trends in California" (Paper presented at the American Studies Association meeting, San Diego, Nov. 1985).

9　Miami

New Immigrant City

Raymond A. Mohl

The United States has become a nation of immigrants once again. During the 1970s, according to one careful study, net immigration—legal and illegal—totaled more than 7 million people, a figure surpassing the previous record high of about 6.3 million between 1900 and 1910. According to the Immigration and Naturalization Service (INS), more than 1.2 million illegal immigrants were apprehended in fiscal 1985, but as many as 4 million successfully eluded capture in entering the country. By the early 1980s specialists were estimating that at current rates, 35 million additional immigrants and refugees would have arrived in the United States by the year 2000.[1]

Much of the new immigration has been directed to the cities of the expanding Sunbelt regions of the South and West. By the early 1980s, for example, the Los Angeles metropolitan area was home not only to more than 2 million Mexicans and Mexican-Americans, but also to hundreds of thousands of new immigrants from Central America, the Middle East, Asia, and the Pacific Islands. As one recent writer has noted, "Los Angeles stands on a frontier between Europe and Asia and between Anglo and Hispanic cultures." With over 27 percent of its 1980 population foreign-born, Los Angeles has become a "racial borderland"—a new immigrant city of incredible diversity.[2]

Over the past twenty-five years, Miami has become one of the most fascinating of the new immigrant cities. Bahamian blacks and east European Jews contributed to the ethnic diversity of Miami's population in the first half of the twentieth century, but the proportion of foreign-born remained relatively stable until the 1960s, ranging from 11.5 percent of the metropolitan population in 1930 to 12 percent in 1960 (see table 9.1). The mass migration of Cuban exiles that began in 1959 upset this population balance dramatically. The Cuban influx has made Miami as much a Latin American as an American city in the short space of twenty-five years. Since the 1970s, growing numbers of immigrants and refugees from other Caribbean and Latin American nations have altered

Table 9.1   Composition of Population of Miami and
Miami Metropolitan Area, 1930–1980

Year	Population	Black	Foreign-Born	Hispanic
1930				
Central city	110,637	22.7	12.5	—
Metropolitan	142,955	20.9	11.5	—
1940				
Central city	172,172	21.4	9.7	—
Metropolitan	267,739	18.5	10.1	—
1950				
Central city	249,276	16.2	12.1	—
Metropolitan	495,084	13.1	11.1	4.0
1960				
Central city	291,688	22.4	17.8	—
Metropolitan	935,047	14.7	12.0	5.3
1970				
Central city	334,859	22.7	41.9	45.4
Metropolitan	1,267,792	15.0	24.2	23.6
1980				
Central city	346,865	25.1	53.7	55.9
Metropolitan	1,625,979	17.2	35.6	35.7

Miami's demographic structure and cultural pattern even more substantially. According to the 1980 census, the foreign-born totaled about 54 percent of the Miami population — twice the percentage of Los Angeles, and more than double that of New York City.

No other major city even approaches Miami's proportion of foreign-born. Among Snowbelt cities only New York, Boston, and Chicago have sizable immigrant populations — 23.6, 15.5, and 14.5 percent, respectively, in 1980 (see table 9.2). Among the major Sunbelt cities, San Diego's foreign-born number 15 percent of the city's population; for Honolulu, the figure is 14.2 percent; for Houston 9.8 percent; San Antonio 8.3 percent; Tampa 6.9 percent; Dallas 6.1 percent; Phoenix 5.7 percent; Albuquerque 4.5 percent; and Atlanta 2.3 percent (see table 9.3). As these statistics suggest, immigrant Miami anchors the eastern Sunbelt just as immigrant Los Angeles anchors the western Sunbelt.[3]

As a result of the unprecedented migration of exiles and refugees from Latin America and the Caribbean, Miami emerged after 1959 as one of the chief immigration ports in the nation. INS annual reports confirm Miami's prominence as a port of entry. From 1960 through 1969, for instance, Miami was second only to New York City as an immigrant port of entry. From 1970 to 1976, reflecting the surging immigration of Asians, Honolulu replaced Miami as the second busiest immigration port. However, in 1977 Miami once again became the nation's second immigration port. INS records also demonstrate that substantial proportions of the newcomers entering through Miami remained in the south Florida region, and particularly in Miami itself (see table 9.4).[4]

A new immigrant city, yes, but Miami also may represent a new model of immigrant adaptation to American society and culture. Few have described Miami as a new melting pot, to borrow the old metaphor describing immigrant adjustment and eventual assimilation. Rather, Miami might be more accurately described as a "boiling pot," a new immigrant city where vibrant ethnic cultures compete and clash with one another while at the same time displacing some of the mainstream American culture. In particular, considerable evidence suggests that the Cuban experience in Miami demonstrates a new pattern of biculturalism, a process of ethnic adjustment without complete assimilation, or perhaps a pattern of assimilation and ethnic cultural maintenance existing side by side. The Miami Cubans are an anomaly among Hispanics in the United States, sociologists Joan Moore and Harry Pachon contend in their 1985 book, *Hispanics in the United States*, and Miami's Cubans are far from assimilated. Whether the Miami model of adjustment without assimilation will apply elsewhere as immigration to the United States intensifies over the next few decades is a question that bears investigation, particularly in those Sunbelt cities and states where the newcomers have settled in such large numbers.[5]

The Contours of Metropolitan Miami

Beginning as a small tourist haven in the mid-1890s, Miami grew quickly in the early twentieth century through the efforts of its chief urban booster, railroad magnate Henry M. Flagler. Miami boomed in the twenties with the rest of south Florida, almost doubled in population in the depression thirties, was positively affected by the big military presence in the area during World War II, and zoomed still further

Table 9.2 Population of Representative Snowbelt Cities, 1950–1980

City	Year	Central City Population	Metropolitan Area Population	Metropolitan Population in Central City	City Population		
					Black	Hispanic	Foreign-Born
Baltimore	1950	949,708	1,337,373	71.0	23.7	—	5.4
	1980	786,775	2,174,023	36.2	54.8	1.0	3.1
Boston	1950	801,444	2,369,986	33.8	5.0	—	18.0
	1980	562,994	2,763,357	20.4	22.5	6.5	15.5
Chicago	1950	3,620,962	5,495,364	65.9	13.6	—	14.5
	1980	3,005,078	7,103,624	42.3	39.8	14.1	14.5
Cleveland	950	914,808	1,465,511	62.4	16.2	—	14.5
	1980	573,822	1,898,825	30.2	43.8	3.1	5.8
Detroit	1950	1,849,568	3,016,197	61.2	16.3	—	14.9
	1980	1,203,339	4,353,413	27.6	63.0	2.4	5.7
New York	1950	7,891,957	12,911,994	61.1	9.5	—	22.6
	1980	7,071,639	16,121,278	43.9	25.3	19.9	23.6
Philadelphia	1950	2,071,605	3,671,048	56.4	18.2	—	11.2
	1980	1,688,210	4,716,818	35.8	37.8	3.8	6.4
Pittsburgh	1950	676,806	2,213,236	30.6	12.2	—	9.6
	1980	423,938	2,263,894	18.7	24.0	.8	5.2
St. Louis	1950	856,796	1,681,281	51.0	18.0	—	4.0
	1980	453,085	2,356,460	19.2	45.5	1.2	2.6

Sources: U.S. Census, 1950 and 1980. All metropolitan area population statistics for 1950 are for "standard metropolitan area." Except for New York, all metropolitan area population statistics for 1980 are for "standard metropolitan statistical area"; New York statistics are for "standard consolidated statistical area."

Table 9.3   Population of Representative Sunbelt Cities, 1950–1980

City	Year	Central City Population	Metropolitan Area Population	Metropolitan Population in Central City	City Population		
					Black	Hispanic	Foreign-Born
Albuquerque	1950	98,815	145,673	67.8	1.2	—	2.6
	1980	331,767	454,499	73.0	2.3	33.8	4.5
Atlanta	1950	331,314	671,797	49.3	36.6	—	1.3
	1980	425,022	2,029,710	20.9	66.6	1.4	2.3
Dallas	1950	434,462	614,799	70.7	13.1	—	1.9
	1980	904,074	2,974,805	30.4	29.3	12.2	6.1
Houston	1950	596,163	806,701	73.9	20.9	—	2.9
	1980	1,595,167	2,905,353	54.9	27.6	17.6	9.8
Los Angeles	1950	1,970,358	4,367,911	45.1	8.7	—	12.5
	1980	2,966,850	11,497,568	25.8	17.0	27.5	27.1
Miami	1950	249,276	495,084	50.4	16.2	—	10.8
	1980	346,865	1,625,781	21.3	25.1	56.0	53.7
Phoenix	1950	106,818	331,770	32.2	4.9	—	6.7
	1980	789,704	1,509,052	52.3	4.8	14.8	5.7
San Antonio	1950	408,442	500,460	81.6	7.0	—	8.0
	1980	785,809	1,071,954	73.3	7.3	53.7	8.3
San Diego	1950	334,387	556,808	60.1	4.5	—	7.0
	1980	875,538	1,861,846	47.0	8.9	14.8	15.0

Sources: U.S. Census, 1950 and 1980. All metropolitan area population statistics for 1950 are for "standard metropolitan area." Except for Los Angeles, all metropolitan area population statistics for 1980 are for "standard metropolitan statistical area"; Los Angeles statistics are for "standard consolidated statistical area."

Table 9.4   Miami as an Immigrant Port, 1972–1977

Year	Total U.S. Entrants N	Total Entering at Miami N	Staying in Florida N	Staying in Florida %	Staying in Miami N	Staying in Miami %
1972	384,689	24,956	12,527	50.2	8,971	35.9
1973	400,063	27,770	17,255	62.1	13,194	47.5
1974	394,861	23,788	13,725	57.7	9,936	41.8
1975	386,194	28,607	17,860	62.4	13,577	47.5
1976	398,613	30,350	19,547	64.4	14,204	46.8
1977	462,315	66,499	50,312	75.7	35,761	53.8

Source: INS Computer tapes, 1972–1977.

ahead in the fifties as the widespread availability of air conditioning drew new people and economic activities to the region. Today Miami is the central city in a metropolitan area rapidly approaching 2 million in population. Local government in the area is divided between metropolitan Dade County, a powerful metropolitan government created in 1957, and twenty-seven separate municipalities, including the city of Miami. Dade County has a commission form of government, with nine commissioners elected at large and an appointed manager. Miami also has a commission form of government, with five commissioners elected at large and an appointed city manager. Although the population of the city itself is relatively small—just under 350,000—few would disagree that Miami has become the vibrant economic, social, and cultural center not only of the Dade County metropolitan area but also of the entire Caribbean basin. As the dozens of new skyscrapers in the central business district suggest, Miami has emerged as one of the rapidly growing and changing cities of the American Sunbelt. The popularity of the television series "Miami Vice," moreover, has added a mythological quality to America's image of the city.

Other factors are important in comprehending the nature of ethnic Miami. First, both the city and the larger metropolitan area are often described as triethnic in character, with blacks, Hispanics, and non-Hispanic whites (or Anglos) making up the three largest and usually competing groups. Blacks comprised a substantial portion of Miami's early population, particularly Bahamian blacks who worked in the local construction industry and in agriculture. By 1920, for instance, Miami's almost 5,000 Bahamians made up 52 percent of the city's entire black population. Between 1940 and 1980 the percentage of blacks in the total metropolitan population declined only marginally, from 18.5 percent in 1940 to 17.2 percent in 1980. Hispanics were historically less numerous, in 1950 totaling about 20,000, or 4 percent of the metropolitan population; most were Puerto Rican and there was only a small Cuban community.[6]

The Cuban revolution in 1959 changed all this, of course. A massive exodus of Cuban exiles began in 1959 and continued sporadically over the next two decades. Between 1959 and 1980 more than 800,000 Cubans left their homeland for the United States. Despite federal government efforts to relocate Cuban exiles throughout the United States, a large proportion eventually settled in the Miami area. By the mid-1980s considerably more than 800,000 Hispanics resided in the area, comprising over 60 percent of the city population and over 43 percent of the population of metropolitan Dade County. By 1980 non-Hispanic whites had actually become a distinct minority in Dade County. In the space of two decades the Cuban influx and other new immigration drastically altered the demographic structure of the Miami metropolitan area.[7]

Cubans make up the great majority of the Hispanics in the Miami metropolitan area, but they are not alone. The 1980 census reported 174,000 non-Cuban Hispanics in Dade County. Recent revolutions and political conflicts in Central America have brought in over 100,000 Nicaraguans since 1979, thousands of Salvadorans, even some Mayan Indians from Guatemala. These newcomers have joined thousands of Puerto Ricans, Colombians, Venezuelans, Peruvians, Chileans, Mexicans, and others who have made new homes in south Florida. In addition, the U.S. Border Patrol in Miami has admitted that "tens of thousands" of illegal aliens, mostly from Latin America, have entered the south Florida area and been absorbed in the populace. Thus the Hispanic population of the Miami area, although mostly Cuban, is actually quite diverse in terms of national origin.[8]

Not only does Miami have a triethnic population, but this population is highly segregated residentially by race and ethnicity. Several sociological studies, for example, demonstrated that of more than one hundred large American cities, Miami had the highest degree of residential segregation by race in 1940, 1950, and 1960.[9] Most of Miami's blacks are concentrated in two large ghettos, Liberty City and Overtown, while others reside in half a dozen smaller black neighborhoods scattered throughout the metropolitan area.[10] Miami's new black immigrants, the Haitians, are also highly segregated residentially. At least 60,000 and possibly as many as 100,000 Haitians, almost all of whom have arrived in Miami in the last decade, are concentrated in several census tracts on the northeastern fringe of the city. About 40 percent Haitian by the mid-1980s, the area is now called Little Haiti.[11]

The Cubans and other Hispanic groups are highly concentrated residentially as well.[12] Miami's Little Havana is well known as an area of Cuban settlement, but the Cubans have pushed out into other sections of the metropolitan area. In 1980 the Hispanic population exceeded 50 percent in 66 of metropolitan Miami's 237 census tracts. Hialeah, Dade County's second largest city, with almost 150,000 people in 1980, was more than 80 percent Hispanic by mid-decade. Sweetwater, a small municipality west of Miami, was well over 80 percent Hispanic by 1985, although not all these were Cubans. Tens of thousands of Nicaraguan exiles from the Sandinista revolution currently reside in Sweetwater and adjacent Fontainbleau Park, earning this section of the Miami metropolitan area the appellation Little Managua. [13]

Turning to another group, Miami's Jews comprise the fifth largest Jewish community of any U.S. metropolitan area. Long heavily concentrated in Miami Beach, the Jews now reside in the densely populated condominium districts of North Miami and North Miami Beach as well.[14]

Thus two decades of demographic revolution have created a high degree of residential segregation in the Miami metropolitan area. As one social scientist put it in 1979, "The Latin American community of Miami has grown so rapidly in population that it has dramatically affected the residential space of other groups within the city." Not only has neighborhood heterogeneity in Miami been reduced substantially since 1950, but according to recent studies residential segregation based on race and ethnicity intensified during the 1980s.[15] Needless to say, a considerable degree of ethnic and racial tension, and occasional open conflict, has accompanied the dramatic transformation of Miami's residential space.

The Cubans in Miami

The Cuban exiles came to the United States in several waves over two decades, an erratic migration flow dictated by the state of U.S.–Cuban relations. They settled first in what is now known as Little Havana, a vast area spreading south and west from the central business district. Little Havana was once a declining section of empty lots, vacant shops, run-down businesses, and aging residential structures. Some Cubans had lived in this section of Miami since the 1930s—exiles of the Cuban revolution of 1933. Attracted by inexpensive property, low rents, and accessibility to downtown Miami, the enormous influx of Cubans in the 1960s began to concentrate in this section. Little Havana grew by absorbing new arrivals from Cuba, along with Cubans who had resettled initially in other parts of the United States. Through a process of population invasion, departing non-Latin whites were quickly replaced by Cubans and other Hispanics. The boundaries of Little Havana pushed outward to accommodate the burgeoning Hispanic influx.[16]

In Miami the Cubans quickly established an active cultural and institutional life, as well as an enclave economy of some 25,000 businesses by the late 1980s—businesses ranging from small shops, factories, and service stations to banks, construction companies, and other large firms. In essence, the first wave of Cuban exile immigration uprooted an entire professional and middle-class population from Cuba to Miami. After a short period of adjustment, the entrepreneurial Cubans energetically pursued economic opportunity and success in America.[17] The import-export business, in particular, has been energized by Hispanic businessmen, who have utilized Miami's Latin ambience and bilingual culture in building international trade links with the nations of Latin America and the Caribbean. As several studies have suggested, the enclave economy provides jobs for Cuban newcomers and contributes in important ways to Spanish-language maintenance.[18]

As the demographic and economic patterns of the Miami metropolitan area changed, so too did the pattern of local politics. When the Cubans first came to Miami in the 1960s, they came as exiles rather than refugees. Almost universally they hoped to depose Fidel Castro and return to their homeland. By the early 1960s almost 200 anti-Castro exile organizations had been established. Thus for many years Castro and Cuba were more important to Miami's newcomers than local political issues. Because they planned to return, few became naturalized citizens. But by the 1970s, most had abandoned the hope of return. As the Cuban exiles increasingly came to view Miami as a permanent place of settlement, they put down roots and became citizens and voters.[19]

The past decade has witnessed a dramatic shift from exile politics to ethnic politics among the Miami Cubans. Urban politics in the metropolitan area are now organized primarily around ethnic and racial issues. By 1985 Hispanics totaled 53 percent of the Miami's registered voters; they controlled the nonpartisan city commission, including the mayor's office; and they held many of the city's major administrative positions and a growing portion of municipal jobs. The at-large election system has prevented similar Hispanic inroads at the metropolitan or county level, where only one Hispanic has achieved a commission seat. Proposed charter changes that would graft new district representation to the existing at-large system would almost certainly open up metropolitan government to Hispanic political leaders. In Hialeah, West Miami, and Sweetwater, Cubans also control local government.[20]

At the level of state and national politics, the Cubans have dramatically altered the political landscape. Traditionally, Florida was an integral part of the one-party Democratic South. But the Miami Cubans blamed President John Kennedy and the Democrats for the failure of the Bay of Pigs invasion. The Republican party has been the beneficiary. Miami's Cubans have strongly supported Republican presidential candidates since the 1968 election. The trend is clear: increasing numbers of Hispanics in Miami are becoming citizens and registered voters, and they vote heavily for Republican state and national candidates. The Miami Cubans have become new players in the old game of ethnic politics. It is also safe to say that exile politics have not died out completely, and Miami is quite possibly the only city in America with its own foreign policy.[21]

The big question, of course, is to what degree Miami's Cubans have assimilated or might be expected to assimilate in the future. What are the prospects for a pluralistic, bilingual culture in Miami for the third generation and later generations of Cuban-Americans? Clearly, the fact that Cubans comprise such a large proportion of the city's population makes Miami somewhat different from the immigrant cities of earlier periods, and different as well from contemporary immigrant cities like Los Angeles or New York, where ethnic diversity prevails. Yet most of the studies of the Cuban immigrants contend that they have not only adjusted but assimilated rapidly to the American mainstream. As early as 1968, Michael G. Wenk, a researcher with the U.S. Department of Immigration, reported that "the majority of Cubans assimilated and adjusted rather quickly," generally within one to three years. Wenk did not define exactly what he meant by assimilation, but it seems clear he was talking mainly about finding a place to live, getting a job, progressing economically, and feeling settled or fulfilled by life in the United States.[22]

Other writers, as well, have taken an assimilationist stance. In the 1980 article on Cubans in the *Harvard Encyclopedia of American Eth-*

nic Groups, Lisandro Pérez conceded that acculturation and assimilation had been slow among the Cubans in Miami, but predicted that "by 1990, when second-generation Cuban Americans come to dominate the Cuban population," the situation would be substantially different. According to this prediction, assimilation should have been achieved by now, but this clearly has not happened. Some other scholars have argued that the Cubans "are assimilating as rapidly as any other non-English-speaking immigrant group in the history of the United States."[23]

These studies may be far more assimilationist in orientation than present evidence warrants. As sociologist Milton M. Gordon suggested in his classic 1964 study, *Assimilation in American Life,* a distinction must be drawn between behavioral assimilation and structural assimilation.[24] There is a big difference between learning the language, getting a job, becoming a citizen, and acquiring skills necessary for survival and success in the new land, on the one hand, and becoming fully integrated or assimilated into the mainstream society, on the other. Clearly, the Cubans in Miami have achieved the first; they have adjusted, and they have done so perhaps faster and more easily than earlier immigrant arrivals. How fully they have abandoned the basic ingredients of their old culture in favor of complete assimilation is quite another question.

The evidence for adjustment is abundant. The Cubans have achieved high levels of citizenship, political participation, educational attainment, occupational success, and socioeconomic mobility. They have adapted to the South Florida economic structure and even shaped it in new and different ways. They are active in American politics, and their voter-participation rates are substantially higher than those of native Americans. English-language competency, however, especially among the older, first generation, remains comparatively low, but studies have shown that Cubans nevertheless have high levels of information about and awareness of American society.[25]

But adjustment is not the same as assimilation. Cuban Miami remains an active and vibrant ethnic community—a bicultural and bilingual community shaped by language, religion, and old-country family, food, and cultural patterns. For example, the predominance of Cubans in the city, along with new patterns of Latin American trade and tourism, has strengthened Spanish-language maintenance. Language scholars have noted that Spanish has been the most persistent of all foreign languages across several generations in the United States. This certainly seems to be true for Miami. The Cubans are perhaps the only immigrant group in American history to perceive an economic value (as opposed to a cultural imperative) to maintaining their language. In the economic enclave of Little Havana, Cubans and other Hispanics can largely avoid speaking English, and apparently most of them do. The 1980 census revealed that about 64 percent of Miami's population above the age of five spoke a language other than English at home. Almost 54 percent of those using other languages in the home were also fluent in English, so Spanish was clearly the language of choice for those families.[26]

Independent research studies have reinforced the census data on language. A 1980 study of Cuban households by the Cuban National Planning Council (CNPC) reported that 92 percent of respondents in Miami spoke only Spanish at home, and 57 percent of Cubans spoke only Spanish or mostly Spanish at work. A 1983 study of 600 Latin heads of household conducted by the Strategy Research Corporation revealed that 89.2 percent of the families spoke only Spanish in the home, while 2.6 percent spoke only English and 8.2 percent spoke both languages. These studies demonstrate that Spanish remains the dominant language among Miami Cubans, a fact probably strengthened by the recent Mariel refugee influx of 1980, which brought an additional 125,000 Cubans to Miami in the space of six months.[27]

Language maintenance in Miami has been enhanced by the mass media. Eight radio stations and two television stations in Miami broadcast in Spanish. According to the CNPC, in 1980 about 64 percent of Miami respondents listened to Spanish or mostly Spanish radio programs. However, fewer Cubans—about 35 percent—watched Spanish-language television exclusively. Two daily and more than thirty weekly Spanish-language newspapers, or *periodiquitos*, serve the Cuban community, along with several local Spanish-language magazines and Spanish translations of popular national magazines. The CNPC survey revealed that less than 20 percent of Miami Cubans read English or mostly English-language newspapers. This evidence seems to suggest that, with the exception of television, the mass media in Miami enhance Spanish-language maintenance.[28]

Although Spanish remains strong among the immigrant generation, bilingualism has become the practice among the younger generation. However, school-aged Cubans and Cuban-Americans use English primarily in school and not at home. The Cuban National Planning Council study, for instance, reported that 75 percent of Cuban students in Miami speak English or mostly English in school. Some observers predict a greater use of English, and a corresponding decline in Spanish, among second and later generations of Cuban-Americans. But a Dade

County study reported in 1980 that less than one percent of Cuban children "used English as the first language between parents and children." Thus, the situation is in flux and the evidence of a declining use of Spanish is hardly conclusive. Indeed, one linguistic scholar recently suggested that the Cubans may be the first immigrant group in American history "to have consolidated and resisted Anglification long enough to compete linguistically with the surrounding majority society." In particular, because Spanish is used extensively in "high domains" such as government and business, as well as in "low domains" such as the family, the language remains "instrumentally valuable."[29]

Leaders in the Cuban community, moreover, have urged Spanish-language maintenance as an important community goal. Hispanics "are simply not melting into the melting pot," writes Frank Soler, editor of the biligual *Miami Mensual*. That Cubans "prefer to function in Spanish" is completely understandable and reflects "their pride in the accomplishments of their native culture and . . . their native language." Taking the argument a bit further, Soler contends that non-Hispanics should become bilingual as well. A recent political controversy over bilingualism in Miami seems to have heightened Cuban cultural consciousness and the sense that the language should be preserved. This feeling has been further strengthened by the militancy of bilingualism opponents, particularly U.S. English, a Washington lobby pushing a constitutional amendment to make English the official language of the United States, and the Florida English Campaign, an affiliated group seeking a state constitutional amendment for the same purpose. Despite the activism of these groups, Spanish remains a vital language in Miami. The continual replenishment of the Hispanic community over twenty-five years, and the likelihood that Florida's Hispanic population will triple in size by the year 2000, suggest a linguistic permanence for Spanish unlike that of earlier mother tongues.[30]

Cubans have maintained their culture to an enormous degree in ways other than language. The Roman Catholic religion has persisted as an important ingredient in Cuban-American culture. Most Catholic parishes in Miami are overwhelmingly Hispanic, and services are usually held in Spanish. The Catholic church played an important part in refugee resettlement and served as an advocate for liberalized immigration laws, earning considerable support from the Cuban community.[31]

It is also true, however, that Cuban-American religious fervor is not so much directed toward the organized church as expressed in devotions to saints and the Virgin Mary. Afro-Indian religious beliefs grafted onto

Catholicism in Cuba persist in the personalized religious practices among Cubans in Miami. A similar pattern can be found in adherence to *santería*, a cult religion of Afro-Cuban origins sometimes described as a Cuban form of voodoo. With its elaborate system of ceremony and ritual, magic and medicine, *santería*, apparently has become more popular in recent years, perhaps because of the massive wave of new Cuban refugees, or perhaps because *santería* serves as a link to the Cuban past. According to Michael McNally, author of a recent study on Catholicism in south Florida, "*Santería* was a way for the Cuban exile to acquire power and security through magic, ritual and symbol. It kept him in touch with the sacred in the midst of the secular, technological culture of America." Adherents of both Catholicism and *santería* often express their devotion by erecting yard shrines, thousands of which adorn front yards throughout Little Havana and Hialeah.[32]

The immigrant family is often viewed as an indicator of cultural change and assimilation. Some Cuban family patterns have changed in America. Notably, Cuban families in America have lower birth rates than was the case in Cuba. A large proportion of Cuban women in Miami, about half of those over age sixteen, work outside the home, a departure from the pattern in Cuba. Similarly, at least one study suggests a high degree of out-marriage among second-generation, American-born Cubans. But exogamous marriage among Cubans is directly related to the degree of residential concentration. Thus in New York City, where Cubans are residentially dispersed, out-marriage is more prevalent than in Miami, where the Cubans have clustered in Little Havana and Hialeah.[33]

Other family patterns have been strengthened in the United States. The extended family household, for instance, is almost three times more prevalent among Cubans than among the U.S. population as a whole. This pattern was enhanced by the Mariel boatlift, which brought in large numbers of relatives. Obviously, when the family is extended with grandparents and other older relatives or recent arrivals, culture and language maintenance are strengthened, particularly when the mother is working.[34]

Cuban culture in Miami has been reinforced in other ways as well. The Cubans have held tenaciously to their old-country cuisine. By the 1980s the Miami area boasted some seven hundred Cuban groceries, or *bodegas*, and over four hundred Cuban restaurants—an institutional pattern that has ensured the preservation of traditional Cuban food habits. An active literary and artistic tradition prevails in Cuban Miami, as does the Cuban musical heritage. Festivals, carnivals, parades, and the like are common events in Little Havana. The Calle Ocho Festival annually brings out half a million people for a day-long celebration of Cuban food, music, dancing, and culture. Colorful Latin architectural and building styles have sprouted in Little Havana, and even the high-rise condominiums along Biscayne Bay have been given technicolor facades.[35]

The organizational life of the Cubans remains strong, with many group activities structured along the lines of old-country municipalities. Of the 126 *municipios*, or townships, in pre-Castro Cuba, some 114 are represented by exile organizations, most of which sponsor a wide range of cultural and social programs. These groups even elect their own mayors-in-exile. And finally, the reality of the Castro regime only a few hundred miles away has kept the anticommunist issue alive and has strengthened the self-consciousness of the Cuban community. The strong local support for Radio Marti, with its anti-Castro theme, suggests that Miami's Cubans have not forgotten the old country.[36]

Thus Miami Cubans have demonstrated obvious patterns of adjustment to American society, but the process can hardly be described as rapid or complete assimilation. The Cubans in Miami, one scholar has concluded, are "a people caught inextricably between two cultures."[37] Continued Hispanic migration to Miami, the possibility of future Cuban boatlifts, and the very real potential of future Latin American revolutions to produce new Hispanic exile communities suggest that Miami will continue to be a bicultural city, at least in the short term, and perhaps considerably longer.

The Haitians in Miami

Another group of Caribbean immigrants, the Haitians, has added to the ethnic complexity of the Miami metropolitan area. Miami's black population has always had a substantial foreign-born component. The early presence of black Bahamian immigrants in Miami has already been mentioned. Although relatively few Cuban blacks came to Florida in the migrations of the 1960s and 1970s, perhaps 20 percent (about 25,000) of the Cubans arriving in the Mariel boatlift of 1980 were blacks. In addition, some 60,000 to 100,000 Haitians and about 20,000 Jamaicans live in the Miami area, along with smaller numbers of other West Indians. According to the 1980 census, over 22 percent of Miami's blacks were foreign-born. The arrival of about 25,000 Haitians in 1980, along with the black Cubans from Mariel, has pushed that figure substantially higher. As a result of this immigration, the black population of the Miami region is much more ethnically diverse than in most metropolitan areas.[38]

Haitian immigrants and refugees began migrating in sizable numbers after 1957, when François Duvalier came to power in Haiti. Haitian political exiles, professionals, and the urban middle class sought to escape the brutality of the Duvalier regime and settled primarily in New York City in the 1960s. Haitian communities eventually sprouted in Miami, Boston, Washington, Philadelphia, and Montreal as well. Beginning in the early 1970s, economic deprivation and political repression under Jean-Claude Duvalier stimulated a further exodus from Haiti of the urban lower classes and the rural poor. These include the thousands of Haitian boat people who have washed up on south Florida beaches after a dangerous seven-hundred-mile journey across open sea in small, rickety, overcrowded boats. According to one recent study of Haitian immigrants, there were about 800,000 Haitians in the United States in 1984, including the American-born children of the immigrants. About 450,000 of these live in New York City, and as noted earlier, perhaps as many as 100,000 have settled in the Miami metropolitan area.[39]

The arrival of the Haitians in south Florida has created tensions; they have received a less-than-enthusiastic welcome. Haitian supporters suggest the existence of a double standard in American immigration policy—one that welcomes mainly white refugees from Cuban communism, but rejects black immigrants from Haiti. The INS has refused to accept Haitian requests for political asylum, claiming they are economic rather than political refugees. As a result, most Cuban "Marielitos" went free almost immediately, but several thousand Haitians were jailed in camps in Miami, Puerto Rico, and elsewhere, in some cases for over a year. In 1982 a federal judge ruled the INS detention policy illegal and forced the release of all Haitians pending individual hearings.[40]

The Haitians in Miami have clustered in the Edison-Little River area, one of the oldest sections of Miami, located north of the central business district. Until the early 1960s Edison-Little River was a solidly white, middle-class district. By the 1970s, however, it had an aging stock of small, wood-frame, single-family homes, and a transitional population. Bounded by the black ghettos of Overtown and Liberty City, the area's population was changing rapidly from working class and elderly white to working-class black and Hispanic. It had become, one investigator noted, "a blighted tri-ethnic community" characterized by "high rates of housing turnover and residential instability." Edison-Little River was 80 percent black by 1980.[41]

The transitional character of the neighborhood, its inexpensive housing, and job opportunities in nearby garment, warehousing, and light-industry districts began attracting Haitian immigrants in the early seventies. As was the case in Little Havana, Edison-Little River became a magnet for the new arrivals. The Haitian newcomers joined settled relatives and friends in a process of chain migration. A study of the 1980 immigrants, for example, revealed that 88 percent of the Haitians knew someone in the United States before their arrival—usually brothers, sisters, or cousins. By 1984 the eight census tracts of Edison-Little River were about 40 percent Haitian, and the area had become known as Little Haiti.[42]

Relatively little is known about this new ethnic group in Miami. Only a handful of studies have been completed, based mainly on survey research. But the research of the past few years has begun to paint a composite picture of a growing ethnic community. The Miami Haitians tend to be relatively young, about 30 percent of them under the age of 15, and over half between the ages of 18 and 29. About 75 percent are males, but the women are in their prime childbearing years. As a result, one researcher predicts, the Haitian population in Miami "could easily double in size from natural increase alone" over the next two decades.[43]

Although poor, the Haitians are neither unskilled nor uneducated peasants, as the popular stereotype suggests. Most are at least one generation removed from rural peasantry, or lived in Haitian cities prior to migration to Florida. One study demonstrated that only 5 percent had been farmers in Haiti, although 62 percent of their fathers worked in agriculture. More often than not, the Haitian immigrants are semiskilled, primarily in tailoring, carpentry, auto mechanics, and similar trades. They achieved an average of 7.6 years of schooling Haiti, a substantial accomplishment in a country where 80 percent of the population has had no formal schooling at all. Migration researchers have argued that the Haitian boat people are positively selected—risk-takers who are ambitious, highly motivated, and anxious to get ahead.[44]

Miami researchers have also noted the "strong education ethic among the Haitians." One study reported that 45 percent of all Haitians in Miami were enrolled in some sort of school, while another noted that 55 percent had received some education after their arrival in the United States. Because language ability is linked to employment, the Haitians are particularly anxious to learn English and even Spanish. About half have already become fluent in English, and another third have picked up rudimentary English skills. Almost half of all employed Haitians work with Cubans, which makes acquisition of Spanish-language skills desirable as well. Fluent in Creole and/or French, some Haitians are well on the way to being trilingual and even quadrilingual—again, hardly consistent with the stereotype.[45]

The Haitians also have a strong work ethic, but they have faced racial prejudice and job discrimination in the United States. In 1982 the Haitian unemployment rate in Miami was a staggering 27 percent, twice the rate for American blacks in the city and four times the overall rate for Miami. Unskilled and semiskilled Haitians with jobs are concentrated in Miami's hotel and restaurant trade, domestic service, and construction, as well as in seasonal agricultural labor on the rural fringes of Miami. However, the Haitians do not dominate in any of these segments of Miami's low-wage labor market. Despite a willingness to work hard, and despite good results when they have found permanent work, they tend to be underemployed or working in temporary and low-paid jobs.[46]

The Haitians have begun to develop their own entrepreneurial sector. At least one hundred Haitian businesses have been established in Miami's Little Haiti. However, they tend to be small retail and service businesses, lacking in capital and employing mostly family members. Dozens of other informal businesses have emerged—lawn services, painting contractors, dressmaking and sewing shops, pest-control services, street-corner vendors—but without access to capital and a wider clientele, these businesses will remain small and marginally profitable. The Cubans have established a self-sufficient economic enclave in Little Havana, but the residents of Little Haiti remain dependent on the larger economy.[47]

Thus the Haitians have not achieved much socioeconomic mobility, at least as compared to the Cubans. Other adjustment problems in Little Haiti include overcrowded housing, inadequate health care, and ineffective social services delivery. Legal difficulties with immigration authorities complicate these poor social conditions. Survey researchers report that regardless of problems and handicaps, the Haitians are highly satisfied with life in the United States. Under the circumstances, the group's adjustment over a short period of time has been remarkable.[48]

Some researchers report an apparent widewpread desire to assimilate to the American mainstream. Haitian parents, for example, want their children to learn only English in school, and do not encourage the use of Creole books. One study revealed that about 40 percent of Miami Haitians read newspapers but almost all reported reading the *Miami Herald* rather than any of the several French or Creole papers. Few Haitians expressed any interest in returning to their home country, suggesting they were here to stay.[49]

Despite this evidence of assimilationist intention, many aspects of Haitian culture remain strong in the United States. Haitian food and music, for instance, are prevalent in Little Haiti. The area is painted in bright colors, and Haitian women dress in colorful native dress, particularly on Sundays. Sociologist Alex Stepick captured something of the cultural vitality of Little Haiti, in this passage from a recent study of the area:

> The store fronts on Little Haiti's commercial streets leap out at passersby. Bright blues, reds, and oranges seem to vibrate to the rousing Haitian music blaring from the sidewalk speakers. The multilingual signs advertise peculiarly Haitian products — rapid money transfer to any village in Haiti, the latest Haitian records, custom tailored, "French-styled" fashions, and culinary delights such as *lambi* and *qriot*. Unlike so many neighborhood shopping areas in the age of the automobile and suburbs, Little Haiti's streets are filled with pedestrians.[50]

As in Little Havana, frequent festivals, celebrations, and parades convey the old-country flavor. Moreover, as is true of the Miami Cubans, the Haitian family serves important functions, ranging from facilitating the chain-migration process to job recruitment.

Haitian Catholic parishes in Miami, with French- and Creole-speaking priests and nuns, provide a form of religious continuity; so also do some 30 storefront Protestant churches in Little Haiti.[51] The Haitians have mixed organized religion with folk religion of African origins. Voodoo, like *santería*, is a mélange of music, magic, ceremony, ritual, natural medicine and even animal sacrifice. The informal voodoo rites, as an indelible part of Haitian culture, are commonly practiced even by those belonging to organized churches.[52]

Like the Cubans in their early years in Miami, the city's Haitians also have been involved in exile politics. In the 1970s and early 1980s a number of groups were organized in Miami with the avowed aim of toppling the Duvalier regime. One such group, the Haitian National People's Party, headed by Bernard Sansaricq, actually conducted an ill-fated invasion in 1982.[53] For many years the Haitian consul in Miami was widely believed to be an agent of the dreaded *tontons macoutes* — the Haitian secret police. Mysterious bombings and fires in Little Haiti were thought to be aimed at silencing outspoken opponents of Jean-Claude Duvalier. Local Haitian leaders regularly blasted U.S. government aid to the Duvalier regime. Miami Haitians had little influence on the events that led Duvalier to flee to France in 1986. Their initial jubilation was dashed after the disastrous 1987 and 1988 Haitian election fiascos, followed soon thereafter by a military coup. Old-country political issues remain predominant in Little Haiti at this early stage, but there are already at least forty-five hundred Haitian voters in Miami, and there could be as many as ten thousand by 1990. Thus a shift to ethnic politics for these new Caribbean immigrants may not be far off.[54]

It is perhaps too early to predict the prospect of pluralism or assimilation among the Miami Haitians. Moreover, new waves of boat people could alter the situation at any moment. Nevertheless, Miami's Little Haiti provides a fascinating glimpse of ethnic dynamics at work in the contemporary Sunbelt city. The fact that these immigrants are black adds a new element to the equation.

Conclusion

It is my argument, then, that ethnicity and biculturalism have become powerful and vital forces in Miami. The arrival of Cubans and other exile and refugee groups since 1959 has dramatically altered the demography and the cultural landscape of the Miami metropolitan area. The Cubans have adjusted rapidly over twenty-five years, and have been successful economically—more so than any other Hispanic group in the United States. The second generation of Cuban-Americans, in particular, has internalized many aspects of mainstream American culture, but it would be difficult to demonstrate their full assimilation. Cubans and other ethnic groups have been thrown together in Miami in a struggle for jobs, residential space, and political power. When ethnic minorities begin competing directly with other groups, sociologist Alejandro Portes has suggested, "awareness of racial and cultural differences will be heightened and [will] form the basis for mobilization."[55] For the Cubans, as for other immigrant groups before them, nationality has been the key variable in determining political attitudes and political behavior. The emergence of a powerful ethnic politics in Miami has stimulated cultural differences and ethnic identification. The maintenance of ethnic mother tongues, in particular Spanish, has had a similar impact. The Miami area almost certainly will continue to serve as a focal point for the arrival and settlement of Caribbean and Latin American exiles, refugees, and immigrants, thus replenishing already strong ethnic communities.

All of these considerations suggest the Miami experience, at least at this stage, to be one of biculturalism—of ethnic adjustment without complete assimilation. With 7 million newcomers arriving in the United States in the 1970s, and with many millions more expected to arrive before the end of the century, now is the right time to begin the systematic study of the new immigrants, particularly in the Sunbelt South and West where so many of them have settled.

What the future holds for Miami, only time will tell. But the character of Cuban and other Latin and Caribbean movement to this new immigrant city suggests that biculturalism will remain a powerful and shaping force in Miami for some time to come.

Notes

1. Douglas S. Massey, "Dimensions of the New Immigration to the United States and the Prospects for Assimilation," *Annual Review of Sociology* 7 (1981): 57–85; Aaron Segal, "The Half-Open Door," *The Wilson Quarterly* 7 (New Year's 1983): 117; *USA Today*, 11–13 Oct. 1985.
2. Kurt Andersen, "The New Ellis Island," *Time* (13 June 1983): 18–25; David L. Clark, "Improbable Los Angeles," in Richard M. Bernard and Bradley R. Rice, eds., *Sunbelt Cities: Politics and Growth since World War II* (Austin: Univ. of Texas Press, 1983), 269.
3. For a general survey of Miami's changing pattern, see Raymond A. Mohl, "Miami: The Ethnic Cauldron," in Bernard and Rice, eds., *Sunbelt Cities*, 58–99.
4. U.S. Immigration and Naturalization Service, *Annual Reports, 1960–1977* (Washington, D.C.: U.S. Government Printing Office, 1960–1977); INS Computer Tapes, 1972–1977.
5. James Kelly, "Trouble in Paradise," *Time* (23 Nov. 1981): 32; Joan Moore and Harry Pachon, *Hispanics in the United States* (Englewood Cliffs, N.J.: Prentice-Hall, 1985), 46; Roberto F. Fleitas, "Adjustment without Assimilation: The Cubans in the United States, 1959–1976" (M.A. thesis, University of Miami, 1976).
6. Paul S. George, "Colored Town: Miami's Black Community, 1896–1930," *Florida Historical Quarterly* 56 (Apr. 1978): 432–47; Raymond A. Mohl, "Race, Ethnicity, and Urban Politics in the Miami Metropolitan Area," *Florida Environmental and Urban Issues* 9 (Apr. 1982): 1–6, 23–25.
7. Sergio Díaz-Briquets and Lisandro Pérez, "Cuba: The Demography of Revolution," *Population Bulletin* 36 (Apr. 1981): 25–28; Thomas D. Boswell, "The Migration and Distribution of Cubans and Puerto Ricans Living in the United States," *Journal of Geography* 83 (Mar.–Apr. 1984): 65–72; Raymond A. Mohl, "Miami: Gateway to America," in *Freedom's Doors: Immigrant Ports of Entry to the U.S.* (Philadelphia: Balch Institute for Ethnic Studies, 1986), 69–80.

8. *Miami Herald*, 7 Sept. 1975, 25 Jan. 1981; *New York Times*, 5 Mar. 1979; *Miami News*, 19 July, 22 Aug. 1984; Clyde B. McCoy et al., "Cuban and Other Latin Immigration to Florida," *Florida Economic Indicators* 12 (May 1980): 1–4; *Hispanic Profile: Dade County's Hispanic Origin Population, 1985* (Miami: Metropolitan Dade County Planning Department, 1986).

9. Donald O. Cowgill, "Trends in Residential Segregation of Non-Whites in American Cities, 1940–1950," *American Sociological Review* 21 (Feb. 1956): 43–47; Karl E. Taeuber and Alma F. Taeuber, *Negroes in Cities: Residential Segregation and Neighborhood Change* (Chicago: Aldine, 1965), 40–41; Annemette Sorenson et al., "Indexes of Racial Residential Segregation for 109 Cities in the United States, 1940–1970," *Sociological Focus* 8 (1975): 125–42.

10. Reinhold P. Wolff and David K. Gillogly, *Negro Housing in the Miami Area: Effects of the Postwar Building Boom* (Coral Gables, Fla.: Bureau of Business and Economic Research, University of Miami, 1951); Harold M. Rose, "Metropolitan Miami's Changing Negro Population, 1950–1960," *Economic Geography* 40 (July 1964): 221–38.

11. Robert A. Ladner et al., *Demography, Social Status, Housing and Social Needs of the Haitian Population of Edison-Little River* (Miami: Behavioral Science Research Institute, 1983), 1–8; Alex Stepick, *The Business Community of Little Haiti* (Miami: Haitian Task Force, 1984), 8.

12. Morton D. Winsberg, "Housing Segregation of a Predominantly Middle-Class Population: Residential Patterns Developed by the Cuban Immigration into Miami, 1950–74," *American Journal of Economics and Sociology* 38 (Oct. 1979): 403–18; Morton D. Winsberg, "Ethnic Competition for Residential Space in Miami, Florida, 1970–80," *American Journal of Economics and Sociology* 42 (July 1983): 305–14; B. E. Aguirre et. al., "The Residential Patterning of Latin American and Other Ethnic Populations in Metropolitan Miami," *Latin American Research Review* 15, no. 2 (1980): 35–63; Rosemary Santana Cooney and Maria Alina Contreras, "Residence Patterns of Social Register Cubans: A Study of Miami, San Juan, and New York SMSAs," *Cuban Studies* 8 (July 1978): 33–49.

13. *Miami Herald*, 17 Jan., 14 Feb., 1 Nov. 1982, 19 July 1984; *Miami News*, 19 July, 22 Aug. 1984; *USA Today*, 10 Sept. 1984.

14. Winsberg, "Housing Segregation," 406, 415; Winsberg, "Ethnic Competition," 306–7; *Miami Herald*, 4 Nov. 1984.

15. Winsberg, "Housing Segregation," 415; Winsberg, "Ethnic Competition," 305, 313–14; Oliver Kerr, *Population Projections: Race and Hispanic Origin, Dade County, Florida, 1980–2000* (Miami: Metropolitan Dade County Planning Department, 1987).

16. "Havana, Fla.," *Newsweek* (1 Sept. 1969): 59; Susan Jacoby, "Miami Si, Cuba No," *New York Times Magazine* (29 Sept. 1974): 28, 103–10, 114, 123: "Miami: New Hispanic Power Base in U.S.", *U.S. News and World Report* (19 Feb. 1979): 66–69.

17. Raymond A. Mohl, "Changing Economic Patterns in the Miami Metropolitan Area, 1940–1980," *Tequesta: The Journal of the Historical Association of Southern Florida* 42 (1982): 63–73; Herbert Burkholz, "The Latinization

of Miami," *New York Times Magazine* (21 Sept. 1980): 45–46, 84; Kenneth L. Wilson and W. Allen Martin, "Ethnic Enclaves: A Comparison of the Cuban and Black Economies in Miami," *American Journal of Sociology* 88 (July 1982): 135–60; Alejandro Portes and Robert L. Bach, *Latin Journey: Cuban and Mexican Immigrants in the United States* (Berkeley: Univ. of California Press, 1985), 200–239.

18. Joel Garreau, *The Nine Nations of North America* (Boston: Houghton Mifflin, 1981), 167–206; Penny Lernoux, "The Miami Connection," *The Nation* 238 (18 Feb. 1984): 186–198; Burkholz, "The Latinization of Miami," 46.

19. William C. Baggs, "The Other Miami—City of Intrigue," *New York Times Magazine* (13 Mar. 1960): 25, 84–87; Lynn Darrell Bender, "The Cuban Exiles: An Analytical Sketch," *Journal of Latin American Studies* 5 (Nov. 1973): 276; "Miami, Haven for Terror," *The Nation* (19 Mar. 1977): 326–31; "Miami's Cubans—Getting a Taste for Politics," *U.S. News and World Report* (5 Apr. 1976): 29.

20. Raymond A. Mohl, "The Politics of Ethnicity in Contemporary Miami," *Migration World* 14, no. 3 (1986): 7–11; Kathy A. Darasz, "Cuban Refugees in Miami: Patterns of Economic and Political Adjustment" (M.A. thesis, Florida Atlantic University, 1982), 70–113; Alejandro Portes, "The Rise of Ethnicity: Determinants of Ethnic Perceptions among Cuban Exiles in Miami," *American Sociological Review* 49 (June 1984): 383–97; Raymond A. Mohl, "Miami's Metropolitan Government: Retrospect and Prospect," *Florida Historical Quarterly* 63 (July 1984): 24–50.

21. Paul S. Salter and Robert C. Mings, "The Projected Impact of Cuban Settlement on Voting Patterns in Metropolitan Miami, Florida," *Professional Geographer* 24 (May 1972): 123–31; Benigno E. Aguirre, "Ethnic Newspapers and Politics: *Diario Las Americas* and the Watergate Affair," *Ethnic Groups* 2 (1979): 155–65; Max Azicri, "The Politics of Exile: Trends and Dynamics of Political Change among Cuban-Americans," *Cuban Studies* 11–12 (July 1981–Jan. 1982): 55–73; Gerald R. Webster, "Factors in the Growth of Republican Voting in the Miami–Dade County SMSA," *Southeastern Geographer* 27 (May 1987): 1–17; Dan Millott, "Cuban Thrust to the GOP," *New Florida* 1 (Sept. 1981): 70–71; Sonia L. Nazario, "Yanqui Si," *Wall Street Journal*, 7 June 1983; *Miami Herald*, 18 Sept. 1984.

22. Michael G. Wenk, "Adjustment and Assimilation: The Cuban Refugee Experience," *International Migration Review* 3 (Fall 1968): 38–49.

23. Lisandro Pérez, "Cubans," in Stephan Thernstrom, ed., *Harvard Encyclopedia of American Ethnic Groups* (Cambridge, Mass.: Harvard Univ. Press, 1980), 256–61; Thomas D. Boswell and James R. Curtis, *The Cuban-American Experience: Culture, Images and Perspectives* (Totowa, N.J.: Rowman and Allanheld, 1984), 191. See also T. D. Allman, *Miami: City of the Future* (New York: Atlantic Monthly, 1987), a journalistic account that argues the case for rapid assimilation. Offering more complex assessments are Silvia Pedraza-Bailey, *Political and Economic Migrants in America: Cubans and Mexicans* (Austin: Univ. of Texas Press, 1985), and Portes and Bach, *Latin Journey*.

24. Milton M. Gordon, *Assimilation in American Life* (New York: Oxford Univ. Press, 1964), 60–83.

25. Pérez, "Cubans," 256–61; Eleanor Meyer Rogg, *The Assimilation of Cuban Exiles: The Role of Community and Class* (New York: Aberdeen, 1974); A. J. Jaffe et al., *The Changing Demography of Spanish Americans* (New York: Academic, 1980), 245–78; Thomas D. Boswell et al., "Socioeconomic Context of Cuban Americans," *Journal of Cultural Geography* 3 (Fall 1982): 29–41.

26. Joshua A. Fishman, *Language Loyalty in the United States* (The Hague: Mouton, 1966), 42–47; Melvyn C. Resnick, "Beyond the Ethnic Community: Spanish Language Roles and Maintenance in Miami," *International Journal of the Sociology of Language* 69 (1988): 103–18; Bureau of the Census, *1980 Census of Population*, vol. 1, *Characteristics of the Population*, PC80–1–C11, *Florida* (Washington, D.C.: Government Printing Office, 1983), 11–15.

27. Guarione M. Diaz, ed., *Evaluation and Identification of Policy Issues in the Cuban Community* (Miami: Cuban National Planning Council, 1981), 48; *Miami Herald*, 29 Apr. 1983.

28. Diaz, *Evaluation and Identification of Policy Issues*, 49–50; Boswell and Curtis, *The Cuban-American Experience*, 115–20.

29. Diaz, *Evaluation and Identification of Policy Issues*, 49; Aida Tomas Levitan, *Hispanics in Dade County: Their Characteristics and Needs* (Miami: Office of the County Manager, 1980), 29; Resnick, "Beyond the Ethnic Community."

30. Frank Soler, "Hispanics in the U.S.: Fact vs. Myth," *Miami Mensual* 5 (Sept. 1985): 8–12; Frank Soler, "Bilingualism a Matter of Survival," *Miami News*, 6 Sept. 1985; Portes, "The Rise of Ethnicity," 394–95; Arlen J. Large, "War of Words," *Wall Street Journal*, 22 June 1985.

31. Michael J. McNally, *Catholicism in South Florida, 1868–1968* (Gainesville: Univ. Presses of Florida, 1984), 127–155; Bryan O. Walsh, "Cubans in Miami," *America* 14 (Feb. 1966): 286–89; Bryan O. Walsh, "The Church and the City: The Miami Experience," *New Catholic World* 225 (May–June 1982): 107–10.

32. McNally, *Catholicism in South Florida*, 160; James R. Curtis, "Miami's Little Havana: Yard Shrines, Cult Religion and Landscape," *Journal of Cultural Geography* 1 (Fall–Winter 1980): 1–15; James R. Curtis, "Santería: Persistence and Change in an Afrocuban Cult Religion," in Ray B. Browne, ed., *Objects of Special Devotion: Fetishism in Popular Culture* (Bowling Green, Ohio: Bowling Green Univ. Popular Press, 1982), 336–51; Juan J. Sosa, "La Santería: A Way of Looking at Reality" (M.A. thesis, Florida Atlantic University, 1981); Joseph M. Murphy, *Santería: An African Religion in America* (Boston: Beacon, 1988).

33. Jaffe et al., *The Changing Demography of Spanish Americans*, 63–68, 252–58, 270–72; B. E. Aguirre, "The Marital Stability of Cubans in the United States," *Ethnicity* 8 (Dec. 1981): 387–405; Margaret S. Boone, "The Uses of Traditional Concepts in the Development of New Urban Roles: Cuban Women in the United States," in Erika Bourguignon, ed., *A World*

of Women (New York: Praeger, 1980), 235–69; José Llanes, *Cuban Americans: Masters of Survival* (Cambridge, Mass.: Abt, 1982), 202; Lourdes Meluza and Maria C. Garcia, "The Changing Cuban Woman," *Miami Herald,* 9 Sept. 1984.

34. Pérez, "Cubans," 259.

35. Boswell and Curtis, *The Cuban-American Experience,* 136–67; Pérez, "Cubans," 258–59; *Miami Herald,* 13 Mar. 1982, 25 Sept. 1984.

36. *Miami Herald,* 18 July 1982; Curtis, "Miami's Little Havana," 4; Dade County, *Needs Assessment Study: Terrorism in Dade County, Florida* (Miami: Dade-Miami Criminal Justice Council, 1979), 128–77; Lourdes Arguelles, "Cuban Miami: The Roots, Development, and Everyday Life of an Emigré Enclave in the U.S. National Security State," *Contemporary Marxism* 5 (Summer 1982): 27–43; Joan Didion, *Miami* (New York: Simon and Schuster, 1987).

37. Curtis, "Miami's Little Havana," 4.

38. Bureau of the Census, *1980 Census of Population,* volume 1, *Characteristics of the Population,* PC80-1–C11, *Florida* (Washington, D.C.: Government Printing Office, 1983), 11–278, 11–281; Dade County, *Cuban and Haitian Refugees, Miami SMSA—1980* (Miami: Metropolitan Dade County Planning Department, 1981), 1–3; Thomas D. Boswell, "The New Haitian Diaspora: Florida's Most Recent Residents," *Caribbean Review* 11 (Winter 1982): 18–21; *New York Times,* 14 May 1980; *Wall Street Journal,* 5 May 1980; *Miami Herald,* 31 July, 5 Sept. 1981; *Palm Beach Post,* 6 Sept. 1981.

39. Michel S. Laguerre, *American Odyssey: Haitians in New York City* (Ithaca, N.Y.: Cornell Univ. Press, 1984), 21–25, 31; Dennis Williams, "Florida's Boat People," *Newsweek* (2 Apr. 1979): 37–38; Kevin Krajick, "Refugees Adrift: Barred from America's Shores," *Saturday Review* (27 Oct. 1979): 17–20; William L. Chaze, "Now It's Haiti's Boat People Coming in a Flood," *U.S. News and World Report* (3 Dec. 1979): 64–66; Bryan O. Walsh, "The Boat People of South Florida," *America* 142 (17 May 1980): 420–21; Alex Stepick, "The New Haitian Exodus: The Flight from Terror and Poverty," *Caribbean Review* 11 (Winter 1982): 14–17; Alex Stepick, "Root Causes of Haitian Migration," in *Immigration Reform,* serial no. 30, pt. 1, Hearings before the Subcomittee on Immigration, Refugees, and International Law of the Committee on the Judiciary, House of Representatives, 97th Cong. (Washington, D.C., 1981), 698–753.

40. The most recent study of the new Haitian immigration is Jake C. Miller, *The Plight of Haitian Refugees* (New York: Praeger, 1984). See also Patrick Lacefield, "These Political Refugees Are from the Wrong Place," *In These Times* (7–13 Nov. 1979): 11, 13; "Haitians, Stay Home!" *America* 144 (16 May 1981): 398; Martin M. Dernis, "Haitian Immigrants: Political Refugees or Economic Escapees?" *University of Miami Law Review* 31 (1976–1977): 27–41; Alex Stepick, "Haitian Boat People: A Study in the Conflicting Forces Shaping U.S. Immigration Policy," *Law and Contemporary Problems* 45 (Spring 1982): 163–196; Alex Stepick, *Haitian Refugees in the U.S.* (London: Minority Rights Group, Report no. 52, 1982), 11–17; Gilburt Loescher and John Scanlan, "Human Rights, U.S. Foreign Policy, and

Haitian Refugees," *Journal of Interamerican Studies and World Affairs* 26 (Aug. 1984): 313–56.

41. Yetta Deckelbaum, "Little Haiti: The Evolution of a Community" (M.A. thesis, Florida Atlantic University, 1983), 39–57; Ladner et al., *Demography, Social Status, Housing and Social Needs*, 2.

42. Dade County, *Social and Economic Problems among Cuban and Haitian Entrant Groups in Dade County, Florida: Trends and Indications* (Miami: Office of the County Manager, 1981), 76; Alex Stepick, *The Business Community of Little Haiti* (Miami: Haitian Task Force, 1984), 8; Ellen Hampton, "Little Haiti: The City Within," *Miami Herald Tropic Magazine* (3 July 1983): 7–26.

43. Alex Stepick and Alejandro Portes, "Flight into Despair: A Profile of Recent Haitian Refugees in South Florida," *International Migration Review* 20 (Summer 1986): 332–33; Ladner et al., *Demography, Social Status, Housing and Social Needs*, 14; Dade County, *Social and Economic Problems* 75; Thomas D. Boswell, "In the Eye of the Storm: The Context of Haitian Migration to Miami, Florida," *Southeastern Geographer* 23 (Nov. 1983): 68.

44. Stepick and Portes, "Flight into Despair," 332–33, 336–37; Alex Stepick, "Haitians in Miami: An Assessment of Their Background and Potential,' *Occasional Papers Series*, Dialogue no. 12 (Miami: Latin American and Caribbean Center, Florida International University, Dec. 1982): 3, 8–11.

45. Ladner et al., *Demography, Social Status, Housing and Social Needs*, 12; Stepick, "Haitians in Miami," 2, 5, 17; Stepick and Portes, "Flight into Despair," 336–38.

46. Ladner et al., *Demography, Social Status, Housing and Social Needs*, 26, 65; Stepick "Haitians in Miami," 4–5; Stepick and Portes, "Flight into Despair," 338–39.

47. Stepick, *Business Community of Little Haiti*, 8–10, 15–16, 20, 30, 36–37, 41–44; Stepick, "The Haitian Informal Sector in Miami" (paper presented at Conference on the Informal Sector, Johns Hopkins University, Baltimore, June 1984), 14–28.

48. *Miami News*, 17 June 1983; *Miami Herald*, 12, 18 Oct. 1981, 11 Apr. 1982, 10 Apr. 1984; Miller, *Plight of Haitian Refugees*, 147–67; Boswell, "Eye of the Storm," 67–68; Ladner et al., *Demography, Social Status, Housing and Social Needs*, 64–67; Alex Stepick, "Haitians Released from Krome: Their Prospects for Adaptation and Integration in South Florida," *Occasional Papers Series*, Dialogue no. 24 (Miami: Latin American and Caribbean Center, Florida International University, March 1984): 12–13, 26–28.

49. Deckelbaum, "Little Haiti," 85; Ladner et al., *Demography, Social Status, Housing and Social Needs*, 62–63; Stepick, "Haitians Released from Krome," 33.

50. Stepick, "Haitian Informal Sector in Miami," 14. See also *Miami News*, 2 Mar. 1981, 23 Apr. 1984; *Miami Herald*, 20 Apr. 1984; *Miami Times*, 2 Oct. 1980, 22 Jan. 1981; Hampton, "Little Haiti," 18–19; Stepick, "Haitians Released from Krome," 27.

51. *Miami Herald*, 15 Aug. 1981, 27 June 1984; Bryan O. Walsh, "Haitians in

Miami," *Migration Today* 7 (Sept. 1979): 44; Deckelbaum, "Little Haiti," 69–79.
52. Michel S. Laguerre, "Haitian Americans," in Alan Harwood, ed., *Ethnicity and Medical Care* (Cambridge, Mass.: Harvard Univ. Press, 1981), 172–210; Patrick Malone, "In Defense of Voodoo," *Miami Herald Tropic Magazine* (20 Sept. 1981): 8–14, 36–37, 40–41; Hugh J. B. Cassidy, "Saturday Night Voodoo; Sunday Morning Mass," *U.S. Catholic* 43 (July 1978): 35–38. On voodoo, see also Robert Tallant, *Voodoo in New Orleans* (New York: Macmillan, 1946), and Michel S. Laguerre, *Voodoo Heritage* (Beverly Hills, Calif.: Sage Publications, 1980).
53. Anthony Summers, "'A Hope and a Doom': Profile of an Invasion," *Miami Magazine* 33 (Apr. 1982): 70–75, 139–144; Miller, *Plight of Haitian Refugees*, 208–15; *Miami Herald*, 1 June 1984; *Miami News*, 19 Mar., 10 July 1982.
54. *Miami Herald*, 31 Jan., 12, 15, 30 Apr., 17 May, 4 June 1984, 13 Dec. 1987, 21 June 1988; *Miami Times*, 11 Feb. 1982, 24 May 1984.
55. Portes, "The Rise of Ethnicity," 385. See also Alejandro Portes et al., "Assimilation or Consciousness: Perceptions of U.S. Society among Recent Latin American Immigrants to the United States," *Social Forces* 59 (Sept. 1980): 200–224.

10   The End of the Long Hot Summer

The Air Conditioner and Southern Culture

Raymond Arsenault

In 1979 *Time* magazine columnist Frank Trippett took the American intellectual community to task for ignoring the social and cultural significance of air conditioning. Scholars and pop sociologists have been keenly aware of "the social implications of the automobile and television," he observed, but for some reason they have not gotten around "to charting and diagnosing all the changes brought about by air conditioning."[1] Trippett's complaint is valid, and strange as it may seem, nowhere is this more evident than in the field of southern history. When the journalist Pat Watters called the air conditioner the "unsung hero" of the modern South in 1963, he knew what he was talking about.[2] With few exceptions, historical works on the twentieth-century South published during the last forty years make no mention of air conditioning or, for that matter, of anything related to climate or climate control.[3] The recently published *Encyclopedia of Southern History* contains 2,900 articles covering everything from "Abbeville" to "Zwaanendael," but, incredibly, it has no article on air conditioning. Even the broader subject of southern climate is dimissed in three paragraphs — less space than is devoted to "reptiles and amphibians."[4]

This scholarly neglect is surprising because it goes against the grain of common sense and popular culture. Ask any southerner over thirty years of age to explain why the South has changed in recent decades, and that person may begin with the civil rights movement or industrialization. But sooner or later he or she will come around to the subject of air conditioning. For better or worse, your informant will tell you, the air conditioner has changed the nature of southern life. Some southerners will praise air conditioning and wonder out loud how they ever lived without it. Others will argue that the South is going to hell, not in a hand basket, but in an air-conditioned Chevy. As one Florida woman recently remarked, "I hate air conditioning; it's a damnfool invention of the Yankees. If they don't like it hot, they can move back up North where they belong."[5]

Southern historians' lack of interest in the social history of climate control cannot be easily explained, but one suspects that, to a great degree, it represents a reaction to the excesses of an earlier generation of scholars. During the first three decades of the twentieth century environmental determinism was a powerful force in American social science. This was the age of Walter Prescott Webb, Ellsworth Huntington, and Ulrich Bonnell Phillips, when the link between climate and culture was often thought to be a simple relationship of cause and effect. The southern climate, in particular, was credited with producing everything from plantation slavery to the southern drawl.[6] "Let us begin by discussing the weather, for that has been the chief agency in making the South distinctive," was the opening line of Phillips's 1929 classic, *Life and Labor in the Old South.* According to Phillips, the hot, humid southern climate "fostered the cultivation of the staple crops, which promoted the plantation system, which brought the importation of negroes, which not only gave rise to chattel slavery but created a lasting race problem. These led to controversy and regional rivalry for power, which produced apprehensive reactions and culminated in a stroke for independence. Thus we have . . . the Confederate States of America."[7] So much for the complexity of history.

Modern scholars have wisely rejected this kind of monocausal climatological determinism, a determinism that was frequently tied to racist and colonialist preconceptions. Unfortunately, they have tended to overreact, throwing out the baby with the bath water.[8] Climate may not be the key to human history, but climate does matter. In some areas, such as the American South, it matters a great deal, or at least it did until the coming of the air conditioner. "Because the air conditioner, the airplane and television have smoothed out harsh differences in climate, nearly abolished distance and homogenized popular taste," a 1970 *New York Times* editorial argued, "Americans are becoming much less regionally diverse. . . . The census sketches a nation that has become one people with much the same problems and expectations everywhere. The regions fade. The urbanized nation strides on."[9] Perhaps so, but the *Times* editor would not be the first person to have been a bit premature in pronouncing the death of southern regionalism. The truth is that no one really knows what impact air conditioning has had on southern life and culture because no one, to this point, has undertaken an in-depth study of the subject. This essay represents a modest first step toward such a study.

When did the "air-conditioning revolution" actually come to the South?

This is not as simple a question as it may seem, because air condition-ing, like most forms of technology, developed in piecemeal fashion. The age of air conditioning, in the broadest sense, was initiated by John Gor-rie, a Florida physician who began experimenting with a crude form of mechanical cooling in the 1830s. In an attempt to lower the body tem-peratures of malaria and yellow fever victims, Gorrie blew forced air over buckets of ice suspended from the ceiling of the U.S. Marine Hospi-tal in Apalachicola, Florida. The experiment yielded mixed results but left Gorrie obsessed with the healing potential of chilled air. His use of the steam-driven compressor to cool air led, in 1851, to a patent for the first ice-making machine. Gorrie eventually was hailed as "the in-ventor of air conditioning," and in 1914 he was memorialized by proud Floridians who placed his statue in Washington, D.C.'s Statuary Hall.[10] But few of his contemporaries appreciated the significance of his achieve-ments. One New York journalist sneered, "A crank down in Florida thinks he can make ice as good as Almighty God."[11]

Despite such skepticism, experimentation in the area of mechanical cooling and refrigeration became widespread during the Civil War and Reconstruction. In the late 1860s the invention of the refrigerated tank car revolutionized the meat-packing industry and spurred new interest in the science of temperature control.[12] A number of inventors, includ-ing several southerners, set out to prove that a technology capable of preserving dead animals could also be used to cool live humans. In 1871 Andrew Muhl of Waco, Texas, designed a room cooling system that used forced air and refrigerated coils suspended from the ceiling. Nine years later two Alexandria, Virginia, engineers, Robert Portner and Edward Eils, invented a cooling apparatus that used a steam-driven ventilating fan to force air over refrigerated pipes. Designed as a quality control de-vice, the Portner-Eils system eventually was installed in several brew-eries. Air conditioning for the masses was still a long way off, but now the American worker could at least cool off with a higher quality of cold beer. The Gilded Age's most celebrated effort at mechanical cool-ing took place during the summer of 1881, when President James A. Garfield's doctors used ventilating fans and 436 pounds of ice per hour to cool his White House bedroom. As the nation watched Garfield ex-pire in relative comfort, the idea of mechanical cooling became a part of American popular culture.[13]

Less dramatic, but probably more important in the long run, was the invention of the electric fan in 1882. Unlike the earlier steam-driven models, which were used primarily to ventilate mines and factories, electric fans soon found their way into homes, hotels, restaurants, barber shops, courthouses, theaters, and other public buildings. By the end of the century ornate brass-fitted ceiling fans graced the lobbies of many southern hotels, while smaller "rocking chair" fans could be found in parlors from Alexandria to San Antonio.[14] Ownership of an electric fan quickly became a badge of middle-class respectability in the urban South. The "whirligig" was a luxury item beyond the reach of most working-class families, although by 1902 small table fans could be purchased from Sears Roebuck for ten dollars.[15] In the rural South, where electrification was almost unknown and farmers and villagers were left to the mercy of natural forces, the electric fan became a symbol of urban opulence—or in some cases decadence. During a 1902 political campaign Governor Jeff Davis of Arkansas had a lot of explaining to do after his opponent pointed out that he had purchased "a whirligig fan at the state's expense, to fan himself with, not being content to use a palm leaf like ordinary people."[16]

The electric fan had some capacity to cool and circulate the air, but it did nothing to alleviate the oppressive humidity that often blanketed the South. To tame the southern climate would take more than ceiling fans and blocks of ice; it would take a true "air conditioner"—a machine that would simultaneously cool, circulate, dehumidify, and cleanse the air.[17] Many years would pass before such a machine was available for domestic use, but at the turn of the century an embryonic air-conditioning technology designed for industrial purposes began to emerge, bringing the promise that someday the era of "muggy air and mosquitoes and ceiling fans" would be over.[18] What is generally acknowledged to be the world's first air-conditioning system was installed in 1902 at the Sackett-Wilhelms Lithographic and Publishing Company in Brooklyn. This system, which controlled both humidity and temperature by pumping air at a set velocity over coils refrigerated at a set temperature, was invented by Willis Haviland Carrier, a twenty-five-year-old Cornell-trained engineer—"air conditioning's Edison."[19] Carrier's ingenuity and vision would guide the air-conditioning industry until his death in 1950.

Although the air-conditioning industry began in the North, most of its early growth took place in the South, thanks to the efforts of two young southern engineers, Stuart W. Cramer and I. H. Hardeman. A textile engineer from Charlotte, North Carolina, Cramer actually coined the term *air conditioning* in 1906. During a long career he designed scores of air-conditioning systems for southern cotton mills.[20] Hardeman, a graduate of the Georgia Institute of Technology working under Carrier, convinced his boss that air conditioning would eventually "revolutionize the textile industry."[21] One of the industry's chronic problems, he pointed out, was its inability to control the moisture content in fibers, which often stiffened and snapped when subjected to the extreme heat generated by spindles. At Hardeman's urging Carrier published an article in *Textile World* in April 1906 describing the benefits air conditioning could bring to the textile industry. By the time the article appeared, Hardeman had already sold a primitive air-conditioning system to the Chronicle Cotton Mills of Belmont, North Carolina. After visiting the Chronicle Mills in the summer of 1906 Carrier added several important refinements to his system. It was during this visit that he discovered the principle of "dew point control," later an axiom of air-conditioning technology. By 1908 air conditioning had been installed in several North Carolina cotton mills and by 1911 in rayon mills, where temperature and humidity problems were especially acute.[22]

In 1909 air conditioning moved into the southern tobacco industry, where it was destined to have a major impact on quality control, marketing, and working conditions. Here the key figure was Irvine Lyle, a Carrier executive who had spent his early years on a Kentucky farm. Lyle was convinced that air conditioning could control the amount of moisture in cut tobacco and thus facilitate accurate weighing and pricing. After an initial system was sold to a Henderson, Kentucky, tobacco dealer, the idea caught on, and air conditioning eventually became a fixture in tobacco warehouses. By 1911 air conditioners were being used in cigar factories and by 1913 in tobacco stemming rooms, where dust had bedeviled workers for centuries. Before the end of the decade, the new technology had spread to paper mills, breweries, bakeries, and a handful of other industries.[23]

Prior to the 1920s air conditioning in the South was restricted almost entirely to industrial uses. The major exceptions were a Baltimore hotel and Montgomery, Alabama's elegant Empire Theater, which added air conditioning in 1917.[24] Even in southern industry the use of air conditioning was severely limited and would remain so for many years. Many southern mills did not install air-conditioning systems until the 1930s or 1940s, and even then the vast majority were only partially air-conditioned.[25]

As late as 1924 most southerners had probably never heard of air conditioning, much less experienced it. But this situation changed abruptly in the mid-1920s, when the primary function of air conditioning shifted from efficient production to human comfort. The breakthrough came in 1922 when Willis Carrier coupled the centrifugal compressor to the air conditioner. By replacing the cumbersome piston-driven compressor, Carrier's innovation reduced the size and increased the efficiency of air conditioners. He also substituted a safer refrigerant, Carrene, for the potentially deadly ammonia gas previously used. The age of "comfort cooling" had dawned.[26]

In the South, as elsewhere, the new age began at the movies. It was through the movie house that air conditioning entered the mainstream of southern life. In the summer of 1924 the Palace Theatre in Dallas and the Texan and Iris theaters in Houston became the first southern movie houses to install air conditioning. Advertising "cool and clear" weather, the Texas theaters were soon bulging with customers.[27] Other theaters, many of which had traditionally closed during the torrid summer months, quickly followed suit. Although most moviegoers welcomed the new technology, not all of the early experiences with chilled theaters were positive. At the grand opening of St. Petersburg's Florida Theatre in 1926, "The proud management had the temperature down so low that ladies in evening dresses almost froze!"[28] Despite such minor setbacks, by 1930 hundreds of southern movie palaces were enticing customers with frost-covered signs boasting "20 degrees cooler inside."[29] The proliferation of comfort cooling in theaters and other public buildings was further accelerated in 1931 with the invention of Freon, a noninflammable refrigerant that made air conditioning safer and less expensive. By the beginning of World War II most southern movies theaters were air-conditioned.[30]

A similar revolution occurred on southern railways during the 1930s. As early as 1884 the Baltimore and Ohio Railroad had made a valiant but futile attempt to cool its passengers by attaching a huge icebox to the front end of one of its coaches. In 1913 the Pullman Company asked Willis Carrier to design an air conditioner for passenger cars, but nothing came of the idea until 1929, when Carrier constructed an experimental system for the Baltimore and Ohio. A year later the Carrier unit was installed in the diner of the "Columbian," which operated between Washington and New York. Air-conditioned dining and passenger cars soon spread to other railroads, especially after Carrier designed an improved unit that used engine steam as its energy source. In 1932 the development of an even better system, the "Frigicar," which took its power from the car axle, opened up vast new markets for railway air conditioning.[31] "Air-conditioned trains . . . have become an accepted fact," *Business Week* reported in 1933. "The novelty has worn off."[32] By the end of the decade most railroad passengers, North and South, were traveling in air-cooled comfort.

The movement of air conditioning into other areas of southern life was much more gradual. The first air-conditioned department store appeared in the North in 1914, but it would be many years before a significant number of stores followed suit.[33] Most big-city department stores in the South continued to depend on ceiling fans until the 1940s. When a large Richmond department store installed air conditioning in 1934, the city buzzed for weeks.[34] In the region's smaller cities and towns many retail stores resisted the lure of air conditioning until the 1960s. S. S. Kresge and Company began air-conditioning its chain stores in 1934, but most chains held out until after World War II.[35] Air conditioning for small retail stores became available in 1928, and by the late 1930s there was a sprinkling of air-conditioned barber shops, hardware stores, funeral homes, drugstores, beauty salons, restaurants, and taverns across the region. Nonetheless, the air-conditioned shop remained an oddity in many areas of the South until the 1950s.[36] Similarly, air-conditioned grocery stores were almost unknown until the International Grocers' Alliance introduced its partially air-conditioned Foodliner stores in 1946.[37]

The introduction of air conditioning in government buildings, banks and office buildings, hotels, and hospitals followed a similar pattern. Air conditioning began to appear in government buildings in the late 1920s, but virtually all of the early installations were in federal buildings. The chamber of the House of Representatives was air-conditioned in 1928; the Senate followed in 1929, the White House and the Executive Office Building in 1930, and the United States Supreme Court Building in 1931.[38] Generally speaking, federal courthouses and military buildings, many of which were air-conditioned by 1950, were the first government buildings in the South to have air conditioning. State and local government lagged far behind; most of the region's state buildings and county courthouses did not become air-conditioned until the 1960s.[39]

In most southern cities and towns, banks were among the first buildings to be equipped with air conditioning. Bastions of progress, the banks often led the way, eventually goading other local establishments into experimenting with the newfangled technology. Yet even the air-cooled bank remained a novelty in many areas of the South until after World War II. In some cases the delay was due to the difficulty of air-conditioning high-rise structures. In 1928 the massive twenty-one-story Milam Building in San Antonio became the world's first fully air-conditioned office block. Unfortunately, the air-conditioning system used in the Milam Building was too expensive and too bulky for general use.[40] During the

1930s Carrier and other engineers tried, with limited success, to develop a practical, efficient air conditioner for skyscrapers. Finally, in 1939, Carrier perfected the Conduit Weathermaster System, which used high-velocity air propelled through narrow tubes. The first buildings to use the new system were the Bankers Life Building in Macon, Georgia; the Durham Life Building in Raleigh, North Carolina; and the United Carbon Building in Charleston, West Virginia. Conduit systems were eventually installed in most of the South's taller office buildings.[41]

Although air conditioning was being used in northern hotels by 1908 and in southern hotels by 1914, all of the early hotel installations were limited to public areas such as lobbies and first-floor restaurants.[42] The first hotel to offer its guests air-conditioned rooms on anything more than an experimental basis was the Detroit Statler in 1934.[43] The newly constructed Statler Hotel in Washington, D. C., was fully air-conditioned in 1941, but the vast majority of southern hotels did not install air conditioning in private rooms until the early 1950s.[44] As late as 1957 the chamber of commerce in one large southern city complained that less than half of the city's hotel rooms were air-cooled.[45] The air-conditioned motel was also a development of the 1950s, though one enterprising Augusta, Georgia, tourist camp offered air-conditioned cabins in 1936.[46] By the 1960s air-conditioned motels and hotels had become so common in the South that most proprietors dropped the traditional one-dollar surcharge for air-conditioned rooms.

Despite Doctor Gorrie's early heroics, the idea of an air-conditioned hospital initially drew a mixed response from the American medical community. A ward for premature babies in a Pittsburgh hospital was successfully air-conditioned in 1914, but several other early experiments in hospital air conditioning ended in disaster when the mechanically circulated air triggered hospital-wide epidemics.[47] Although numerous operating rooms and special wards were air-conditioned by 1940, fully air-conditioned hospitals did not become common until much later. By the late 1950s virtually all new hospital buildings were equipped with air conditioning.[48] Nevertheless, as late as 1962 only 15 percent of the nation's hospital rooms were air-conditioned.[49]

In southern educational institutions, even more than in hotels and hospitals, the proliferation of air conditioning was surprisingly slow. Except for a few libraries, air-conditioned university buildings were rare until the late 1950s. Louisiana State University's Fine Arts Building was air-conditioned by 1931, but it remained an academic oddity for decades.[50] A similar situation prevailed in primary and secondary schools. In 1948 air conditioning was installed in three Louisiana schools "as a national experiment to find out how much it benefits school children."[51] Although the experiment was hailed as a success, most southern school boards continued to view air conditioning as an overpriced luxury. Air-conditioned classrooms began to appear in a few affluent school districts in the early 1950s, but in most areas of the South school air conditioning did not become common until at least a decade later. A large majority of the university buildings and public schools constructed after 1960 were air-conditioned, generally with rooftop units specially designed for educational buildings. Many older buildings, however, continued to rely on electric fans and open windows. Even today thousands of southern schools have yet to install air conditioning.[52]

Although air conditioning could be found in a growing number of southern factories, banks, shops, and office buildings by 1930, it had yet to invade the southern home. An air conditioner was installed in a Minneapolis mansion in 1914, but few people took the idea of home air conditioning seriously until after the invention of the centrifugal compressor in the early 1920s.[53] In 1928 Willis Carrier introduced the Weather-maker—a "winter air conditioner" that could heat and humidify a home during cold weather. Later the same year Carrier and Irvine Lyle formed a special corporation to develop the residential air-conditioning market. In 1929 Frigidaire began marketing an expensive, four-foot-high room cooler, and by the early 1930s several companies were working feverishly on the development of a practical residential air conditioner.[54] In 1931 The Aerologist, an environmentalist magazine published in Chicago, ran the headline, "Wanted, an Air-Conditioning Flivver!"[55] A year later Carrier came out with the Atmospheric Cabinet, a fairly compact, self-contained room cooler. Unfortunately, the unit did not sell very well, and the company soon discontinued production.[56] Despite this setback, at the depths of the depression in 1933, a writer in Business Week predicted that "the day is not far when the home air-conditioning plant will be as universally accepted as the furnace."[57] With the same spirit of optimism the Crosley Corporation introduced an air-conditioned canopy bed called the Coolrest in 1934. For some reason—perhaps because the unit looked like a pup tent attached to a refrigerator—the idea never quite caught on.[58]

During the mid-1930s several types of home air conditioners—all as cumbersome as they were expensive—went on the market. But by the end of the decade fewer than two hundred thousand units had been sold.[59] One of the biggest markets was in the Southwest, where people were desperate to protect their homes from the worst dust storms of the century.[60] By the beginning of World War II most southern cities boasted a handful of air-conditioned homes, almost all of which were owned by the wealthy.[61] Very few homes added air conditioning during the war, but several technological advances—including experimentation with the heat pump—brought the age of home cooling closer to reality.[62] In 1945, in a preview of things to come, shipping magnate Henry Kaiser announced plans to build "complete communities of mass-produced air conditioned homes."[63] Room air-conditioner sales climbed to over forty thousand by 1947, but at that period residential air conditioning still accounted for only 2 percent of the industry's business. By 1950 the figure had risen to 5 percent, but in most areas the air-conditioned home remained a novelty.[64]

In 1951 the inexpensive, efficient window unit finally hit the market, and sales skyrocketed, especially in the South.[65] Within a year the Carrier Corporation had set up model tract houses in Louisiana, Texas, and Virginia in an effort to convince consumers that the air conditioner had made porches, basements, attics, and movable windows obsolete.[66] By 1955 one out of every twenty-two American homes had some form of air-conditioning. In the South the figures were closer to one in ten.[67] Five years later census takers found air conditioners in 18 percent of the region's homes (see table 10.1).[68] By that time central air-conditioning systems—scaled-down versions of those used to cool offices and factories—had begun to compete with window units in the South's more affluent neighborhoods. Over four hundred thousand southern homes had central units in 1960; by the mid-1960s more than 40 percent of the new homes being built in the region were equipped with "central air."[69] In 1966 Texas became the first state to have more than half of all its homes and apartments air-conditioned, but by the end of the decade half of the homes and apartments in the South were air-conditioned.[70] During the early 1970s, despite a severe energy crisis, millions of additional southern homes were air-conditioned for the first time. Many other southern families traded in their window or central units for reverse-cycle heat pumps.[71] The age of the push-button "climate-conditioned" home had arrived.

The saga of the air-conditioned automobile closely paralleled that of the air-conditioned home. The world's first air-conditioned car was owned by a wealthy Houston businessman. A chronic hay fever sufferer, he outfitted his new 1930 Cadillac with a unique cooling system. With a condensing unit mounted on the trunk and an evaporator blower be-

Table 10.1   Residential Air Conditioning in the South, 1960–1980

| | Percentage of Households with Air Conditioning | | | | | |
| | Total Households | | | Black Households | | |
	1960	1970	1980	1960	1970	1980
U.S.	12.4	35.8	55.0	4.1	18.0	42.7
Urban	14.2	39.7	58.4	4.7	19.8	44.1
Rural	7.7	24.6	44.8	2.2	8.8	32.6
South	18.2	50.1	73.2	3.9	20.8	52.1
Urban	—	59.3	79.9	—	25.8	58.0
Rural	—	33.0	59.2	—	8.4	32.4
Alabama	16.7	49.0	70.7	2.6	15.3	44.0
Arkansas	14.0	46.5	71.3	1.9	14.7	46.2
Delaware	16.9	48.4	64.6	—	19.8	45.3
D.C.	21.4	49.4	67.1	7.3	36.8	58.5
Florida	18.3	60.5	84.0	1.9	13.3	47.0
Georgia	12.3	43.0	66.0	1.9	13.0	42.7
Kentucky	8.4	32.8	61.7	3.7	17.6	51.3
Louisiana	23.1	58.8	82.2	3.0	23.6	60.6
Maryland	14.9	50.6	70.1	4.4	23.9	58.3
Mississippi	15.7	47.5	69.9	1.5	11.6	40.0
North Carolina	8.9	32.7	59.6	2.4	11.7	40.3
Oklahoma	29.8	58.7	81.5	12.9	34.3	69.2
South Carolina	12.2	40.0	68.0	2.3	10.4	39.9
Tennessee	20.5	52.5	74.0	4.8	33.6	68.4
Texas	30.3	64.2	83.2	9.9	38.5	71.3
Virginia	12.2	43.3	64.8	2.8	17.4	50.9
West Virginia	5.8	17.8	38.5	—	8.5	28.3

Sources: Bureau of the Census, *U.S. Census of Housing:1960*, vol. 1, *States and Small Areas*, p. 1, *United States Summary* (Washington, 1963), tables 7, 13, 26, and 29; "Detailed Housing Characteristics," in Bureau of the Census, *Census of Housing:1970*, vol. 1, *Housing Characteristics for States, Cities, and Counties*, p. 1, *United States Summary* (Washington, 1972), tables 20, 21, 27, and 37; "Detailed Housing Characteristics," in Bureau of the Census, *Census of Housing:1980*, vol. 1, Chap. B. *Characteristics of Housing Units*, p. 1, *United States Summary* (Washington, 1982), tables 78, 79, 84, and 123: and ibid., p. 2, 5, 9–12, 19–20, 22, 26, 35, 38, 42, 44–45, 48, 50, table 64.

a The "census" South includes eleven states of the ex-Confederacy, plus Delaware, the District of Columbia, Kentucky, Maryland, Oklahoma, and West Virginia.

hind the driver's seat, he cruised the Texas highways in pollen-free comfort.[72] The Packard Motor Car Company began experimenting with a less cumbersome system in 1933; six years later Packard became the first automobile line to offer air conditioning as a factory-installed accessory.[73] During World War II the War Production Board all but prohibited comfort cooling, but after the war there was renewed interest in automobile air conditioning.[74] In the early 1950s several luxury cars began offering "factory air," and many lower-priced lines soon followed suit. Wealthy southerners accounted for the vast majority of the early sales, but by 1955, 10 percent of the new cars sold in the United States had factory-installed air conditioners. A decade later the figure was 23 percent; in most areas of the South the figure approched 50 percent. By 1973 more than 80 percent of the cars in the South were equipped with air conditioning.[75] During the energy crisis of 1974 the Environmental Protection Agency warned consumers that air conditioning increased automobile fuel consumption by as much as 20 percent. But this had little effect on the soaring demand for factory air.[76]

Other forms of mobile air conditioning had a similar history. Air-conditioned public transportation vehicles did not become common in the South until the late 1950s, although Atlanta experimented with an air-conditioned trackless trolley car as early as 1944.[77] Air-conditioned taxis, intercity buses, and trucks appeared in most southern cities around 1953 and became routine by the end of the decade.[78] By 1968 Teamsters Union president Jimmy Hoffa was demanding that Teamsters be provided with air-conditioned truck cabs on all long-distance southern runs — not an unreasonable demand in an age when thousands of southern farmers were plowing their fields in air-conditioned tractors.[79]

The so-called air-conditioning revolution, then, was actually an evolution — a long, slow, uneven process stretching over seven decades. The air conditioner came to the South in a series of waves, and only with the wave of the 1950s was the region truly engulfed. What had been largely a curiosity in the pre–World War II South became an immutable part of southern life in the postwar era. After the air conditioner invaded the home and the automobile, there was no turning back. By the mid-1970s air conditioning had made its way into more than 90 percent of the South's high-rise office buildings, banks, apartments, and railroad passenger coaches; more than 80 percent of its automobiles, government buildings, and hotels; approximately two-thirds of its homes, stores, trucks, and hospital rooms; roughly half of its classrooms; and at least a third of its tractors.[80] Virtually all of the region's newer buildings, regardless of type or function, were equipped with air conditioning. The South of the 1970s could claim air-conditioned shopping malls, domed stadiums, dugouts, green houses, grain elevators, chicken coops, aircraft hangars, crane cabs, off-shore oil rigs, cattle barns, steel mills, and drive-in movies and restaurants.[81] In Chalmette, Louisiana, aluminum workers walked around with portable air conditioners strapped to their belts.[82] In Nashville a massive air-conditioning plant was fueled by a steady flow of city garbage.[83] And in Richmond local officials could control the air conditioning in scores of public buildings from a single console.[84] Farther north in Virginia, at Lake Anne Village, an entire town was fully air-conditioned by one central cooling plant.[85] At several amusement parks in Texas and Florida even the outdoor queuing areas were air cooled.[86] Predictably, the South's most air-conditioned state was Texas, where even the Alamo had central air.[87] In Houston alone the annual cost ($666 million) of air conditioning exceeded the annual gross national product of several Third World nations in 1980.[88]

It is little wonder that southeners and many other Americans came to regard air conditioning as a requirement for civilized living. "People no longer think of interior coolness as an amenity," Frank Trippett observed in 1979, they "consider it a necessity, almost a birthright, like suffrage."[89] As Secretary of Commerce Frederick H. Mueller put it in 1960, "People have just decided that it's part of the American standard of living, something we're all entitled to, just as we're entitled to heat in the winter and food on the table."[90] Governor Richard W. Riley of South Carolina took this idea to its logical extreme when, at the 1980 National Governor's Conference, he insisted that federal assistance programs should operate under the assumption that air-conditioning a home in the South is no less essential than heating a home in the North.[91] Many people living below the Mason-Dixon line undoubtedly agreed. In some southerners the preoccupation with indoor cooling reached the level of addiction. According to one business analyst, many southern shoppers simply refused to patronize non-air-conditioned stores: "Any merchant, the customers figure, that can't supply them with air-conditioned comfort, isn't worthy of their patronage."[92] As early as 1955 one southern newspaper columnist concluded that most customers feel that air-conditioned shopping "is their legal right. They feel insulted when they don't find it."[93] For many southerners—especially those born after 1960—the truly inalienable right is the right to live in an air-conditioned home. "Our children are raised in an air-conditioned culture," an air-conditioning executive explained in 1968. "They attend air-conditioned schools, ride air-conditioned buses. You can't really expect them to live in a home that isn't air-conditioned."[94]

This attitude was encouraged not only by the air-conditioning industry—which kept up a steady barrage of promotional "cool air clinics" and "beat the heat week" campaigns—but also by governmental and financial institutions.[95] In 1959 the General Services Administration issued a glowing endorsement of air-conditioned living, and throughout the 1950s and 1960s the policies of the Internal Revenue Service encouraged homeowners to install air conditioners.[96] In 1962 a Federal Housing Administration official flatly declared, "Within a few years, any house that is not air-conditioned will probably be obsolescent."[97] Two years later a Florida mortgage company began penalizing customers whose homes did not have central air conditioning.[98] A more subtle influence was exerted by the National Weather Bureau, which began issuing its "discomfort index" in 1959. A composite of heat and humidity, the index, as interpreted by the air-conditioning industry, was a good way to tell when it was time to go indoors and turn up the dial to "hi cool."[99] Another sign of the times was the term "heat storm," which became a part of meteorological jargon in the mid-1960s.[100] What had once simply been a "hot day" had suddenly turned into a menacing aberration.

It is important to keep the air conditioning revolution in perspective. Despite the best efforts of government, industry, and Madison Avenue, the air conditioner has not conquered all. The South still has more than its share of sun and sweat. And contrary to the claim of one air-conditioning industry spokesman, it is still possible to "escape air conditioning."[101] Not all southerners live in air-conditioned homes, ride in air-conditioned cars, or work in air-conditioned buildings. Among rural and working-class blacks, poor whites, migrant laborers, and mountaineers, air-conditioned living is not the norm.[102] On the other hand, nearly everyone in the region spends at least part of his or her life in an air-conditioned environment. In varying degress virtually all southerners have been affected, directly or indirectly, by the technology of climate control. Air conditioning has changed the southern way of life, influencing everything from architecture to sleeping habits. Most important, it has contributed to the erosion of several regional traditions: cultural isolation, agrarianism, poverty, romanticism, historical consciousness, an orientation toward nontechnological folk culture, a preoccupation with kinship, neighborliness, a strong sense of place, and a relatively slow pace of life. The net result has been a dramatic decline in regional distinctiveness. In combination with other historical forces—such as the civil rights movement, advances in communication and transportation technologies, and economic and political change—the air conditioner has greatly accelerated what John Egerton has called "the Americanization of Dixie."[103]

Perhaps most obviously, air conditioning has had a major impact on southern population growth. The population density of the South (86.3 persons per square mile in 1980) has doubled since 1930.[104] Some of this growth can be attributed to a high birth rate, some to a declining death rate, and some to migration. For the most part, the demographic impact of air conditioning has been limited to the latter two phenomena. Although a number of southerners have adopted the colloquialism "heir conditioning," and during the early 1960s one survey researcher reported a positive correlation between air-conditioned living and fertility, there is no reason to believe that air conditioning has had a significant impact on the region's fertility. A high birth rate was characteristic of the South long before the advent of mechanical cooling. Moreover, despite the rising popularity of air-conditioned bedrooms, the southern birth rate, like the national birth rate, has declined in recent decades.[105]

The link between air conditioning and declining mortality is much more substantial. Prior to the twentieth century the nonmountain South was a relatively unhealthy place. Generally speaking, southern mortality rates were much higher than those of other areas of the United States. And as David Hackett Fischer has pointed out, the southern climate, which fostered yellow fever, malaria, and other semitropical diseases, was a primary determinant of the region's high mortality.[106] Significantly, since the beginning of the twentieth century regional mortality rates have converged, and the southern population is much healthier today than it was a century ago.[107] The proliferation of air conditioning is one of the reasons. In addition to making millions of hospital patients more comfortable, air conditioning has reduced fetal and infant mortality, prolonged the lives of thousands of patients suffering from heart disease and respiratory disorders, increased the reliability and sophistication of microsurgery, facilitated the institutionalization of public health, and aided the production of modern drugs such as penicillin.[108] On the other side of the ledger, critics of air conditioning claim that it causes allergies and that it is partially responsible for the pervasiveness of the common cold. Some researchers have even argued that air conditioning contributes to mental illness by disturbing the balance between positive and negative ions in the air.[109] Nevertheless, even if these charges have some merit, the net effect of air conditioning on southern health and life expectancy has been positive.

Climate control has had an even greater impact on migration patterns. In a variety of ways the air conditioner has helped to reverse an almost century-long southern tradition of net out-migration. Between 1910 and 1950 alone, the South's net loss was more than 10 million people.[110] It is more than a coincidence that in the 1950s, the decade when air conditioning first engulfed the South, the region's net out-migration was much smaller than in previous decades and that in the 1960s, for the first time since the Civil War, the South experienced more in-migration than out-migration. Although the net gain during the 1960s was modest—less than half a million people—its very existence was startling. This sudden demographic reversal was partly a function of the success of the civil rights movement and the decline of massive resistance.[111] But it was also a by-product of air conditioning. The 1970 census, according to the *New York Times*, was "the air-conditioned census." "The humble air-conditioner," a 1970 *Times* editorial concluded, "has been a powerful influence in circulating people as well as air in this country. In the last ten years it has become almost as common a device in the warmer sections of the United States as the automobile and the television set. Its availability explains why increasing numbers of Americans find it comfortable to live year around in the semitropical heat."[112] The 1960s were, of course, only the beginning. Between 1970 and 1978, 7 million people migrated to the South, twice the number that left the region.[113] By the end of the decade the Sunbelt era was in full swing.

Because of air conditioning, an undetermined but clearly substantial number of southerners who might otherwise have left the South have remained in the region. Insofar as it has promoted personal contentment and employment opportunities, and improved working conditions, the air conditioner has helped to stem the tide of out-migration. This reduction in out-migration has influenced southern political and economic life. But its qualitative impact on regional culture has been somewhat limited. The cultural transformation that has rocked the South in recent years is essentially an outgrowth of the other side of the migration equation. Abetted by millions of tourists, northern migrants have brought new ideas and new lifestyles to the South, disrupting the region's long-standing cultural isolation. The cultural intrusions of the New Deal and World War II that shocked so many southerners fifty years ago have been expanded and deepened by the massive northern influx of the 1960s and 1970s. During the last twenty years the southern population has become increasingly heterogeneous, and the concept of the "solid South"—long a bulwark of regional mythology—has all but faded from view.[114]

Air conditioning also has played a key role in the industrialization of the modern South. After decades of false starts and inflated promises, industry came to the South in a rush after World War II. The number of southerners employed in manufacturing exceeded those in agriculture for the first time in 1958, and by 1980 the region's manufacturing work force was more than three times as large as its agricultural work force.[115] For better or worse, Henry Grady's "New South" had finally arrived. Some commercial and industrial growth would have occurred in the post–World War II South with or without the air conditioner. But the magnitude and scope of economic change in a non-air-conditioned South would have been much smaller. "Can you conceive a Walt Disney World over in the 95-degree summers of central Florida without its air-conditioned hotels, attractions and shops?" a southern columnist asked in 1978. "Can you see a Honeywell or Sperry or anyone else opening a big plant where their workers would have to spend much of their time mopping brows and cursing mosquitoes?"[116] Climate control has not only brought new factories and businesses to the region; it has also brought improved working conditions, greater efficiency, and increased productivity. As numerous controlled studies have demonstrated, an air-conditioned workplace invariably means higher productivity and greater job satisfaction.[117] One of air conditioning's most telling effects has been its positive influence on southern economic growth.

This economic growth has led in turn to a rising standard of living for many southern families. Real wages have increased substantially during the postwar era, and per capita income in the South has risen from 52 percent of the national average in 1930 to almost 90 percent today. Although this increased income has been unevenly distributed across the region—Texas, Florida, and Virginia registered the biggest gains— few areas have been left unaffected.[118] Maldistribution of wealth remains a serious regional problem, but the proportion of southerners living in Tobacco Road–style poverty has declined significantly in recent decades. Thus, in an indirect way, air conditioning has helped to ameliorate one of the post–Civil War South's most distressing characteristics. The social and cultural implications of the decline in southern poverty are immense because, as C. Vann Woodward noted in 1958, "Generations of scarcity and want constitute one of the distinctive historical experiences of the Southern people."[119]

Air conditioning has also fostered the urbanization of the South. Since 1940 the South "has been the most rapidly urbanizing section of the country."[120] During this period the proportion of southerners living in urban areas has nearly doubled, from 36.7 percent in 1940 to almost 70 percent today.[121] Although the South remains the most rural area of the United States, the gap between the region and the rest of the nation is closing fast. How much of this recent urbanization can be attributed to air conditioning is difficult to say. But a number of observers have credited the air conditioner with being a major factor behind the rise of the urban South. According to the journalist Wade Greene, "Two of the country's fastest growing cities, Houston and Dallas, would probably be provincial backwaters today without air conditioning."[122] In a similar vein, Frank Trippett has argued that "Sunbelt cities like Phoenix, Atlanta, Dallas, and Houston . . . could never have mushroomed so prosperously without air conditioning."[123]

Air conditioning has promoted the growth of the urban South in a variety of ways: by encouraging industrialization and population growth; by accelerating the development of large public institutions, such as universities, museums, hospitals, sports arenas, and military bases; by facilitating the efficient use of urban space and opening the city to vertical, high-rise development; and by influencing the development of distinctively urban forms of architecture. Without air conditioning, skyscrapers and high-rise apartments would be less prevalent (indeed, they would not exist in their present form); urban populations would be smaller; cities would be more spread out; and the physical and architectural differences between inner cities and suburbs would be less striking (even though as an integral component of enclosed shopping malls, air conditioning has contributed to urban sprawl). In sum, the size, shape, and character of urban centers would be vastly different.[124]

In the South urbanization is a matter of no small importance. The stakes go well beyond aesthetics, economics, and demographics. Although its influence has sometimes been exaggerated, few historians would deny that self-conscious agrarianism has been a key element of southern distinctiveness. With the passing of the rural South such things as the Populist heritage, the plantation experience, and the mythic world of the Vanderbilt Agrarians have lost much of their meaning.[125] The region's rural legacy is still a force to be reckoned with, but it is no longer the prime mover of southern life. The locus of power and activity in the South has moved to Main Street, and air conditioning is one of the reasons why.

In a related development, climate control has altered southern attitudes toward nature and technology. Specifically, air conditioning has taken its toll on traditional folk culture, which, as David Potter once pointed out, "survived in the South long after it succumbed to the onslaught of urban-industrial culture elsewhere. It was an aspect of this culture that the relation between the land and the people remained more direct and more primal in the South than in other parts of the country."[126] The South has always been an elemental land of blood, sweat, and tears—a land where personalism and a curious mixture of romance and realism have prevailed. As W. J. Cash noted in 1941, southern elementalism and romanticism have been mutually reinforcing traditions. "The influence of the Southern physical world" was, in Cash's words,

> a sort of cosmic conspiracy against reality in favor of romance. The country is one of extravagant colors, of proliferating foliage and bloom, of flooding yellow sunlight, and, above all perhaps, of haze. Pale blue fogs hang above the valleys in the morning, the atmosphere smokes faintly at midday, and through the long slow afternoon cloud-stacks tower from the horizon and the earth-heat quivers upward through the iridescent air, blurring every outline and rendering every object vague and problematical. I know that winter comes to the land, certainly. I know there are days when the color and the haze are stripped away and the real stands up in drab and depressing harshness. But these things pass and are forgotten. The dominant mood, the mood that lingers in the memory, is one of well-nigh drunken reverie.[127]

Cash's idyllic statement is part hyperbole, but his central point is well taken. If we remove climate from the historical equation, the South is not the South. At the very least, climate control has taken the edge off of the region's romantic elementalism. As the southern climate has been artificially tamed, pastoralism has been replaced by technological determinism. In escaping the heat and humidity, southerners have weakened the bond between humanity and the natural environment. In the process, they have lost some of what made them interesting and distinctive. Of course, not all southerners would agree that air conditioning has removed them from the natural world. A 1961 profile of a Florida household claimed that "living an air-conditioned life doesn't mean shutting oneself off from beautiful Florida summers. It means enjoying them more. . . . Air conditioning provides relaxing intervals between the recreational, business and household activities that take them outdoors." As the father of the house explained, "Our living is about the same as before, only more comfortable and enjoyable. We go swimming as often but it's for the fun of being in the water, not just to cool off."[128] Similarly, a couple in Washington, D.C., insisted that air conditioning added new meaning to their flower garden. "We enjoy gardening," they said, "but even more we enjoy being able to sit indoors comfortably and look out at our garden."[129] Although such testimonials are revealing, it seems clear that, on balance, human interaction with the natural environment has decreased significantly since the advent of air conditioning. To confirm this point, one has only to walk down almost any southern street on a hot summer afternoon, listen to the whir of compressors, and look in vain for open windows or human faces. As Frank Trippett put it, air conditioning has "seduced families into retreating into houses with closed doors and shut windows, reducing the commonalty of neighborhood life and all but obsoleting the front-porch society whose open casual folkways were an appealing hallmark of the sweatier America."[130]

In many cases the porch is not simply empty, it's not even there. To the dismay of many southerners, air conditioning has impinged on a rich tradition of vernacular architecture. From the "dogtrot cabin" with its central breezeway, to the grand plantation house with its wraparound porch, to the tin-roofed "cracker" house up on blocks, traditional southern architecture has been an ingenious conspiracy of passive cooling and cross-ventilation.[131] "You look at what the Crackers were doing 75 or 100 years ago," one southern architect recently remarked, " . . . and when you analyze it, they had the right answers."[132] The catalog of structural techniques developed to tame the hot, humid southern climate is long and varied: high ceilings, thin walls, long breezeways, floors raised three or more feet off the ground, steeply pitched roofs vented from top to bottom, open porches, broad eaves that block the slanting sun, massive doors and windows that sometimes stretched from floor to ceiling, louvered jalousies, transoms placed above bedroom doors, dormers, groves of shade trees blanketing the southern exposure, and houses situated to capture prevailing breezes, to name a few.[133] Historically, these techniques have been an important element of an aesthetic and social milieu that is distinctively southern.

The science of passive cooling, which was refined over several centuries of southern history, was rendered obsolete in less than a decade, or so it seemed before the onset of the energy crisis. With the proliferation of residential air conditioning, vernacular architecture gave way to the modern tract house, with its low ceilings, small windows, and compact floor plan. As early as 1959 the South's largest home builder proclaimed that air conditioning had made the traditional "Florida room" unnecessary. "I figured that for the cost of building a Florida room," he explained, "I could air condition the whole house."[134] It was this kind of calculus that ushered in the age of mass-produced, homogeneous architecture. As the architectural historian Reyner Banham described the situation, since the lightweight air-conditioned tract house "is the house that the U.S. building industry is geared to produce above all others, it is now endemic from Maine to California, Seattle to Miami, from the Rockies to the bayous."[135] Many southerners, of course, continue to live in traditionally designed houses. But their numbers are thinning with each passing year.

Residential air conditioning has not only affected architectural form; it has also influenced the character of southern family life. Since strong family ties have long been recognized as an integral characteristic of southern culture, this is a matter of some importance.[136] During the 1950s and 1960s the air conditioner was often portrayed as the savior of the American family. In 1955, for example, one observer claimed that residential air conditioning was changing "the family living pattern back to the days before the automobile took Americans out of their homes." "With comfort in its own living room," he argued, "the family tends to stay home and enjoy each other's society in relaxed evenings of reading, sewing, television, or card-playing."[137] This rosy picture of the air-conditioned family was confirmed by several controlled studies conducted in the late 1950s and early 1960s. A 1962 report was typical: "More than an hour's extra sleep at night during the summer for each member of the family. Daytime naps for children that stretch out three times longer. Hot meals — 40 per cent more nutritious — enthusiastically eaten despite soaring outdoor temperatures. A $5.80 average weekly saving on outside entertainment. Laundry time cut in half; house-cleaning time cut by one-third. Dreams of the future? Not at all. These were some of the actual effects of air conditioning on families in Austin, Tex., and Levittown, Pa."[138]

The alleged benefits of residential air conditioning ranged from better dispositions to increased family privacy.[139] In retrospect, such expansive claims seem naive and misleading. Air-conditioned living may have made many individual family members happier, but it does not necessarily follow that the family unit was strengthened in the process.

As numerous social critics have pointed out, endless hours of television watching often detract from meaningful family life.[140] In any event, the popularity of the air-conditioned living room was soon counterbalanced by the lure of air-conditioned shopping malls, bowling alleys, and other amusements. Of course, even if, on balance, residential air conditioning strengthened the nuclear family, the impact on wider kinship networks probably went in the opposite direction. One suspects that as family members withdrew into air-cooled privatism, interaction with grandparents, aunts, uncles, and cousins sometimes suffered. As more than one observer has noted, the vaunted southern tradition of "visiting" has fallen on hard times in recent years.[141] This is an important point, because the essence of southern family life has always been its semi-extended nature. Thus, the overall effect of chilled air on traditional ties of blood and kin has been, at best, contradictory.

The same could probably be said for air conditioning's effect on patterns of aggression and violence. Throughout much of its history, the South has been the most violent section of the United States. In 1934 H. C. Brearley aptly described the South as "that part of the United States lying below the Smith and Wesson line."[142] More recently, Sheldon Hackney and Raymond D. Gastil have used homicide and suicide rates to document the South's "regional culture of violence."[143] Interestingly, few students of southern violence have paid much attention to climatic forces. Instead, they have concentrated on such factors as a lingering frontier tradition, adherence to an aristocratic code of honor, white supremacist ideology, racial demography, rurality, poverty, and an endemic "siege mentality" related to the nature of southern history.[144] On occasion, however, climate has been cited as an important determinant of southern violence. In 1969 the historian Albro Martin insisted that the region's propensity for violence was largely a function of climate.[145] And in 1977 Joseph C. Carroll's statistical analysis of homicide and suicide rates in 100 American cities uncovered a strong positive correlation between heat and humidity and both homicide and suicide.[146] If these assessments are accurate, what does one make of the fact that southern homicide rates have increased since the advent of air conditioning? Would the rates have increased even more rapidly in a non-air-conditioned South? Unfortunately, the answers to these questions await further study. We know that southern and nonsouthern homicide rates have converged in recent decades, but at this point it is almost impossible to determine the extent to which this convergence is a function of climate control.[147] Available evidence is contradictory and consists of little more than speculation. Proponents of indoor cooling have often argued that air conditioning invariably makes people less irritable and hence less violent.[148] On the other hand, several critics of air conditioning, including René Dubos and Frank Lloyd Wright, have claimed that artificial cooling is a physiologically dangerous process that reduces human adaptability to stress.[149] According to Wright:

> The human body is able continually to adjust itself—to and fro. But if you carry these contrasts too far too often, when you are cooled the heat becomes more unendurable; it becomes hotter and hotter outside as you get cooler and cooler inside. . . . I think it far better to go with the natural climate than try to fix a special artificial climate of your own. Climate means something to man. It means something in relation to one's life in it. Nature makes the body flexible and so the life of the individual invariably becomes adapted to environment and circumstance. . . . I doubt that you can ignore climate completely, by reversal make a climate of your own and get away with it without harm to yourself.[150]

If Wright is correct, climate control may be one of the factors behind the rising tide of violence that has engulfed the United States in recent years.

The air conditioner has had a more straightforward impact on the basic rhythm of southern life. To a significant degree, air conditioning has modulated the daily and seasonal rhythms that were once an inescapable part of southern living. As Charles Roland once noted, "The climate of the South affected the rhythm of life, slowed its beat. Farmers could hardly be blamed for taking naps on shady porches or under sheltering oaks at the height of the sun; nor city dwellers, for pausing frequently to sip iced drinks under the fans."[151] Although a southern summer is still a force to be reckoned with, thanks to air conditioning the "siesta mentality" has declined in recent years, and the summer sun is no longer the final arbiter of daily and yearly planning. As one observer put it, the southern "summer has ceased to be a long siesta, with Wednesday afternoon store-closings and the like."[152] In addition to these mundane changes the declining importance of climatic and seasonal change may have profound long-term consequences. Climate control may eventually dull southerners' sense of time, and perhaps even their sense of history.

A more immediate threat is the air conditioner's assault on the South's strong "sense of place." Southerners, more than most other Americans, have tied themselves to local geography. Their lives and identities have been rooted in a particular piece of turf—a county, a town, a neighborhood, a homestead, a family graveyard.[153] Yet in recent years, thanks in part to air conditioning, southern particularism has been overwhelmed by an almost endless string of look-alike chain stores, tract houses, glassed-in high rises, and, perhaps most important, enclosed shopping malls. The modern shopping mall is the cathedral of air-conditioned culture, and it symbolizes the placelessness of the New South. As William S. Kowinski recently observed, "these climate-controlled bubbles" are designed "to create timeless space. Removed from everything else and existing in a world of its own, a mall . . . is a placeless space."[154] As such, it is the antithesis of traditional southern culture. To quote Kowinski, "can you imagine William Faulkner writing about the Yoknapatawpha Mall?"[155]

At one level or another, air conditioning has affected nearly every aspect of southern life. But it has not changed everything. Although climate control has done its best to homogenize the nation and eliminate regional consciousness, the South remains a land apart—a land that still owes much of its distinctiveness to climatic forces. Of course, how long this will remain so is an open question. Perhaps, as it has done so often in the past, the southerner's special devotion to regional and local traditions will ensure the survival of southern folk culture. But this time it will not be easy: General Electric has proved a more devastating invader than General Sherman. As long as air conditioning, abetted by immigration, urbanization, and broad technological change, continues to make inroads, the South's distinctive character will continue to diminish, never to rise again.

Notes

1. Frank Trippett, "The Great American Cooling Machine," *Time* 114 (13 Aug. 1979): 75. The author wishes to thank Kathleen Arsenault and Gary Mormino for their help in the preparation of this article.
2. *Air Conditioning, Heating, and Refrigeration News* (26 Aug. 1963): 1 (hereinafter cited as *ACHR News*).
3. Two exceptions are Charles P. Roland, *The Improbable Era: The South since World War II* (Lexington: Univ. Press of Kentucky, 1975), 2–3, 185; and Fred Hobson, "A South Too Busy to Hate?" in *Fifteen Southerners, Why the South Will Survive* (Athens: Univ. of Georgia Press, 1981), 45, 51.
4. David C. Roller and Robert W. Twyman, eds., *The Encyclopedia of Southern History* (Baton Rouge: Louisiana State Univ. Press, 1979), 1, 242–43, 1047–49, 1371.
5. Anonymous interview, St. Petersburg, Florida, 12 Mar. 1982. Since 1974 I have discussed the South's "air-conditioning revolution" with more than two hundred individuals. Some of these discussions took place during ex-

tended conversations or formal interviews. Others (hereinafter cited as "misc. interviews") were nothing more than brief, casual conversations, though these conversations often rendered valuable information on the proliferation and impact of air conditioning in the South.

6. Ellsworth Huntington, *Civilization and Climate* (New Haven: Yale Univ. Press, 1915); Walter Prescott Webb, *The Great Plains* (Boston: Ginn and Company, 1931); Ulrich Bonnell Phillips, *Life and Labor in the Old South* (Boston: Little, Brown, 1929). On the historiography of southern climate see James C. Bonner, "Plantation and Farm: The Agricultural South," in Arthur S. Link and Rembert W. Patrick, eds., *Writing Southern History: Essays in Historiography in Honor of Fletcher M. Green* (Baton Rouge: Louisiana State Univ. Press, 1965), 150–52; William A. Foran, "Southern Legend: Climate or Climate of Opinion," South Carolina Historical Association *Proceedings, 1956* (Columbia, S.C., 1957), 6–22; Edgar T. Thompson, "The Climatic Theory of the Plantation," *Agricultural History* 15 (Jan. 1941): 49–50; and C. Vann Woodward, *The Burden of Southern History* (Baton Rouge: Louisiana State Univ. Press, 1968), x–xi.

7. Phillips, *Life and Labor in the Old South,* 3.

8. For a good introduction to the continuing controversy over the relationship between climate and culture, see David Hackett Fischer, "Climate and History: Priorities for Research," *Journal of Interdisciplinary History* 10 (Spring 1980): 821–30. See also Emmanuel Le Roy Ladurie, *Times of Feast, Times of Famine: A History of Climate Since the Year 1000,* trans. Barbara Bray (Garden City, N.Y.: Doubleday, 1971); H. H. Lamb, *Climate, History, and the Modern World* (London: Methuen, 1982); and T. M. L. Wigley, M. J. Ingram, and G. Farmer, eds., *Climate and History: Studies in Past Climates and Their Impact on Man* (Cambridge, Eng.: Cambridge Univ. Press, 1981).

9. *New York Times,* 6 Sept. 1970.

10. Raymond B. Becker, *John Gorrie, M.D.: Father of Air Conditioning and Mechanical Refrigeration* (New York: Carlton, 1972); *St. Petersburg Times,* 5 Aug. 1963; Margaret Ingels, *Willis Haviland Carrier, Father of Air Conditioning* (Garden City, N.Y.: Country Life, 1952), 110; Wade Greene, "Air-Conditioning," *New York Times Magazine* (14 July 1974): 12, 16, 18; James Burke, *Connections* (Boston: Little, Brown, 1978), 238–41, 291.

11. Greene, "Air-Conditioning," 18; *St. Petersburg Times,* 5 Aug. 1963, 15 July 1966.

12. Daniel J. Boorstin, *The Americans: The Democratic Experience* (New York: Random House, 1973), 316–31; Harper Leech and John Charles Carroll, *Armour and His Times* (New York: Appleton-Century, 1938), 125–62; Burke, *Connections,* 241–44.

13. Ingels, *Willis Haviland Carrier,* 14, 114, 117–18; *ACHR News* (20 Sept. 1976): 5; Bolling Flood (grandson of Robert Portner), interview, St. Petersburg, Florida, 28 Sept. 1982; Alan Peskin, *Garfield: A Biography* (Kent, Ohio: Kent State Univ. Press, 1978), 601–2; Robert Friedman, "The Air-Conditioned Century," *American Heritage* 35 (Aug.-Sept. 1984): 20, 22.

14. The electric fan was invented by Dr. Schuyler Skaats Wheeler. Joseph Na-

than Kane, *Famous First Facts* . . . (New York: Wilson, 1981), 236; *ACHR News* (18 Oct. 1976): 28; "Baker's Rocking Chair Fan," *Scientific American* 67 (15 Oct. 1892): 242; "A Substitute for Fresh Air," *Literary Digest* 45 (7 Dec. 1912): 1058; Reyner Banham, *The Architecture of the Well-Tempered Environment* (London: Architectural Press, 1969), 51–54, 176–77.

15. *The 1902 Edition of the Sears Roebuck Catalogue* (New York, 1969), 663.

16. *Arkansas Gazette* (Little Rock), 29 Jan. 1902; Raymond Arsenault, *The Wild Ass of the Ozarks: Jeff Davis and the Social Bases of Southern Politics* (Philadelphia: Temple Univ. Press, 1984), 143.

17. Ingels, *Willis Haviland Carrier,* 17; Banham, *Architecture of the Well-Tempered Environment,* 82.

18. Greene, "Air-Conditioning," 16.

19. Ingels, *Willis Haviland Carrier,* 1–19; "Blow, Cool Air," *Time* 80 (27 July 1962): 42; Carrier Corporation, *The Two Faces of Janus: The Story of Carrier Corporation* (Syracuse, N.Y., 1977), 1–28.

20. Ingels, *Willis Haviland Carrier,* 26, 124, 136–39; Friedman, "The Air-Conditioned Century," 25–26. Carrier Corporation, *Two Faces of Janus,* 3, notes that the process of "keeping textile fibers dampened during spinning and weaving" was commonly called "yarn conditioning."

21. Ingels, *Willis Haviland Carrier,* 26.

22. Ibid., 26–30, 40, 48.

23. Ibid., 37–43, 48–49; Carrier Corporation, *Two Faces of Janus,* 17; *ACHR News* (20 Sept. 1976): 6; "Tobacco Air Conditioning Cuts Curing Time in Half," *Newsweek* 14 (24 July 1939): 23; Banham, *Architecture of the Well-Tempered Environment,* 30–31; P. R. Moses, "Heating, Ventilating, and Air Conditioning of Factories," *Engineering Magazine* 39 (Aug.-Sept. 1910): 697–712, 865–80; Friedman, "The Air-Conditioned Century," 26.

24. Ingels, *Willis Haviland Carrier,* 142; Banham, *Architecture of the Well-Tempered Environment,* 171, 174.

25. "Keeping Cool," *Business Week,* no. 997 (9 Oct. 1948): 108–110; F. R. Ellis, "Getting Away From the Handicap of Climate," *Industrial Management* 73 (May 1927): 274–78; Ingels, *Willis Haviland Carrier,* 145, 153, 156; "Cool Age," *Time* 82 (2 Aug. 1963): 60; *ACHR News* (20 Sept. 1976): 114; Friedman, "Air-Conditioned Century," 26.

26. Ingels, *Willis Haviland Carrier,* 61–63; *ACHR News* (20 Sept. 1976): 5–6, 8; Banham, *Architecture of the Well-Tempered Environment,* 171, 175; Carrier Corporation, *Two Faces of Janus,* 5.

27. Ingels, *Willis Haviland Carrier,* 64–68; Banham, *Architecture of the Well-Tempered Environment,* 176–78.

28. *St. Petersburg Times,* 15 July 1966 (quotation), 17 July 1952; *St. Petersburg Evening Independent,* 7 June 1955. See also "Overdone Theater Cooling," *Literary Digest* 103 (26 Oct. 1929): 32.

29. Ingels, *Willis Haviland Carrier,* 68, 147; *St. Petersburg Times,* 17 July 1952; "Home-Made Weather," *Literary Digest* 104 (15 Feb. 1930), 28.

30. Boorstin, *Americans: The Democratic Experience,* 356; *ACHR News* (20 Sept. 1976): 8; misc. interviews.

31. Ingels, *Willis Haviland Carrier,* 78–81; "Hot Steam for Cooling Trains,"

Scientific American 145 (Nov. 1931): 348; *ACHR News* (20 Sept. 1976): 14.

32. "R. R. Air Conditioning," *Business Week*, no. 208 (26 Aug. 1933): 12; see also "Air Conditioning," *Business Week* no. 247 (26 May 1934): 11–12; Banham, *Architecture of the Well-Tempered Environment*, 185; and *Tampa Tribune*, 2 Feb. 1934.

33. Ingels, *Willis Haviland Carrier*, 42, 63; *ACHR News* (20 Sept. 1976): 6, 8; Carrier Corporation, *Two Faces of Janus*, 7.

34. "Air Conditioning," *Business Week*, no. 247 (26 May 1934): 12; misc. interviews; *St. Petersburg Times*, 7 June 1955; *St. Petersburg Evening Independent*, 7 June 1955.

35. *ACHR News* (28 June 1976): 22; "Air Conditioning," *Business Week* no. 247 (26 May 1934): 11; "Cooling for 13,000 Stores, the Alamo, and a Harem," *Architectural Forum* 114 (Apr. 1961): 134; misc. interviews. *Chain Store Age* has conducted annual air-conditioning surveys since the 1950s.

36. Ingels, *Willis Haviland Carrier*, 76, 85; *St. Petersburg Times*, 17 July 1952; *ACHR News* (20 Sept. 1976): 16; misc. interviews.

37. *ACHR News* (31 May 1976): 26, (9 Aug. 1976): 8; (16 Aug. 1976): 16.

38. Ingels, *Willis Haviland Carrier*, 71–73, 91; Friedman, "Air-Conditioned Century," 28–29; "Air Conditioning Starts Fast," *Business Week*, no. 292 (6 Apr. 1935): 11–12; *ACHR News* (9 Feb. 1976): 12. A number of politicians and political pundits have commented on the far-reaching implications of the coming of air conditioning to Washington. Republican Congressman Joseph W. Martin of Massachusetts wrote in 1960: "The installation of air conditioning in the 1930s did more, I believe, than cool the Capitol: it prolonged the sessions. The members were no longer in such a hurry to flee Washington in July. The southerners especially had no place else to go that was half as comfortable." From Joseph W. Martin (as told to Robert J. Donovan), *My First Fifty Years in Politics* (New York: McGraw-Hill, 1960), 49.

In 1978 *New York Times* columnist Russell Baker offered a tongue-in-cheek appraisal of air-conditioned government: "If I were a conservative, having given the big taxers a taste of the axe, I would now forget the death penalty and the crusade against homosexuality for a while and attack one of the taproots of waste and big government. I refer to air conditioning in Washington. Air conditioning has contributed far more to the decline of the Republic than unexecuted murderers and unorthodox sex. Until it became universal in Washington after World War II, Congress habitually closed shop around the end of June and did not reopen until the following January. Six months of every year, the nation enjoyed a respite from the promulgaton of more laws, the depredations of lobbyists, the hatching of new schemes for Federal expansion and, of course, the cost of maintaining a government running at full blast. Once air conditioning arrived, Congress had twice as much time to exercise its skill at regulation and plucking the population. . . . The custom of sitting year round in Washington was begun, not surprisingly, by the Southern bloc that dominated Congress during the 1950s. Until air conditioning arrived, they had made it a point to schedule business so they could take relief from Washington summers in the shade of the catalpa and the magnolia. With an air conditioned Capitol, however, the necessity for perspiring into their juleps abruptly ended. Instead of wilting by the swamps, they could now stay crisp as lettuce in the cool splendor of the Capitol. For voters accustomed to seeing them working the home turf during the steam season, of course, they had to offer justifications for remaining in Washington, and the best of all justifications was the pressing duty of toil for the national good." From Russell Baker, "No Sweat," *New York Times Magazine* (9 July 1978): 6.

More recently, Gore Vidal has written, "I date the end of the old republic and the birth of the empire to the invention, in the late Thirties, of air conditioning. Before air conditioning, Washington was deserted from mid-June to September. . . . But after air conditioning and the Second World War arrived, more or less at the same time, Congress sits and sits while the presidents—or at least their staffs—never stop making mischief at the White House or in the spendid old State and War Departments building, now totally absorbed by the minions of President Augustus." Gore Vidal, "The Ruins of Washington," *The New York Review of Books* 29 (29 Apr. 1982): 10.

39. *ACHR News* (9 Aug. 1976): 8, (16 Aug. 1976): 16, (20 Sept. 1976): 21; misc. interviews.

40. Banham, *Architecture of the Well-Tempered Environment*, 178–79; Kane, *Famous First Acts*, 137; misc. interviews. In 1956 the twenty-four-story Bank of the Southwest in Houston became the "first large commercial building" to have air conditioning "controlled from a single central panel." *ACHR News* (9 Aug. 1976): 8.

41. Ingels, *Willis Haviland Carrier*, 88–94; Banham, *Architecture of the Well-Tempered Environment*, 180–81; *ACHR News* (14 June 1976): 18; "Cool Age," *Time* 82 (2 Aug. 1963): 60.

42. "Hotel Conditioning," *Business Week*, no. 252 (30 June 1934): 10; Ingels, *Willis Haviland Carrier*, 42, 94–95; *ACHR News* (19 Apr. 1976): 3, (20 Sept. 1976): 6.

43. "Hotel Conditioning," 10.

44. Ingels, *Willis Haviland Carrier*, 94–95; *ACHR News* (19 Apr. 1976), 3.

45. *St. Petersburg Times*, 22 July 1957; see also *St. Petersburg Times*, 29 May 1954. In 1962 approximately 60 percent of the nation's hotel rooms were air-conditioned. From "Blow, Cool Air," *Time* 80 (27 July 1962): 42.

46. *St. Petersburg Times*, 22 July 1957, 20 Aug. 1978; *ACHR News* (22 Mar. 1976): 8; misc. interviews.

47. Ingels, *Willis Haviland Carrier*, 40; Carrier Corporation, *Two Faces of Janus*, 13; John Reese, "The Air-Conditioning Revolution," *Saturday Evening Post* 233 (9 July 1960): 100; "Air-Conditioning of Hospitals," *Science* 80 (28 Sept. 1934), supp. 7; Max F. Meyer, "The South and the North," *Science* 80 (9 Nov. 1934): 428; A. S. Bacon, "Doing Away with the Open Window in the Hospital," *American Journal of Public Health* 22 (Dec. 1932): 1301.

48. David Kenerson, interview, St. Petersburg, Florida, 19 Mar. 1982; misc. interviews; *ACHR News* (20 Sept. 1976): 21, (6 Sept. 1976): 8.

49. "Blow, Cool Air," 42.
50. Ingels, *Willis Haviland Carrier*, 91; misc. interviews; *ACHR News* (20 Sept. 1976): 21 and (6 Sept. 1976): 8; "Central Heating and Cooling of College Campuses," *Architectural Record* 134 (Aug. 1963): 162–64.
51. *ACHR News* (14 June 1976): 18.
52. "Cool Age," 60; Carrier Corporation, *Two Faces of Janus*, 14–15; *ACHR News* (19 Jan. 1976): 2, (12 July 1976): 24, (9 Aug. 1976): 8, (23 Aug. 1976): 1, (20 Sept. 1976): 20–21, (6 Sept. 1976): 8; misc. interviews; *St. Petersburg Times*, 23 Jan. 1964; *St. Petersburg Evening Independent*, 27 Sept. 1984, 17 Sept. 1982.
53. The Minneapolis home was that of Charles G. Gates, the son of industrialist John W. "Bet-a-Million" Gates. Carrier designed the massive system, which was twenty feet long, six feet wide, and seven feet high. Carrier Corporation, *Two Faces of Janus*, 13; "Blow, Cool Air," 42; S. R. Winters, "Hook Your Electric Fan to a Humidifier to Keep the Home and Office Cool," *Illustrated World* 38 (Sept. 1922): 132–33; "Air Conditioning," *Business Week*, no. 247 (26 May 1934): 12. In 1893 Robert Portner adapted a brewery "cooling aparatus" for use in his home in Manassas, Virginia. Bolling Flood, interview, St. Petersburg, Florida, 28 Sept. 1982.
54. Ingels, *Willis Haviland Carrier*, 76–77, 149; Willis Haviland Carrier and Margaret Ingels, "Making Weather to Order in the Home," *Good Housekeeping* 92 (Mar. 1931): 92–93; *ACHR News* (2 Feb. 1976): 32, (23 Feb. 1976): 22; "A 'House of Perpetual Spring,'" *Literary Digest* 110 (11 July 1931): 39; Banham, *Architecture of the Well-Tempered Environment*, 184–85.
55. Banham, *Architecture of the Well-Tempered Environment*, 184.
56. Ingels, *Willis Haviland Carrier*, 85; *ACHR News* (20 Sept. 1976): 14; Banham, *Architecture of the Well-Tempered Environment*, 185.
57. "Air Conditioning," *Business Week*, no. 204 (29 July 1933): 12.
58. *ACHR News* (8 Mar. 1976): 21.
59. *ACHR News* (15 Mar. 1976): 20, (22 Mar. 1976): 8, (5 Apr. 1976): 10; Reese, "Air-Conditioning Revolution," 97.
60. *ACHR News* (15 Mar. 1976): 20, (20 Sept. 1976): 14.
61. Banham, *Architecture of the Well-Tempered Environment*, 184; misc. interviews; *St. Petersburg Evening Indepedent*, 7 June 1955. In 1936 the Kelvinator corporation announced plans "to set up 100 'Kelvin homes' across the country to demonstrate the feasibility of complete air conditioning for low cost homes ($5,000 to $6,000 ranges, including air conditioning)." From *ACHR News* (22 Mar. 1976): 8.
62. *ACHR News* (21 Sept. 1959), special issue on heat pumps), (17 May 1976): 20, (24 May, 1976): 8, (31 May 1976): 26, (7 June 1976): 16, (20 Sept. 1976): 14–15; Banham, *Architecture of the Well-Tempered Environment*, 181, 185.
63. *ACHR News* (24 May 1976): 8.
64. "Booming Like Television," *Newsweek* 36 (10 July 1950): 64, 67.
65. Banham, *Architecture of the Well-Tempered Environment*, 185–87; Arthur Carson, *How to Keep Cool* (Greenlawn, N.Y., 1954), 56; "Now for Small Homes," *Newsweek* 40 (8 Sept. 1952): 73.
66. "Now for Small Homes," 73; see also *ACHR News* (19 July 1976): 20, (26

July 1976): 12; and F. Lopez, "Your New Home Can Be Designed for Air Conditioning," *Better Homes and Gardens* 27 (Feb. 1949): 37.

67. *ACHR News* (2 Aug. 1976): 8; misc. interviews.

68. Bureau of the Census, *U.S. Census of Housing, 1960*, vol. 1, *States and Small Areas*, pt. 1: *United States Summary* (Washington, D.C.: Government Printing Office, 1963), 28.

69. Ibid.; *New York Times*, 14 Aug. 1960, 6R and 28 July 1963, 1F; "Cool Age," *Time* 82 (2 Aug. 1963): 60; *ACHR News* 1959–1965, especially (6 July 1959): 1, (14 Sept. 1959): 12, (12 July 1965): 18.

70. "Detailed Housing Characteristics," in Bureau of the Census, *Census of Housing: 1970*, vol. 1, *Housing Characteristics for States, Cities, and Counties*, pt. 1, *United States Summary* (Washington, D.C.: Government Printing Office, 1972), 1–235; *St. Petersburg Times*, 15 July 1966; *ACHR News* (18 Aug. 1969): 4.

71. *ACHR News* (20 Sept. 1976): 5, 23, 116–26; "Profiting from Misery," *Time* 110 (1 Aug. 1977): 35; "Reverse-Cycle Electric Air Conditioning—The Answer to Florida's Temperature Control Problem," *Florida Contractor and Builder* 20 (Jan. 1965): 20; *New York Times*, 14 July 1974.

72. *ACHR News* (9 Feb. 1976): 12 and (16 Feb. 1976): 7; see also "First Air-Conditioned Auto," *Popular Science* 123 (Nov. 1933): 30.

73. *ACHR News* (12 Apr. 1976): 12; Kane, *Famous First Facts*, 51–52; "Automotive Air Conditioning," *Business Week*, no. 208 (26 Aug. 1933): 12.

74. *ACHR News* (3 May 1976): 14, (17 May 1976): 20. In May 1942 the board issued Limitation Order L-38, which prohibited installations of commercial refrigeration on air conditioning "for personal comfort." The order was relaxed somewhat in 1943. The Frigikar Corporation began its production of automobile air conditioners in 1950. See *ACHR News* (28 June 1976): 38.

75. "Air Conditioned Cars," *Newsweek* 40 (1 Sept. 1952): 54; Devon Francis, "Car Air Conditioning: Is This Your Year?" *Popular Science* 183 (July 1963): 82–83; "Cool Cars," *Time* 81 (22 Mar. 1963): 55; "Cool Age," *Time* 82 (2 Aug. 1963): 60; *ACHR News* (20 Sept. 1976): 5, 23, (12 July 1976): 24, (26 July 1976): 12, (2 Aug. 1976): 8; *St. Petersburg Times*, 29 Nov. 1965; "Keeping Cool at the Wheel," *Business Week* no. 1767 (13 July 1963): 32.

76. J. Fuchs, "Economy and Air Conditioning: Separating the Hot Air from the Cold Facts," *Motor Trend* 26 (July 1974): 46; D. Seligman, "Keeping Cool While Fighting OPEC," *Fortune* 100 (27 Aug. 1979): 27.

77. *ACHR News* (16 May 1976): 20; misc. interviews. In 1938 Santa Fe (New Mexico) Trailways became the first American bus company to make extended use of air-conditioned buses. Carrier Corporation, *Two Faces of Janus*, 7.

78. *ACHR News* (19 July 1976): 20, (2 Aug. 1976): 8, (16 Aug. 1976): 16; *St. Petersburg Evening Independent*, 17 Sept. 1982; misc. interviews. The city of St. Louis had 100 air-conditioned buses in operation by 1957.

79. "Hot Times in a Cool Business," *Time* 92 (2 Aug. 1968): 62; *ACHR News* (20 Sept. 1976): 10. Hoffa initially made this demand in 1962. Trippett, "The Great American Cooling Machine," 75; Greene, "Air-Conditioning," 12; N. Willatt, "Mobile Air Conditioning," *Barron's* 40 (24 Oct. 1960), 11ff.

80. *ACHR News* (20 Sept. 1976): 5; Greene, "Air-Conditioning," 12; *New York Times*, 12 July and 8 Aug. 1976.

81. *ACHR News* (17 Aug., 1959): 18, (14 Sept. 1959): 10–11, 32–33, (11 Sept 1961): 12, (14 June 1976): 18, (23 Mar. 1964): 26, (30 Aug. 1976): 18; John Reese, "The Air-Conditioning Revolution," 100; *St. Petersburg Times*, (4 May, and 7 July 1955, 11 July, 1962; Hobson, "A South Too Busy to Hate?" 51.

82. *New York Times*, 23 Jan. and 13 Feb. 1964.

83. *New York Times*, 10 Dec. 1973.

84. Ibid., 11 May 1969.

85. *St. Petersburg Times*, 28 Feb. 1965.

86. Greene, "Air-Conditioning," 12; *ACHR News* (22 July 1963): 19, (16 Aug. 1957): 16. In 1957 a San Antonio shopping center was touted as the first shopping center in the nation to offer "air-conditioned sidewalks."

87. *ACHR News* (12 June 1961): 18–19; "Cooling for 13,000 Stores, the Alamo, and a Harem," *Architectural Forum* 114 (Apr. 1961): 134. According to Wade Greene: "In Texas, the automobile air-conditioner has become a status symbol so powerful that some who cannot afford it have been known to drive in sufferance under the hot sun with all their windows rolled up, to give at least the appearance of air-conditioning." Greene, "Air-Conditioning," 16.

88. John M. Crewdson, "How a Hot Town Manages to Maintain Its Cool," *St. Petersburg Times*, 16 Aug. 1981; see also *New York Times*, 21 July 1980; *ACHR News* (29 Apr. 1963): 2.

89. Trippett, "The Great American Cooling Machine," 75. See also Lewis Grizzard, "Air Conditioning's 'Cooled' Traditions," *Alabama Journal and Advertiser* (Montgomery), 10 July 1983; and Lisanne Renner, "Air Conditioning—a Fact of Southern Life," *Orlando Sentinel*, 9 May 1984.

90. John Reese, "The Air-Conditioning Revolution," 100.

91. *New York Times*, 27 Feb. 1980.

92. Milton Beckerman, "Air Conditioning and the Open Door Policy," *St. Petersburg Times*, 3 Aug. 1963. See also Greene, "Air-Conditioning," 16; *St. Petersburg Times*, 5 June 1962; and Ingels, *Willis Haviland Carrier*, 102.

93. Dick Bothwell in the *St. Petersburg Times*, 7 June 1955.

94. "Hot Times in a Cool Business," *Time* 92 (2 Aug. 1968): 61.

95. *ACHR News* (18 May 1959): 1, (25 May 1959): 12, (29 May 1961): 1ff, (9 Oct. 1961): 31, (8 Apr. 1963): 10, (30 Aug. 1976): 18, (13 Sept. 1976): 10; *St. Petersburg Times*, 28 June 1959. In the 1950s one Florida power company offered electricians a fifty-dollar bounty for each ceiling fan removed from private residences or businesses. Phil Deluca, interview, St. Petersburg, Florida, 19 Aug. 1981.

96. *ACHR News* (27 Apr. 1959): 1, (4 May 1959): 18–19, (30 Aug. 1976): 18. Greene, "Air-Conditioning," 20, notes that the Internal Revenue Service allows "substantial tax write-offs for air-conditioning expenses if a doctor says you need it."

97. *St. Petersburg Times*, 14 June 1962. See also *ACHR News* (16 Aug. 1957): 16.

98. *St. Petersburg Times*, 21 Aug. 1964; *ACHR News* (7 Sept. 1964): 1.

99. "Measuring the Misery," *Newsweek* 53 (15 June 1959): 29; "DI," *New Yorker* 35 (6 June 1959): 33–35; "Now It's the Weather Bureau in a Storm Center," *U.S. News and World Report* 46 (22 June 1959): 98–99; *ACHR News* (1 June 1959): 24, (5 Oct. 1959): 5.

100. *St. Petersburg Times*, 15 July 1966.

101. F. J. Versagi, quoted in *ACHR News* (26 Aug. 1968): 21.

102. See table 10.1 in text; Greene, "Air-Conditioning," 22; *New York Times*, 21 July 1980; misc. interviews; *ACHR News* (9 Mar. 1964): 23.

103. John Egerton, *The Americanization of Dixie: The Southernization of America* (New York: Harper's Magazine Press, 1974).

104. Bureau of the Census, *Statistical Abstract of the United States: 1981* (Washington, D.C.: U.S. Government Printing Office, 1981), 11; Greene, "Air-Conditioning," 16; *New York Times*, 6 Sept. 1970.

105. Jake Vonk, interview, St. Petersburg, Florida, 6 Sept. 1981; Trippett, "The Great American Cooling Machine," 76; Reese, "The Air-Conditioning Revolution," 97; John M. Maclachlan and Joe S. Floyd, Jr., *This Changing South* (Gainesville: Univ. of Florida Press, 1956), 122–33; Bureau of the Census, *Statistical Abstract of the United States: 1981*, 60.

106. Fischer, "Climate and History," 829; and David Hackett Fischer, "The Climatic Determinants of American Regionalism" (Paper presented at the annual meeting of the Organization of American Historians, Philadelphia, 1 Apr. 1982). On the general relationship between climate and disease, see René Dubos, *Mirage of Health: Utopias, Progress, and Biological Change* (New York: Harper, 1959), 95–128; René Dubos, *Man Adapting* (New Haven: Yale Univ. Press, 1965); and Lamb, *Climate, History, and the Modern World*, 301–5. See also Thomas C. Angus, *The Control of Indoor Climate* (Oxford: Pergamon, 1968).

107. Maclachlan and Floyd, *This Changing South*, 133–40; Bureau of the Census, *Statistical Abstract of the United States: 1981*, 72–73, 75.

108. *ACHR News* (16 July 1942), passim, (8 Mar. 1976): 20, (10 May 1976): 22, (9 Mar. 1964): 40, (7 Oct. 1968): 1, (2 Aug. 1976): 8, (13 Sept. 1976): 10; Greene, "Air-Conditioning," 20, 22; *St. Petersburg Times*, 7 July 1955, 23 June 1960, 14 June 1962.

109. J. C. Furnas, "How Healthy is Air Conditioning?" *Today's Health* 36 (July 1958): 17–19; *ACHR News* (12 Aug. 1968): 8, (7 July 1969): 22, (20 Oct. 1969): 2–3; Greene, "Air-Conditioning," 22; Friedman, "Air-Conditioned Century," 25; Angus, *Control of Indoor Climate*, passim. On the ionization controversy, see Fred Soyka, with Alan Edmonds, *The Ion Effect: How Air Electricity Rules Your Life and Health* (New York: Dutton, 1978); and Dubos, *Man Adapting*, 59. In 1978 mysterious mental and physical illnesses among employees at the R. A. Gray Building (the new home of the Florida State Archives) in Tallahassee, Florida, were attributed to an electrical imbalance caused by overpurified air. The state installed negative-ion generators to solve the problem, but many employees and other observers questioned the effectiveness of the generators. *New York Times*, 15 Aug. 1978.

110. Maclachlan and Floyd, *This Changing South*, 66–79; Jack Temple Kirby, "The Southern Exodus, 1910–1960: A Primer for Historians," *Journal of Southern History* 49 (Nov. 1983): 585–600.

111. *St. Petersburg Times*, 13 Dec. 1981. On black migration patterns, see Daniel M. Johnson and Rex R. Campbell, *Black Migration in America: A Social Demographic History* (Durham, N.C.: Duke Univ. Press, 1981); Flora Gill, *Economics and the Black Exodus: An Analysis of Negro Emigration from the Southern United States, 1910–1970* (New York: Garland Publishing, 1979); and Neil Fligstein, *Going North: Migration of Blacks and Whites from the South, 1900–1950* (New York: Academic, 1981).

112. *New York Times*, 6 Sept. 1970. See also *ACHR News* (20 Sept. 1976): 5.

113. *St. Petersburg Times*, 13 Dec. 1981. See also Bureau of the Census, *Statistical Abstract of the United States: 1981*, 13. On the emergence of the Sunbelt, see Richard M. Bernard and Bradley R. Rice, eds., *Sunbelt Cities: Politics and Growth since World War II* (Austin: Univ. of Texas Press, 1983); Egerton, *The Americanization of Dixie*; Carl Abbott, *The New Urban America: Growth and Politics in Sunbelt Cities* (Chapel Hill: Univ. of North Carolina Press, 1981); Kirkpatrick Sale, *Power Shift: The Rise of the Southern Rim and Its Challenge to the Eastern Establishment* (New York: Random House, 1975); and James R. Adams, "The Sunbelt," in John B. Boles, ed., *Dixie Dateline: A Journalistic Portrait of the Contemporary South* (Houston: Rice University Studies, 1983), 141–57.

114. See Egerton, *The Americanization of Dixie*, passim. In a 1948 speech in Pittsburgh, William B. Henderson, executive vice president of the Air Conditioning and Refrigerating Machinery Association, stated: "We see mass migration of peoples and industries, affecting large areas of our country, made possible through the use of refrigeration and air conditioning. The movement of industry and people from the crowded industrial areas of the north to the spacious areas and kindlier climates of the south is profoundly affecting our national industrial and political economy and, directly or indirectly, the lives of all of us." *ACHR News* (20 Sept. 1976): 20. In 1960 an official of the Air Conditioning Institute claimed that the recent proliferation of central air conditioning had "broken down regional barriers." *St. Petersburg Evening Independent*, 7 Aug. 1960.

115. *St. Petersburg Times*, 13 Dec. 1981; Maclachlan and Floyd, *This Changing South*, 91–98.

116. Clayton Reed, quoted in the *St. Petersburg Times*, 20 Aug. 1978.

117. *ACHR News* (4 May 1959): 18–19, (13 Feb. 1961): 6, (20 Aug. 1976): 18, (20 Sept. 1976): 114; Reese, "The Air-Conditioning Revolution," 97; Greene, "Air-Conditioning," 20, 22; Friedman, "The Air-Conditioned Century," 24, 26, 29; *St. Petersburg Times*, 14 June 1962; "Home-Made Weather," *Literary Digest* 104 (15 Feb. 1930): 28; "General Services Study Evaluates Influence of Air Conditioning on Production," *Fuel Oil and Oil Heat* 18 (Nov. 1959): 179. In 1935 Clarence Cason predicted, "Air conditioning cannot be a grand success in the South for the reason that the honest natives of the region recognize the natural summer heat as a welcome ally in that it makes the inside of houses and offices agreeably uninviting, if not ac-

tually prohibited territory." Clarence Cason, *90° in the Shade* (Chapel Hill: Univ. of North Carolina Press, 1935), 10. Twenty years later, the *St. Petersburg Times*, on 7 June 1955, noted that "air conditioning has become of major importance for the night-shift worker, who needs to sleep during the day unbothered by heat or outside noises."

118. Maclachlan and Floyd, *This Changing South*, 99–118; Bureau of the Census, *Statistical Abstract of the United States: 1981*, 428–29; *St. Petersburg Times*, 13 Dec. 1981.
119. Woodward, *Burden of Southern History*, 17.
120. Roller and Twyman, eds., *The Encyclopedia of Southern History*, 1264.
121. Ibid., 1266; Bureau of the Census, *Statistical Abstract of the United States: 1981*, 12.
122. Greene, "Air-Conditioning," 16. See also Trippett, "Great American Cooling Machine," 75; *ACHR News* (6 Apr. 1959): 12–14, (29 Apr. 1963): 2; and Friedman, "The Air-Conditioned Century," 24–25.
123. Trippett, "The Great American Cooling Machine," 75.
124. Ibid.; *New York Times*, 3 June 1960, and 2 September 1962; Reese, "The Air-Conditioning Revolution," 100; Greene, "Air-Conditioning," 20; Banham, *Architecture of the Well-Tempered Environment*, 72, 162–63, 209–28.
125. See Twelve Southerners, *I'll Take My Stand: The South and the Agrarian Tradition* (New York: Harper Brothers, 1930); C. Vann Woodward, "The Populist Heritage and the Intellectual," in Woodward, *Burden of Southern History*, 141–66; Lawrence Goodwyn, *Democratic Promise: The Populist Moment in America* (New York: Oxford Univ. Press, 1976); and John Shelton Reed, "The Same Old Stand?" in Fifteen Southerners, *Why the South Will Survive*, 13–34.
126. David M. Potter, *The South and the Sectional Conflict* (Baton Rouge: Louisiana State Univ. Press, 1968), 15–16.
127. W. J. Cash, *The Mind of the South* (New York: Knopf, 1941), 48. See also Malcolm Jones, "Sure, It's Hot Out, But Summer Weather Has Its Diehard Fans," *St. Petersburg Times*, 10 June 1984.
128. *St. Petersburg Times*, 15 June 1961. See also Trippett, "The Great American Cooling Machine," 76.
129. "What Does Climate-Conditioning Mean to Family Living?" *Living for Young Homemakers* 14 (Oct. 1961): 131.
130. Trippett, "The Great American Cooling Machine," 75. See also Robert Bowden, "Turn off the A/C; Listen to Nature," *St. Petersburg Times*, 4 Apr. 1977; and Lewis Grizzard, "Air Conditioning's 'Cooled' Traditions," *Alabama Journal and Advertiser* (Montgomery), 10 July 1983.
131. Suzanne Stephens and Janet Bloom, "Before the Virgin Met the Dynamo," *Architectural Forum* 139 (July-Aug. 1973): 76–87; Otis White, "The Home of the Future Needs a New Foundation," *Florida Trend* 24 (Jan. 1982): 79–84; *St. Petersburg Evening Independent*, 20 July 1977. See also Sigfried Giedion, *Mechanization Takes Command* (New York: Oxford Univ. Press, 1948).
132. Dwight E. Holmes, quoted in White, "The Home of the Future Needs a New Foundation," 79.

133. Ibid., 79–84; Banham, *Architecture of the Well-Tempered Environment*, 23–24; Greene, "Air-Conditioning," 16, 18; *St. Petersburg Evening Independent*, 20 July 1977; Curt Besinger, "Sensible Way to Control Climate," *House Beautiful* 56 (Aug. 1964): 67–75; "How to Live Happily Ever After in a Warm, Sunny Climate," *House Beautiful* 56 (Jan. 1964), 59–110; *New York Times*, 30 Nov. 1975; Vivian Loftness, "Climate and Architecture," *Weatherwise* 31 (Dec. 1978): 214–15; Stephens and Bloom, "Before the Virgin Met the Dynamo," 77–87; James Marston Fitch, *Architecture and the Esthetics of Plenty* (New York: Columbia Univ. Press, 1961), 244–45; Henry H. Glassie, *Folk Housing in Middle Virginia* (Knoxville: Univ. of Tennessee Press, 1975), 136–40.

134. Herbert Heftler, quoted in "Home Air Conditioning Said 'Must,'" *Florida Builder* 14 (Nov. 1959): 11; Banham, *Architecture of the Well-Tempered Environment*, 100–102, 190.

135. Banham, *Architecture of the Well-Tempered Environment*, 190.

136. Rupert Vance, "Regional Family Patterns: in The Southern Family," *American Journal of Sociology* 53 (May 1948): 426–29; Bertram Wyatt-Brown, *Southern Honor: Ethics and Behavior in the Old South* (New York: Oxford Univ. Press, 1982), passim; Richard H. King, *A Southern Renaissance: The Cultural Awakening of the American South, 1930–1955* (New York: Oxford Univ. Press, 1980), 26–38; Anne Firor Scott, *The Southern Lady: From Pedestal to Politics, 1830–1930* (Chicago: Univ. of Chicago Press, 1970), 213–14.

137. *St. Petersburg Times*, 7 July 1955.

138. Ibid., 14 June 1962.

139. Ibid., 7 July 1955, 23 June 1960, 14 June 1962; "What Does Climate-Conditioning Mean to Family Living?" 130–32; Reese, "The Air-Conditioning Revolution," 97; *ACHR News* (6 May 1963): 34–36, (9 Aug. 1976): 8; "Guinea Pigs in Luxury," *Business Week*, no. 1290 (22 May 1954): 60; A. Nicholson, "Lock Hot Weather Out,"*Saturday Evening Post* 238 (16 June 1956): 36ff; *ACHR News* (9 Mar. 1959): 6ff.

140. See Jerry Mander, *Four Arguments for the Elimination of Television* (New York: Morrow, 1978); Gregor T. Goethals, *The TV Ritual: Worship at the Video Altar* (Boston: Beacon, 1981); Leland W. Howe and Bernard Solomon, *How To Raise Children in a TV World* (New York: Hart, 1979); Kate Moody, *Growing Up On Television, The TV Effect: A Report to Parents* (New York: Time Books, 1980); George Comstock et al., *Television and Human Behavior* (New York: Columbia Univ. Press, 1978); Carl Lowe, ed., *Television and American Culture* (New York: Wilson, 1981).

141. Misc. interviews; Trippett, "The Great American Cooling Machine," 75; Joe Gray Taylor, *Eating, Drinking, and Visiting in the South: An Informal History* (Baton Rouge: Louisiana State Univ. Press, 1982), 156–57.

142. Sheldon Hackney, "Southern Violence," *American Historical Review* 84 (Feb. 1969): 906.

143. Ibid., 906–25; Raymond D. Gastil, "Homicide and a Regional Culture of Violence," *American Sociological Review* 36 (June 1971): 412–27. For a critique of this view, see Colin Loftin and Robert H. Hill, "Regional Subcul-

ture and Homicide: An Examination of the Gastil-Hackney Thesis," *American Sociological Review* 39 (Oct. 1974): 714–24.

144. See Gastil, "Homicide," 412–27; Hackney, "Southern Violence," 908–25; John Hope Franklin, *The Militant South, 1800–1861* (Cambridge, Mass.: Harvard Univ. Press, 1956); Dickson D. Bruce, Jr., *Violence and Culture in the Antebellum South* (Austin: Univ. of Texas Press, 1979); John Shelton Reed, *The Enduring South: Subcultural Persistence in Mass Society* (Lexington, Mass.: Lexington Books, 1972), 45–55; and Edward L. Ayers, *Vengeance and Justice: Crime and Punishment in the Nineteenth-Century American South* (New York: Oxford Univ. Press, 1984).

145. See Martin's letter to the editor, *American Historical Review* 75 (Oct. 1969): 325–26.

146. Joseph C. Carroll, "The Effect of Climate on Homicide and Suicide" (Paper presented at the annual meeting of the Society for the Study of Social Problems, Chicago, 1977).

147. Hackney, "Southern Violence," 913; Bureau of the Census, *Statistical Abstract of the United States: 1981*, 174.

148. Misc. interviews; *St. Petersburg Evening Independent*, 15 June 1961; *ACHR News* (16 May 1960): 24–25.

149. Trippett, "The Great American Cooling Machine," 75; Friedman, "Air-Conditioned Century," 25; Greene, "Air-Conditioning," 22; Frank Lloyd Wright, *The Natural House* (New York: Bramhall House, 1954), 176, 178; René Dubos, *A God Within* (New York: Scribner, 1972), 53–54.

150. Wright, *Natural House*, 176, 178.

151. Roland, *Improbable Era*, 3; Helen Muir, *Miami, USA* (New York: Holt, 1953), 291–99; *St. Petersburg Times*, 5 June 1962, 20 Aug. 1978. On the biological importance of daily and seasonal rhythms, see Dubos, *A God Within*, 48–55.

152. *St. Petersburg Times*, 5 June 1962.

153. See Willie Morris, *North Toward Home* (Boston: Houghton Mifflin, 1967); Woodward, *Burden of Southern History*, 22–24; and Paul Hemphill, *The Good Old Boys* (New York: Simon and Schuster, 1974), 11.

154. William S. Kowinski, "The Malling of America," *New Times* 10 (1 May 1978): 34, 41. Air-conditioned shopping malls first appeared in the South in the late 1950s. See *ACHR News* (14 Sept. 1959): 32–33, (11 Jan. 1960): 20, (9 July 1962): 2, (28 Jan. 1963): 7, (4 May 1964): 1; and *Chain Store Age* 35 (Nov. 1959): 23; 41 (Mar. 1965): 31.

155. Kowinski, "Malling of America," 45. In a similar vein, Fred Hobson has written: "Can one imagine Faulkner writing *Absalom, Absalom!* under the spell of central air? One might, indeed, discover a direct relationship between the rise of air-conditioning and the decline of the creative fury of the Southern writer." Hobson, "A South Too Busy to Hate?" 51.

11   Searching for the Sunbelt

Bradley R. Rice

Explaining the historical significance of the Sunbelt phenomenon of the 1970s and early 1980s is a difficult task. It is made even more so by the fact that defining the Sunbelt is nearly as much of a challenge as explaining it. It has been evident since 1980 that there is no generally agreed upon definition of the Sunbelt—there is not even a consensus as to whether the new region should be named with one word or two, although *Sunbelt* does seem to edge out *Sun Belt*. Some commentators have wanted to dispense with the term altogether. Eminent southern historian George Tindall, of the University of North Carolina at Chapel Hill, called the whole concept a "snow job." Two geographers from the same institution declared the use of *Sunbelt* "a case of sloppy regionalizing." They had set out to define the Sunbelt using ten variables in four groupings (sunshine, population change, federal involvement, and economic well being), but their efforts failed to identify a statistically distinct region. Despite their findings, however, they admitted that the Sunbelt was "a notion whose time has come." The idea of the Sunbelt, they wrote, "has become fixed firmly in the minds of many Americans: *the image is the reality.*"[1]

That image is now a historical as well as a present reality. For better or worse, the word *Sunbelt* has been in general use for more than a decade and has acquired a generally understood, if also generally vague, meaning. Perception matters, and it especially matters for those who can turn perception to their own advantage, as many entrepreneurs of the Sunbelt have.

Key word searches of data bases turn up hundreds of entries about the Sunbelt. Television news commentators have tossed the term about, as Bill Moyers did when he referred to the Dallas skyline as "a symbol of Sunbelt power and wealth." The three big weekly newsmagazines, *Time, U.S. News and World Report,* and *Newsweek,* have found *Sunbelt* a handy term that quickly and easily communicates a complex concept to their readers. The *Wall Street Journal, Business Week, Industry Week,*

Forbes, and many others have used *Sunbelt* in article titles. *Variety*, the entertainment trade paper, found *Sunbelt* a useful term to describe a theater chain's expansion in the South and Southwest. The emerging region even developed its own new publication, *Sunbelt Executive Magazine*.[2]

Of course, the most influential early description, and still probably the best, was Kirkpatrick Sale's "southern rim," which lay below the 37th parallel.[3] On the other hand, the most convenient Sunbelt is that found by simply taking the U.S. Census Bureau's South and West regions and adding them together. That approach neatly excludes the North Central and Northeast regions, even if it does include the questionable Sunbelt areas of the upper South, the Rocky Mountains, and the Pacific Northwest. It may be inexact, but it has the advantage of being a quick and dirty way to present data.

The principal states of definitional difficulty, therefore, have been those of the upper south, the Rocky Mountains, and the Pacific Northwest. One other point of contention involves those states or cities below the 37th parallel that have not performed up to the Sunbelt image of rapid population growth and economic expansion. Some definitions, notably Carl Abbott's, have excised at least parts of Alabama, Mississippi, Louisiana, Arkansas, Tennessee, and even Oklahoma. Abbott in turn includes the Pacific Northwest in his definition. One widely circulated booklet has further muddled the situation by including Missouri in its Sunbelt. The map of the Sunbelt is therefore not one map but in fact many maps, depending on whose book or article one is reading. Bernard L. Weinstein, coauthor of an early book on the Sunbelt, told a conference of journalists and business experts that the South is not so much a sun "belt" as it is a region with some sun "spots."[4]

At least there has been consensus about what is *not* in the Sunbelt — or so it appears. I ended a brief 1981 article in *American Demographics* with the line, "As yet, no one has nominated Alaska as a Sunbelt state." Even that assertion was not safe. In the *Wall Street Journal*, columnist Sam Allis wrote, "Wrong, Mr. Rice," for he knew of an Advisory Commission on Intergovernmental Relations staffer who had declared that "from a fiscal standpoint . . . [the Sunbelt] should include Alaska."[5] This exchange aside, there is, of course, general agreement that the states of the Northeast and North Central regions are not in the Sunbelt, although the use of other "belt" terms such as Frostbelt, Snowbelt, or Rust Belt, may not be appropriate either.

In 1983 I collaborated with Richard M. Bernard in editing the anthology *Sunbelt Cities: Politics and Growth since World War II*. Using public and business perceptions as the principal criterion, the introduction to that work defined the Sunbelt as that part of the nation lying below the 37th parallel.[6] This essay updates the technique on which that definition was based, and uses a case study of an Atlanta economic development campaign to illustrate how businesses have taken advantage of the Sunbelt image to boost regional fortunes.

The business-and-public-perceptions method of defining the elusive Sunbelt was derived from the work of John Shelton Reed. Wanting to define the South, in Howard Odum's words, as "an extension of the folk," and operating from the assumption that the South is "that part of the country where the people think they are Southerners," Reed used a "convenient and inexpensive" way to measure that perception. He searched telephone directories for white-pages listings beginning with *southern* and *Dixie*, using *American* as a control. He titled the work "The Heart of Dixie," and he found that the heart was right were one would have expected—in the areas of the Deep South states least affected by national economic growth. In the tradition of good social science, Reed called on scholars to try his technique with other regions.[7]

A search of 1979 and 1980 telephone directories resulted in a fairly neat convergence of attitude and latitude that tended to endorse Sale's 37th parallel definition of the southern rim, or Sunbelt. There were Sunbelt listings for many cities below the 37th parallel, including all dozen of the metropolitan areas included in *Sunbelt Cities*. In contrast, entrepreneurs in the large metropolitan regions of the upper South, the Rocky Mountains, and the Pacific Northwest were not naming their businesses "Sunbelt" this or "Sun Belt" that.

One thing that Reed suggested but did not pursue in his essay was that directory listings could be used not only to identify regions at a particular point in time but also to track changes in regional perception over the years. In the case of the Sunbelt it is possible to make such a comparison on at least a limited basis by comparing 1979–80 findings with more recent listings. Directories were checked for 1984–85 and 1987–88 to see if the perception of the Sunbelt and its boundaries had changed over eight years. Because of the breakup of American Telephone and Telegraph (AT&T), frequent changes in directory composition, overlapping listings, and limitations on the data available, especially in 1979–80, the comparisons are not as complete or as precise as one would prefer.[8]

Still, two points are clear: first, the public perception of the Sunbelt does not generally include the upper South or the Pacific Northwest; and second, the term came into much wider use in the first few years of the 1980s and has remained in general currency.

Most of the cities of the Pacific Northwest appearing in some Sunbelt definitions had no Sunbelt-named businesses for any of the three periods observed. There were no such entries for Seattle, Spokane, or Portland. The Oregon metropolis, for example, had businesses named Sunbrite, Sunburst, Sunrise, and Sunset, but not Sunbelt. Northern California had a tiny sprinkling of Sunbelt-named businesses, but certainly not enough to place it firmly in the region.

The upper South states also lacked any significant number of Sunbelt businesses. The search of Virginia directories failed to turn up any Sunbelt listings for Norfolk, Roanoke, or the northern Virginia-Washington, D.C. area. Richmond had no Sunbelt listings in the first two periods and only one in 1987–88. Norfolk, for example, was home to businesses named Sunbird, Sunbeam, and even Sunbums, but not Sunbelt. Like Richmond, Louisville lacked any Sunbelt entries in the first two checks and had only one in the most recent observation. Baltimore started out with one listing, a trucking company, and added Sunbelt Motivation in the newer listings. In short, by this measure the upper South hardly belongs in the Sunbelt definition.

The most obvious change from 1980 to 1985 was in Colorado. In the first search Denver had no Sunbelt listings, but five years later it had five and Colorado Springs had three. Two years later Denver still had five, but Colorado Springs was down to one. Based on these findings, the front-range cities of the Rockies might qualify for associate Sunbelt status.

The sheer increase in the number of Sunbelt-named businesses in a mere half decade was impressive. In the directories selected for 1984–85 there were 665 Sunbelt entries, 642 of them in the 54 cities below the 37th parallel. In those cities for which reasonably direct comparisons could be made, there were 157 listings in 1979–80 and 587 in 1984–85 — an increase of 374 percent. The growth rate in the number of Sunbelt-named businesses slowed after 1985, but there was still a healthy increase in raw numbers from 587 in 1984–85 to 749 in 1987–88.

The cities that the media have most often associated with the Sunbelt are indeed those that continue to have the most Sunbelt listings. Throughout the late 1970s and most of the 1980s the majority of these cities were expanding in population and adding new businesses. One

may assume that most of the Sunbelt listings are new, since it is un-
likely, although not impossible, that a going concern would change its
name simply to capitalize on the Sunbelt image. Consequently, cities
that gave birth to many new businesses had more opportunity to name
them *Sunbelt* something-or-other. Of the cities with ten or more Sunbelt listings in 1984–85, only Birmingham had a metropolitan statistical area that grew more slowly than the national average of 3.9 percent
from April 1980 through December 1983.[9]

Dallas-Fort Worth, Houston, and Atlanta stand out as the Sunbelt
buckles, according to the business-name technique. From mid-1980 to
the end of 1983 the Dallas population expanded 11.5 percent, and from
the period 1979–80 to 1984–85, its Sunbelt-named businesses increased
in number from 16 to 69. The increase was from 21 to 92 if Dallas and
Fort Worth—which grew 11.6 percent—are combined. Houston's growth
from 1980 to 1983 was 15.2 percent, and its five-year Sunbelt-name count
advanced from 22 to 78. Metropolitan Atlanta grew 8.5 percent, and its
Sunbelt businesses leaped from 18 to 53.

Other cities with large numbers of Sunbelt businesses include Tampa–
St. Petersburg, which had only 2 listings as the decade opened, but sported
21 five years later. Boosters on one side of the bay used the slogan, "St.
Pete: Where the Sunbelt Buckles Down!" Charlotte also had only 2
Sunbelt-named businesses in the first search, but it had 18 by midde-
cade and 20 three years after that. Orlando went from none to 14 and
then to 17, Miami from 2 to 11 and then to 12, and Jacksonville from
1 to 13 but then down to 9.

Oklahoma City and Tulsa were also Sunbelt leaders early in the 1980s.
Each city grew about 11 percent from 1980 to 1983, and their Sunbelt
listings increased from 12 to 29 and from 8 to 26, respectively, in the first
half of the decade. The 1987–88 count, however, reflects the crisis in
the oil patch as the state's capital city dropped from 29 to 17 listings
and the one-time oil capital slipped from 26 to 14. Oklahoma City and
Tulsa experienced booms in 1979–80 and in the early stages of petroleum
price adjustment in 1984–85. Business failures and bankruptcies have
since become commonplace, as T-shirts proclaim, "Oklahoma: Home
of the FDIC." In *Funny Money*, an account of the oil-related failure of
Oklahoma City's Penn Square National Bank, author Mark Singer caught
the flavor of those halcyon times when northern banks were pouring
capital into the Southwest. "'Sunbelt,'" he wrote, "was the word of the day."[10]

In 1981 Blaine Liner, executive director of the Southern Growth Policies Board, said that the term *Sunbelt* "is ludicrous and should be stricken

from our vocabulary."[11] Obviously, however, it has not been. With over 600 Sunbelt-named businesses in the selected cities below the 37th parallel, and undoubtedly more in the smaller cities not studied here, it is clear that in the term's short history it has firmly established itself. As Carl Abbott notes in his essay in this volume, in less than a decade the term *Sunbelt* went "from coinage to cliché"

Many of the Sunbelt entries are for businesses in real estate, recreation, research and development, and high technology—activities often associated in the public mind with the Sunbelt phenomenon. Thus one finds Sunbelt Research and Development Consortium in Jackson, Mississippi; Sunbelt Computer Systems in Atlanta; and Sunbelt Real Estate Showcase in Fort Lauderdale. Louisiana, Texas, and Oklahoma had Sunbelt banks with numerous branches. Atlanta had one business called Sunbelt Growth Stocks and another known simply as Sun Belt.

On the other hand, the term is not the exclusive province of such white-collar activities. Jackson not only had the research-and-development firm named above but also had the Sunbelt Bolt and Screw Co. New Orleans was home to Sunbelt Stud Welding. Among Fort Worth's Sunbelt businesses was Sunbelt Pipe Threaders. Agribusiness was represented by Lubbock's Sunbelt Delinting and by Atlanta's Sunbelt Forest Products.

If referring to the Sunbelt constitutes "sloppy regionalizing," and in some ways it does, its sloppiness has not prevented the term from coming into general use in business and journalistic vocabularies. If the use of the word Sunbelt has been a "snow job," as Tindall asserted, it has been an effective snow job. In a prize-winning article, James C. Cobb declared that "the enigmatic nature of life in Sunbelt Georgia. . .has produced a society that all but defies regional categorization." Yet Cobb still found himself using *Sunbelt* to describe a city like Atlanta, where he could find both "cracklin's and caviar" within a few blocks of each other. In 1981 geographer Clyde Browning confessed to using the term *Sunbelt* "not because of its adequacy as a region, but because it is constantly referred to in discussions of regional rivalry."[12]

Imprecise or not, *Sunbelt* allows a speaker or writer to communicate a general image quickly without digressing into qualifiers and details. When a person hears the term on radio or television, or reads it in a magazine or book, or sees it in the telephone book or on a firm's letter-head, it is likely to conjure up an image of growing cities and booming economies in southern or southwestern cities with pleasant climates. The fact that the image may be a bit fuzzy, that it may not accurately apply to the entire South and Southwest, and that it may also describe some places in other parts of the country does not make it an unreasonable characterization of much of the area generally thought to be in the Sunbelt.

The positive image and the imprecise definition have actually proved to be a boon for southern boosters seeking to emphasize their purported rise into the national economic mainstream. These chamber-of-commerce types did not coin the word, but they were more than happy to use it. "Sun Belt sophistry," David R. Goldfield wrote accurately but somewhat cynically, "has replaced the New South Creed as the prevailing rhetorical ruse in the region." Cobb expressed a similar conclusion. "The Sunbelt ballyhoo of the late 1970s suggested that the realization of Henry Grady's dreams might at last be close at hand."[13] The president of Fantus, a business relocation firm, was blunt in his assertion that the use of Sunbelt was mainly a tool of boosterism. "It's a public relations coup. It's used whenever and wherever it serves a purpose."[14] Many enterprises found that it served their purposes well.

One study based on a survey of black students at Bowling Green State University in Ohio revealed that the alluring image of the Sunbelt cities was effective in attracting educated young blacks from the North. About 40 percent of the sample planned to leave Ohio and migrate to the Sunbelt. The author, who later moved to the Atlanta area himself, wrote, "Knowledge of Sunbelt cities' positive attributes is of primary importance in terms of predicting a student's plan to migrate to the Sunbelt." High-status university faculty were also "lured by the Sun Belt," according to U.S. News and World Report.[15]

For many southern promoters the use of Sunbelt seems to have been a conscious effort to reject confrontational sectionalism. Howard Odum's classic distinction between "sectionalism" as divisive and evil and "regionalism" as benign and healthy may help explain the word's popularity for boosterism. Reed has observed that Dixie is "unambiguously" a term of sectionalism, while southern mixes regional and sectional imagery.[16] Sunbelt goes a step further. Despite some arguments over federal funding formulas, Sunbelt remains almost wholly a concept of regionalism rather than sectionalism.

In his Southerners All, Nash Boney took on many students of southern identity and distinctiveness and contended that even in the past regional differences were all too often exaggerated. He persuasively argued that the differences are becoming smaller still, and implied that the positive popular perception of the Sunbelt has accelerated the transition. "The bulk of the contemporary 'Sun Belt,'" he predicted, will move even more into the national mainstream.[17]

Entrepreneurs who wanted to communicate, accurately or not, that they were involved in exciting growth could name their companies Sunbelt. Marketing professionals and economic development specialists found the use of *Sunbelt* handy because, explicitly or implicitly, they could present the Sunbelt in ways that contrasted with the traditional image of the South. For example, some Texans and Floridians might have been uncomfortable thinking of themselves as part of the South, but they probably did not mind being included in the Sunbelt.

The South was known to be hot and muggy; the Sunbelt was portrayed as sunny, mild, and mechanically cooled. The South was unsophisticated and backward; the Sunbelt was seen as cosmopolitan and forward looking. The South had cheap labor and shotgun houses; the Sunbelt was said to offer a lower cost of living and affordable homes. The picture of the South was of a rural region dotted with beautiful but declining plantations and laced with endless tobacco roads; the vision of the Sunbelt was of sprawling metropolitan areas covered with pleasant suburban subdivisions. The South was sharecroppers and lintheads; the Sunbelt spoke of high tech. Yankee executives might balk at moving to the South, but they might seek to locate in the Sunbelt.

The rhetoric of Atlanta's boosters, as exemplified in the promotional materials produced by the Metropolitan Atlanta Council for Economic Development (MACFED), provides a useful case study of what Goldfield called "Sunbelt sophistry." The council was a cooperative effort of Atlanta's Chamber of Commerce and the chambers of the major suburban counties: Clayton, Cobb, DeKalb, Douglas, and Gwinnett. The multicounty booster effort was symbolic of the fact that the central city's chamber could no longer singlehandedly market the metropolis as it had in its effective Forward Atlanta campaigns of the 1920s and 1960s. If entrepreneurs were searching for the Sunbelt, Atlanta's promoters wanted them to find it in Georgia's capital city. One of MACFED's booklets crowed, "The Sun Belt, with Atlanta as its centerpiece, has surged into overwhelming economic significance." The booklet urged business people to "come find your place in the Sun Belt." An ad placed in numerous business-oriented periodicals carried on the theme, saying, "If you're looking for a place in the Sunbelt, you really can't afford to go anywhere else."[18]

MACFED's promotional literature emphasized the mild climate in an article on trucking. "The year-round moderate weather is yet another factor in distributors' decisions to locate in Atlanta. Since snow and sleet are rare, reliability of shipping and receiving is enhanced, at least to other Sun Belt points." As one trucking executive put it, "Weather is extremely important. Sure, we get our ice storm every so often, but compared to what goes on up North, it's a pink tea party."[19] For years the southern image had suffered because of the oppressive summers, but with air conditioning available, warm summers became attractive rather than oppressive.

Raymond Arsenault's influential study of the impact of air conditioning on the South (Chapter 10) describes how refrigeration helped turn the southern climate from a liability into an asset. Arsenault writes that "the Sunbelt era" could not get into "full swing" until air conditioning became widespread in the region. Ironically, the population shift to the Sunbelt may have actually saved the country $500 million annually in net energy costs. Commerce Department figures show that between 1970 and 1980 the Sunbelt migration saved an average of $1.3 billion a year in heating costs and only cost an extra $800 million in air-conditioning expenditures.[20]

When combined with lower living costs, climate can be marketed as even more of an advantage. "We chose Atlanta. And let me tell you we couldn't be happier," the chairman of the Equitable Real Estate Group declared in one MACFED report. "Even the case-hardened New Yorkers, who sent out Bronx cheers at the thought of having to leave the sophisticated East, and the Big Apple, with all its trappings of power and prestige, are singing the praises of warmer winters, and neighborhoods close to work that offer a lifestyle which was out of reach in New York." He viewed Atlanta as "the strongest city in the Sun Belt, with only Dallas offering any competition."[21]

The Sunbelt's image of prosperity and growth has suffered some assaults, especially during the 1981–82 recession. A *Wall Street Journal* reporter's assessment was typical. "Though its economy is still probably in better shape than most of the country's, the Sun Belt isn't any longer the job seekers' paradise it was a year ago and for much of the 1970s." The South's boosters were undaunted, however. In early 1982 the business section of the Sunday *Atlanta Journal and Constitution* was headlined "How the Sun Belt will keep right on shining." Cobb and others have emphasized that a critical population mass was essential to the Sunbelt's takeoff and that continued in-migration is important to sustained economic growth—especially, of course, in real estate. In 1985

MACFED boosters cited the growth rates of Atlanta, Dallas, Houston, Tampa, and San Diego and then boldly asserted, "Increases like that are expected to continue throughout the Sunbelt." A U.S. Census Bureau branch chief agreed, declaring, "I don't see any real sign of abatement. There might be a little, but not an awful lot."[22]

A 1985 article in the *Christian Science Monitor* charted a diplomatic middle ground between the glowing accolades of the region's most ardent spokespeople and the gloomy predictions of some observers. "The Sunbelt isn't what it used to be," Ruth Walker wrote. "But then it never was. . . . That is not to say that what we might call 'the Sunbelt phenomenon' isn't continuing. Rather, what was always true is just becoming more evident: the Sunbelt is not a monolithic region of snow-free posperity. . . . The Sunbelt today appears to be neither the backwater that some northerners considered it nor the economic mecca that some Sunbelt boosters would claim."[23]

The later part of the 1980s witnessed something of a rejuvenation in the Northeast—especially in suburban Boston and New York. Using tax data to track population, two geographers documented the Northeast improvement and asked, "How do the IRS statistics on migration mesh with the common perception of Frostbelt to Sunbelt migration?" The answer was that "they confirm the regional deconcentration for which the 1970s are known, but they also reveal that migration patterns are changing." In a recent article, Bernard Weinstein and Harold T. Gross, both of Southern Methodist University in Dallas, stressed how quickly economic situations can change due to outside forces. They asserted, "A strong argument can be made that the Sunbelt is today the most distressed economic region in the United States."[24] This point is probably overplayed, but for parts of the Sunbelt it is not too far off base.

The boomers of Atlanta and many of the other cities below the 37th parallel could not have been unaware of the regional readjustments evident by the mid-1980s, but they professed not to be worried. MACFED declared, "Even turnarounds in the so-called Rust Belt cities won't make that much difference to Atlanta."[25] Sunbelt boosters undoubtedly were also aware that their newly named region was not uniformly prosperous—although it is hard to document that awareness from their optimistic rhetoric. Positive perception of the Sunbelt is their stock-in-trade. After all, boosterism is a booster's job.

Notes

1. George B. Tindall, "The Sunbelt Snow Job," *Houston Review* (Spring 1979): 3–13; Clyde E. Browning and Wil Gesler, "Sun Belt-Snow Belt: A Case of Sloppy Regionalizing," *Professional Geographer* 31 (Feb. 1979): 66.
2. CBS-TV, 3 Sept. 1985; *Time* (22 July 1985): 63; *Variety*, 19 Sept. 1984; on *Sunbelt Executive Magazine*, see *New York Times*, 22 Sept. 1982.
3. Kirkpatrick Sale, *Power Shift: The Rise of the Southern Rim and Its Challenge to the Eastern Establishment* (New York: Random House, 1975).
4. Carl Abbott, *The New Urban America: Growth and Politics in Sunbelt Cities* (Chapel Hill: Univ. of North Carolina Press, 1981); Jeanne C. Biggar, "The Sunning of America: Migration to the Sunbelt," *Population Bulletin* 34 (Mar. 1979): 1–42; *Atlanta Journal and Constitution*, 22 July 1984, quoting Weinstein.
5. Bradley R. Rice, "Searching for the Sunbelt," *American Demographics* 3 (Mar. 1981): 22–23; Sam Allis, "Regions," *Wall Street Journal*, 14 Apr. 1981.
6. Richard M. Bernard and Bradley R. Rice, eds., *Sunbelt Cities: Politics and Growth since World War II* (Austin: Univ. of Texas Press, 1983).
7. John Sheldon Reed, "The Heart of Dixie: An Essay in Folk Geography," *Social Forces* 54 (June 1976): 925–39. Reprinted as chapter 4 of Reed's *One South: An Ethnic Approach to Regional Culture* (Baton Rouge: Louisiana State Univ. Press, 1982).
8. The counts are based on businesses listed in the white pages under "Sunbelt" or "Sun Belt." Firms such as banks that had several branches in one metropolitan were counted only once for that city. The 1979–80 count was made from directories available at the University of Texas Library in the summer of 1980. Most of the 1984–85 and 1987–88 listings were obtained from the Bell and Howell Phonefiche collection. Hard copies were consulted for some cities unavailable in Phonefiche. Travis Rice kindly helped his father compile the 1987–88 figures.
9. *Rand-McNally Commercial Atlas*, 1985.
10. Mark Singer, *Funny Money* (New York: Knopf, 1985), 70.
11. Allis, "Regions."
12. Tindall, "Sunbelt Snow Job"; James C. Cobb, "Cracklin's and Caviar: The Enigma of Sunbelt Georgia," *Georgia Historical Quarterly* 58 (Spring 1984): 19; Clyde E. Browning, "The Role of the South in the Sunbelt-Snowbelt Struggle for Federal Funds," in Merle Black and John Shelton Reed, eds., *Perspectives on the American South*, vol. 1 (New York: Gordon and Breach, 1981), 253.
13. David R. Goldfield, *Cotton Fields and Skyscrapers: Southern City and Region, 1607–1980* (Baton Rouge: Louisiana State Univ. Press, 1982), 192; James C. Cobb, *The Selling of the South: The Southern Crusade for Industrial Development, 1936–1980* (Baton Rouge: Louisiana State Univ. Press, 1982), 208.
14. Allis, "Regions."
15. Bruce H. Wade, "Migration to the Sunbelt: Plans and Aspirations of Black

Students at BGSU" (M.A. thesis, Bowling Green State University, 1980), 39. See James H. Johnson and Walter C. Farrell, Jr., "Implications of the Black Move to the South," *Black Enterprise* 12 (Jan. 1982): 21. "Now It's College Faculty Lured by the Sun Belt," *U.S. News and World Report* (4 Feb. 1985): 58.

16. Reed, "The Heart of Dixie." On Odum, see George B. Tindall, *The Ethnic Southerners* (Baton Rouge: Louisiana State Univ. Press, 1976), chap. 5; and Robert B. Downs, *Books That Changed the South* (Totowa, N.J.: Little-field, Adams, 1977), chap. 23.

17. F. N. Boney, *Southerners All* (Macon, Ga.: Mercer Univ. Press, 1984), 199.

18. Metropolitan Atlanta Council for Economic Development, *Advantage Metro Atlanta* (MACFED, 1983). MACFED has dissolved, but it laid ground-work for continuing cooperation. On Atlanta's earlier promotion efforts see Bradley R. Rice, "Atlanta," in Bernard and Rice, eds., *Sunbelt Cities*, 29–57; and Rice, "Urbanization, 'Atlanta-ization,' and Suburbanization: Three Themes for the Urban History of Twentieth-Century Georgia," *Georgia Historical Quarterly* 58 (Spring 1984): 40–59.

19. MACFED, *Metropolitan Atlanta Business Report* (Apr.–May 1985).

20. See Raymond Arsenault's essay in this volume; *Wall Street Journal*, 2 Apr. 1982.

21. MACFED, *Metropolitan Atlanta Business Report* (Dec. 1984–Jan. 1985).

22. *Wall Street Journal*, 25 Mar. 1982; *Atlanta Journal and Constitution*, 14 Feb. 1982; Cobb, *Selling of the South*, chap. 7; Cobb, *Industrialization and Southern Society, 1877–1894*, (Lexington: Univ. Press of Kentucky, 1984), chap. 3; MACFED, *Metropolitan Atlanta Business Report* (Feb.–Mar. 1985). One study noted that the physical as well as the economic health of the Sunbelt had slipped: Michael R. Greenberg, "Sunbelt, Frost-belt, and Public Health," *Society* 21 (July–Aug. 1984): 75.

23. Ruth Walker, "Sunbelt Success a Dappled Pattern," *Christian Science Monitor*, 18 Mar. 1985.

24. Peter A. Rogerson and David A. Plane, "Monitoring Migration Trends," *American Demographics* 7 (Feb. 1985): 27–29; Bernard L. Weinstein and Harold T. Gross, "National Change and the Regional Conundrum," *Society* 25 (Nov.–Dec. 1987): 55–61. See also Gary Gappert, ed., *The Future of Winter Cities* (Newbury Park, Calif.: Sage Publications, 1987).

25. MACFED, *Metropolitan Atlanta Business Report* (Feb.-Mar. 1985).

12   Epilogue
The Vanishing Sunbelt
David R. Goldfield
and Howard N. Rabinowitz

This volume is more an epitaph than a herald of a new era in regional scholarship. In a way this is appropriate, since most of the contributors are historians accustomed to picking up after lost civilizations. The lifespan of the Sunbelt, at least its reality, was relatively brief. It emerged in the 1970s as journalistic shorthand for the economic, political, and demographic trends occurring in an ambiguous zone somewhere below the 37th parallel. For people living in this zone, the designation doubtless came as a surprise. As *Texas Monthly* editor Nicholas Lemann suggested, "Millions of people were living in the Sunbelt without one of them realizing it. They thought of themselves as Southerners or Texans or Los Angelenos."[1] Now the era has passed them by. Its lifespan was remarkably short. In 1980 economist Bernard Weinstein extolled the broad prosperity of the Sunbelt. Five years later, in a *Wall Street Journal* editorial, he announced that the Sunbelt had "collapsed into only a few 'sunspots.'"[2] Call it death by reality or death by convergence, the Sunbelt is vanishing.

The Sunbelt, thanks to some of its component parts, retains a measure of utility as a research framework. Like "modernization," it is difficult to define and defend, but it can offer a perspective. At the least it is better for urbanists to talk about regions than about individual cities, even if the region is only an image or a state of mind. The essays in this collection demonstrate the slippery nature of that image. Definitions vary widely, though it seems wise to accept Carl Abbott's suggestion to disaggregate the Sunbelt into at least three components. The South and West remain uneasy partners, even conceptually. As several authors note, the West, especially California, Arizona, and Texas, has had less difficulty meeting the criteria for Sunbelt inclusion. The irony is that the South, the nation's "number one economic problem" a half century ago, is now the synonym for prosperity.

Disengaging the South, however, reveals that southern states still share top billing in the least-likely-to-succeed categories. In terms of il-

224

literacy, high school dropout rates, per capita income, industrial wages, infant mortality, and poverty, southern states continue to bring up the rear nationally. The prosperity of limited areas within states and within the region mask persistent economic problems. Take the Atlanta metropolitan area out of Georgia, and Georgia lags behind even Mississippi. Rural unemployment is roughly three times as high as metropolitan unemployment and heavily skewed toward blacks and women. In the small, one-industry textile communities of the Piedmont, the retail trade, the mills, and the young people have gone. These are the silver-mining ghost towns of the 1990s. As James Cobb suggests, even within prosperous metropolitan areas the two-tiered post-industrial work force has meant upward mobility for some and flipping hamburgers and making beds for many others.[3]

Scrutinizing the Sunbelt image is especially important for the South, a region historically prone to believing publicity rather than the world around it. It doesn't take much of a crystal ball to figure out whether the suburbia extolled by *Southern Living* or the labor, racial, and economic tensions uncovered by *Southern Exposure* will triumph in the public mind. Sobriety is needed to countervail the excessive hyperbole. Indeed, organizations such as the Southern Growth Policies Board and the Southern Regional Council exist in large part to offer strong doses of reality for inflamed regional egos.

Of course, the South has never taken criticism well, even when offered by native sons and daughters. The danger is that the more southerners become taken in by the Sunbelt, the less southern they become. The essayists note this irony: although the Sunbelt emerged in the mid-1970s media hype as a distinctive region, many of its distinctions turned out merely to move the region (wherever it was) closer to the national norm. As Roger Lotchin demonstrates, the South is no longer a have-not region as far as defense installations are concerned. In political terms, the transition from business-oriented, low-tax, low-service municipalities to a pluralistic local government with strong neighborhood and ethnic involvement moves Sunbelt cities into closer alignment with urban administrations elsewhere. The essays by Richard M. Bernard, Amy Bridges, and Ronald H. Bayor make this point. They cite external forces such as the civil rights movement and the federal government as instrumental in bringing urban Sunbelt politics closer to the national norm. Not only in politics, but in ethnicity as well, the Sunbelt is coming to parallel the experience of northern cities. Elliott Barkan's Miami-Honolulu axis represents America's new "golden door." At

least on the mainland portion of this axis there seems to be a gradual
return, in terms of population, to the sixteenth century, when these
areas were under Spanish domination. Because southerners like to consider themselves traditionalists, this is perhaps appropriate.

Florida, of course, is different. It has already transcended convergence
and has embarked on a new course. It would not be unexpected if, in
a few years, the Laws of the Indies became the state's legal foundation
and the bar mitzvah the most important form of ceremonial investiture.
In Miami there are several shops with English Spoken Here signs prominently displayed in the window, and at some hotels it is possible to get
huevos rancheros with lox. *Rolling Stone* magazine summarized the
state as "afterlife for Ohio, surrogate for Cuba, landing strip for Colom-
bia, laundromat for the mob, [and] beach for Brooklyn."[4] Raymond A.
Mohl's suggestion that Miami's ethnic pattern represents a case of adjustment without assimilation accurately reflects the Hispanic dominance in the city and the unique role of Cubans. Pluralism hardly describes the case for Miami any longer.

But Florida aside (and many Americans would prefer it that way), the
trend toward convergence is evident in other ways as well. As Raymond
Arsenault demonstrates, technology can be a great equalizer. The steamy
Faulknerian summers might have made good literature, but they made
for uncomfortable living and working. Air conditioning gave the Sunbelt (South and Southwest) a climatic trump on the North. Central
heating tamed northern winters, to be sure, but you had to go outside
eventually and then you had to consider layers of clothing, blasts of arc-
tic wind, colds and respiratory illnesses, and negotiating snow and ice.
Depending on residence below the 37th parallel, some of these wintry
elements may appear from time to time. But the Sunbelt's red-nose season
is mercifully short as compared with the North's. How many northern
executives have been lured into opening southern or western branches
or even into moving lock, stock, and briefcase after boarding a plane in
Detroit on a cold January morning and arriving in the splendid warmth
of Phoenix or Tampa by lunchtime? Technology has conquered not only
climate but space as well.

Technology, like many beneficial drugs, has some negative side effects. Air conditioning effectively eliminated the front porch, that story-
telling, generation-gathering center that traditionally had adorned southern homes. Television, magazines, and junk mail have told southerners
what they have been missing. High-speed highways, regional airports,
and subdivisions have spawned shopping malls, shopping strips, and

more highways. For southerners who have been away for a while, the culture shock must be similar to that experienced by Will Barrett, the young hero of Walker Percy's *The Last Gentleman.* "The South he came home to was different from the South he had left. It was happy, victorious, Christian, rich, patriotic, and Republican."[5] The Sunbelt veneer does not fit very well over aspects of the old South, as cartoonist Doug Marlette noted in his "Kudzu" strip.

Booger Red: Hey Dub! [Dub is a car mechanic and service station owner]
Dub: Booger Red! I didn't recognize you without your overalls!
Booger Red: Well, I just wanted to let you know after all these years just sittin' around the station here I finally got a job. I'm in computer sales now. The benefits are just super! Dental and everything.
Dub: Good Booger. Good for you.
Booger Red: Well . . . gotta run. Let's do lunch sometime! . . . Ciao!
Dub: Pitiful.
Rev. Will B. Dunn: Booger got his only tooth capped![6]

But it is not only the Sunbelt that has changed; since 1980 the rest of the nation has undergone a transformation as well. A major impetus for the journalistic shorthand of the mid-1970s was the corresponding demise of northeastern and midwestern cities. The Sunbelt-Frostbelt dichotomy, though overdrawn, offered a summary presentation of the major economic and demographic shifts underway as the national economy became more oriented toward services. The dichotomy also summarized the lifestyle differences of the two regions — the warm, open, relaxed Sunbelt, and the closed, cold, uptight Frostbelt. While decay, bankruptcy, and racial antagonism plagued northern cities, the biggest dilemma confronting Sunbelt metropolises was where to place the next shopping mall. As the chamber of commerce advertisements noted, where else could you play tennis outdoors in December and go to sleep listening to crickets instead of police sirens? It is not surprising, as Bradley R. Rice discovered, that most of the enterprises employing the Sunbelt name were connected with such "lifestyle" activities as real estate, recreation, and research and development.

The Sunbelt, in other words, required an opposite to retain its validity not only in reality but partly in image as well. But the Frostbelt has thawed in recent years. Since 1984 states such as New York, Massachusetts, and Ohio have been among the nation's leaders in job creation. New York has hauled itself up from the brink of bankruptcy; Boston is the hub of a far-reaching high-tech empire; Pittsburgh has been touted

as a great place to live; Cleveland has gone from being a joke to a jugger-
naut; and New Jersey is being transformed from wasteland to promised
land. And northern urban officials are adopting the aggressive development tactics of their southern and western counterparts, offering tax
incentives and land write-downs, opening recruitment offices abroad,
launching splashy advertising campaigns, and seeking partnerships with
businesses and universities. The recovery has been uneven, of course,
just as in the Sunbelt. But the old dichotomy no longer holds. And a
cursory check of major magazines and newspapers indicates that although
there are few articles on the Sunbelt miracle any more, a considerable
amount of ink is being expended on various aspects of the Frostbelt re-
vival. So the convergence implied by many of the essays here in terms
of politics, ethnicity, and technology is even stronger given recent demographic and economic events up north. Future regional research will
need to keep this comparative element in mind to present a fuller account of regional development.

Regional convergence affords some insights into the urban process.
What has been occurring in the Sunbelt is a maturation process, stimulated by growth and federal policy, that has further narrowed the regional
distinctions among cities. In his classic work *Southern Politics in State
and Nation* (1949), political scientist V. O. Key, Jr., argued that "the growth
of cities contains the seeds of political change for the South."[7] The rapid
demographic and geographic expansion of Sunbelt cities during and after the Second World War brought to power a new generation of leaders
anxious to generate a second coming of Progressive Era efficiency combined with more modern concerns about the quality and level of services. In the South, these new urban leaders helped to initiate a region-
wide political transformation by supporting such progressive politicians
as Georgia governor Ellis Arnall, Governor Sid McMath of Arkansas,
and senators Claude Pepper of Florida and Frank Porter Graham of North
Carolina; and newcomers such as Francis Pickens Miller of Virginia,
who challenged the powerful Byrd machine, and James Folsom of Alabama, who broke the grip of the large planters and Birmingham steel
barons. The transformation spurred the old liners (or, as Bernard calls
them, "Old Guardsmen") to use red-baiting and race-baiting tactics to
recover the southern electorate. By the early 1950s, even before the *Brown*
decision, they were generally successful in recapturing the machinery
of southern politics.[8]

But the cities retained their progressive entrepreneurial leadership.
By the 1960s this leadership belatedly concluded that segregation was

bad business, and cautiously supported desegregation of public accommodations. In some cities, such as Birmingham and New Orleans, battles royal ensued between political and business leaders, but for the most part the transition to integrated public accommodations proceeded smoothly in the urban South even before the passage of the 1964 Civil Rights Act. Population growth and the consumer demand it generated combined with racial accommodation to enhance the economic potential of southern cities. And by the 1970s the impact of growth, the 1965 Voting Rights Act, and the 1974 Community Development Act had helped to create political pluralism in Sunbelt cities. By the 1980s, as in the West, environmental issues related to traffic congestion, service delivery, and real estate development further dampened the entrepreneurial thrust of local government, and limited-growth advocates found widespread political support, even in such free enterprise bastions as Dallas and Houston. An urban political system that had been predicated on a relatively narrow electorate, low taxes, minimal services, and an exclusive elite has — as Key predicted — become more open and diverse due to the process of urban development.

But the urban process historically has also created disparities — between citizens, between city center and suburb, and between metropolis and hinterland. The Sunbelt cities, as we have indicated, have not been immune to these disparities. Nor have they had any greater success than their northern counterparts in modifying them. The fact that Sunbelt cities are newer has not necessarily made them better. And the problems they face are a further link with the Frostbelt cities, lessening the differences between the two regions.

The impact of the urban process on space has had significant import for the distribution of these disparities. The older cities of the Northeast and Midwest grew up during the electric age; the trolley lines converged at the city center, lending importance and density to the core. Sunbelt cities have emerged during the automobile age and reflect the spread-out, leisurely, low-density profile that the car culture has helped to generate. Here would seem to be a *divergence* from the national urban spatial norm, especially since annexation and far-flung subdivisions and shopping malls have maintained this profile through the 1980s. But in an ironic twist, metropolitan spatial arrangements are actually converging, only now it is the North that is following the Sunbelt's example.

Northern metropolitan areas are beginning to resemble in some respects the dispersed cities of the South and West. One of the most significant spatial trends of the 1980s has been the emergence of "out-

towns": concentrated, multiuse developments on the periphery of metropolitan areas. These communities exist beyond the beltways and have
tenuous connections to the core city. They are, in effect, cities in
themselves. Concentrations outside Princeton, New Jersey, or Dallas, or
in Orange County, California, are the most rapidly growing urban areas
today. They are not suburbs: they are not primarily residential communities whose residents commute to jobs in core cities or even in other
suburbs. The new towns are likely to be farther out and to contain many
more employment opportunities. They are going so far out, in fact, that
the out-towns are becoming links in a vast metropolitan chain drawing
metropolitan areas together. In North Carolina people refer to "Char-
leigh" and "Ralette" along Interstate 85. In Florida there is a spreading
conurbation extending from Dade County to beyond Palm Beach. Although the core cities, North and South, remain distinctive in their
spatial configurations, their respective peripheral areas are taking on a
similar aspect.[9]

Of course, there are differences in scale in the megametropolitan
areas, especially between the southern portion of the Sunbelt and the
North. The four largest metropolitan areas in the South, for example,
are Dallas, Houston, Atlanta, and Miami. Nationally these cities rank
8th, 9th, 16th, and 21st, respectively. The typical southern metropolitan area is modest in size, with a population of five hundred thousand
to one million (for example, Memphis, Nashville, Jacksonville, Birmingham, Charlotte, Norfolk). In addition, the South still has more people living in small cities and towns with fewer than fifty thousand people than does any other region. But the disparities of scale may narrow
as Sunbelt metropolitan areas continue to outspace metropolitan growth
nationally.[10]

The convergence implied in the essays in this volume may be part
of a more general phenomenon reported in John Egerton's *The Americanization of Dixie: The Southernization of America* (1974). Perhaps after all the premature obituaries the South is dying at last. First it melted
into the Sunbelt, and now along with other parts of the Sunbelt it appears to be blending into America. "Which is worse," the title character
asks rhetorically in Walker Percy's 1977 novel *Lancelot*, "to die with T. J.
Jackson at Chancellorsville or live with Johnny Carson in Burbank?"[11]

But the South is resilient. Its distinction has survived numerous
traumas, and it will survive the lure of the Sunbelt and the example of
the rest of America. As sociologist John Shelton Reed notes, southerners
remain distinctive in a number of areas including religious commitment,

family orientation, political conservatism, attachment to past and place, and adherence to manners. Surprisingly, he argues, the characteristics of distinction are often strongest among metropolitan southerners—those who have had an opportunity to travel widely in the country and who are therefore more sensitive to differences and more appreciative of the threats to tradition.[12] Rather than treating the South as a homogenized part of the Sunbelt that has become part of a homogenized America, observers might profit from an emphasis on distinction; on how southern culture bends, seduces, and assimilates newcomers, whether foreigners or Yankees; and on how the economy and technology of postindustrial America can fit in with a regional culture without changing that culture. The Sunbelt may be dead, except as a flickering image on the journalist's word processor or on the marquee of a health spa, but the South lives.

So too does the West. As Carl Abbott and others suggest, it is the traditional West rather than the New South that best fits the stereotype of the Sunbelt. Yet if the South, despite its resilience, is beginning to look more like the North by following in that region's footsteps, the convergence of North and West is due more to the North acting as follower, though the West retains its unique orientation due to land and water issues, demography, Native American relations, and the like. As Gerald Nash has argued, the post–World War II West, especially California, has often been the nation's pacesetter, whether in matters of the economy, in politics, or in lifestyle.[13] And the virtues that Frederick Jackson Turner long ago claimed to be peculiarly American—individualism, equality, innovation, faith in progress, and widespread abundance—most clearly correspond to western characteristics (certainly when compared to C. Vann Woodward's famous depiction of a South plagued by defeat, pessimism, and poverty).[14]

In the end it is the uneasy alliance of South and West in the Sunbelt and the equally oversimplified view of the Frostbelt that exposes the weakness of the concept. Recent trends in the South and West have been making those areas more, not less, like the rest of the country. Just try to find a town anywhere in the United States without a McDonald's or a television happy-news format featuring an anchorperson with an unidentifiable accent. Even the shift of political power to the Sunbelt will not change the country as much as once thought. Ironically, while discovering the richness and complexity of reality in the Sunbelt, the authors of these essays have exposed the barrenness of a concept that obscures more than it reveals. In short, in the future we can more profitably understand America in terms of North, South, and West, or urban, rural, and suburban. Either of these more traditional models works better than the Sunbelt stereotypes of more recent theorists. Still, it was fun while it lasted, and perhaps at least now the South and West will get the attention they deserve from scholars too long preoccupied with the Northeast and Midwest.

Notes

1. Quoted in Deborah Dash Moore, "Jewish Migration to the Sunbelt," in Randall M. Miller and George E. Pozzetta, eds., *Shades of the Sunbelt: Essays on Ethnicity, Race, and the Urban South* (Westport, Conn.: Greenwood, 1988), 43.
2. Quoted in Stuart Rosenfeld, "A Divided South," *Southern Exposure* 14 (Nov.–Dec. 1986): 10.
3. In 1986 the Southern Growth Policies Board, a research organization supported by southern states, issued several reports detailing economic and social disparities within the South. The reports, authored by the 1986 Commission on the Future of the South, include "The Report of the Committee on Human Resource Development"; "Equity: The Critical Link in Southern Economic Development"; and "Rural Flight-Urban Might: Economic Development Challenges for the 1990s." (Research Triangle Park, N.C.: Southern Growth Policies Board, 1986).
4. Quoted in Raymond Arsenault and Gary R. Mormino, "From Dixie to Dreamland: Demographic and Cultural Changes in Florida, 1880–1980," in Miller and Pozzetta, eds., *Shades of the Sunbelt*, 161.
5. Walker Percy, *The Last Gentleman* (New York: Farrar, Straus and Giroux, 1966), 185–86.
6. *Charlotte Observer*, 29 May 1986.
7. V. O. Key, Jr., *Southern Politics in State and Nation* (New York: Knopf, 1949), 673–74.
8. For a discussion of the political thaw in the South during the years immediately after World War II, see David R. Goldfield, *Promised Land: The South since 1945* (Arlington Heights, Ill.: Harlan Davidson, 1987), 33–49.
9. There has been relatively little discussion of the out-town phenomenon. See Neal Peirce, "Can Urban Villages Become Real People Places?" *Washington Post*, 17 Aug. 1985; and Peter O. Muller, "The Suburbanization of the Sunbelt City: Metropolitan Restructuring in the South and West" (Paper presented at conference on "The Sunbelt: A Region and Regionalism in the Making?" Miami, Nov. 1985).
10. On the low-density character of southern metropolitan development and its costs and benefits, see "Development Threatens Farmers," *Charlotte Observer*, 31 May 1987. See also Robert G. Healy, *Competition for Land in the American South: Agriculture, Human Settlement, and the Environment* (Washington, D.C.: Conservation Foundation, 1985), chap. 5.
11. Walker Percy, *Lancelot* (New York: Farrar, Straus and Giroux, 1977), 158.

12. John Shelton Reed, *Southerners: The Social Psychology of Sectionalism* (Chapel Hill: Univ. of North Carolina Press, 1983).
13. Gerald D. Nash, *The American West in the Twentieth Century: A Short History of an Urban Oasis* (Englewood Cliffs, N.J.: Prentice-Hall, 1973); Gerald D. Nash, *The American West Transformed: The Impact of the Second World War* (Bloomington: Indiana Univ. Press, 1985).
14. Frederick Jackson Turner, *The Frontier in American History* (New York: Holt, 1920); C. Vann Woodward, *The Burden of Southern History*, enlarged ed. (Baton Rouge: Louisiana State Univ. Press, 1968).

Contributors

Carl Abbott is professor of urban studies and planning at Portland State University. He is the author of numerous books, including *The New Urban America: Growth and Politics in Sunbelt Cities* (Univ. of North Carolina Press, 1981, rev. ed., 1987); *Portland: Planning, Politics, and Growth in a Twentieth-Century City* (Univ. of Nebraska Press, 1983); and *Urban America in the Modern Age: 1920 to the Present* (Harlan Davidson, 1987).

Raymond Arsenault is professor of history at the University of South Florida, St. Petersburg. He is the author of *The Wild Ass of the Ozarks: Jeff Davis and the Social Bases of Southern Politics* (Temple Univ. Press, 1984); *St. Petersburg and the Florida Dream, 1888–1950* (Donning, 1988); and other publications.

Elliott Barkan is professor of history at California State University at San Bernardino. He is the author of numerous articles on twentieth-century immigration and ethnicity, which have appeared in the *Journal of American Ethnic History, Journal of Urban History, Ethnic Forum, Ethnicity,* the *Harvard Encyclopedia of American Ethnic Groups,* and other publications.

Ronald H. Bayor is professor of history at the Georgia Institute of Technology. He is the author of *Neighbors in Conflict: The Irish, Germans, Jews, and Italians of New York City, 1929–1942* (Johns Hopkins Univ. Press, 1978); editor of *Neighborhoods in Urban America* (Kennikat, 1982); and editor of the *Journal of American Ethnic History.*

Richard M. Bernard is professor of history and dean of the faculty at Bethany College, West Virginia. He is the author of *The Melting Pot and the Altar: Marital Assimilation in Early Twentieth-Century Wisconsin* (Univ. of Minnesota Press, 1980), coeditor of *Sunbelt Cities: Politics and Growth since World War II* (Univ. of Texas Press, 1983), and editor of *Snowbelt Cities: Metropolitan Politics in the Northeast since World War II* (Indiana Univ. Press, 1990).

Amy Bridges is associate professor of political science at the University of California at San Diego. She is the author of *A City in the Republic: Antebellum New York and the Origins of Machine Politics* (Cambridge Univ. Press, 1984).

Blaine A. Brownell is professor of history, and provost and vice-president for academic affairs, at the University of North Texas. He is the author of *The Urban Ethos in the South, 1920–1930* (Louisiana State Univ. Press, 1975); and coauthor of *Urban America: A History* (Houghton Mifflin, 1979, 2nd ed., 1990) and *The Urban Nation, 1920–1980* (Hill and Wang, 1981).

James C. Cobb is Bernadotte E. Schmidt Professor of American History at the University of Tennessee, Knoxville. He is the author of *The Selling of the South: The Southern Crusade for Industrial Development, 1936–1980* (Louisiana State University Press, 1982) and *Industrialization and Southern Society, 1877–1984* (University Press of Kentucky, 1984).

David R. Goldfield is Robert Lee Bailey Professor of History at the University of North Carolina at Charlotte. He is the author of *Urban Growth in the Age of Sectionalism: Virginia, 1847–1861* (Louisiana State University Press, 1977); *Cotton Fields and Skyscrapers: Southern City and Region, 1607–1980* (Louisiana State University Press, 1982); and *Promised Land: The South since 1945* (Harlan Davidson, 1987); and he is coauthor of *Urban America: A History* (Houghton Mifflin, 1979, 2nd ed., 1990); and editor of the *Journal of Urban History*.

Roger W. Lotchin is professor of history at the University of North Carolina, Chapel Hill. He is the author of *San Francisco, 1846–1856: From Hamlet to City* (Oxford University Press, 1974) and the editor of *The Martial Metropolis: U.S. Cities in War and Peace* (Praeger, 1984).

Raymond A. Mohl is professor and chairman of the Department of History at Florida Atlantic University in Boca Raton. He is the author of *Poverty in New York, 1783–1825* (Oxford University Press, 1971) and *The New City: Urban America in the Industrial Age, 1860–1920* (Harlan Davidson, 1985); coauthor of *Steel City: Urban and Ethnic Patterns in Gary, Indiana, 1906–1950* (Holmes and Meier, 1986); and editor of *The Making of Urban America* (Scholarly Resources, 1988).

Howard N. Rabinowitz is professor of history at the University of New Mexico in Albuquerque. He is the author of *Race Relations in the*

Urban South, 1865–*1890* (Oxford University Press, 1978) and editor of *Southern Black Leaders of the Reconstruction Era* (University of Illinois Press, 1982).

Bradley R. Rice is professor of history at Clayton State College, Morrow, Georgia. He is the author of *Progressive Cities: The Commission Government Movement in America, 1901–1920* (University of Texas Press, 1977); coeditor of *Sunbelt Cities: Growth and Politics since World War II* (University of Texas Press, 1983); and editor of *Atlanta History: A Journal of Georgia and the South.*

Index

Searching for the Sunbelt was designed
by Dariel Mayer, composed by Lithocraft, Inc.,
and printed and bound by BookCrafters, Inc.
The book is set in Trump and printed on
50–lb Glatfelter Natural.